GOD WHO ARE YOU?

I NEED TO KNOW

WRITTEN BY PHYLLIS COOK

COPYRIGHT

Contents

AUTHOR'S COMMENT

——◆——

For God so loved the world, that he gave his only begotten Son (John 3:16).

First of all, I want to say that I am very thankful that I have someone special in my life, who is here for me no matter what is going on, good or bad. I can trust him to keep me through all troubles, trials and temptations that may come up against me. We don't live in a perfect world as of yet and we all face some kind of issues almost on a daily basis.

There are so many stories in the bible that help us to understand who God is, why he did the things that he did, and what he has planned for our future.

Throughout these lessons, I may go back and forth through the different stories to show their connection or relationship to one another. As I do, I try to add more depth to the stories as I go through each lesson.

I believe that the bible is the inspired, living word of God and he gave it to us to reveal himself. It has survived throughout history to assist us in knowing him even though he is invisible.

He promises that if we seek him, we can have a happy and eternal life now and in the forever! He may be invisible, but we can truly see and hear him in our own imagination, as we learn about him in his historical stories. As we put His-story all together like we would do with a jigsaw puzzle, we can see the whole picture more perfectly. Each lesson goes a little deeper to reveal who God is.

As part of my investigation, I wanted to know who God was, and how is it that he loved me and you. With some of the things that happened in the bible, I did not understand how God seemed so cruel at times and at other times full of mercy. But as I studied different stories, I realized my thoughts about him were somewhat distorted. After reading through some of the stories and asking God some question about why things happened the way they did, he gave me answers that made more sense. I found out that all the things that he has done are things that prove his love.

The spiritual environment around us is just as real as we are, and more so! We might as well get used to the idea, and that there will be a time when we will fully be a part of the invisible realm that we can't see right now. It is better to learn about it now and be prepared. We can know without any doubt that there is something more to look forward to in the future that comes from the spiritual environment.

There is an invisible enemy that we can't see. He wants us to be afraid or weirded out by supernatural and spiritual things, so that we will not seek God. He wants us to be so fearful of God that we will avoid him altogether. I have found that God is awesome and loving. I hope to reveal to you all that God, the Father and his Son went through to eliminate any fear you may have of him, as well as any fear brought on by the invisible spiritual enemy.

I am learning that everything God does has a purpose. He is revealing his plan to us through what we learn about Jesus. We have power to live forever because of Jesus! The whole book centers around Jesus, who is the answer to all life's questions. He truly is the savior of the world and I want to prove it! I hope you will be blessed by some of my finding!

INTRODUCTION

Like a script playing out on stage, God has written out his dream plan and chooses us to live it out if we accept. It is an awesome plan that will be done to give us everlasting peace and joy. The more we seek out the truth about our existence, the more we gain an understanding or revelation of why we do exist and how to live out his plan for our lives to the fullest.

There are good and bad forces that work behind the scenes of our realm of existence that we can't see. It is a realm were angels look into the affairs of mankind for our creator, while godless creatures work to wipe us out. Do you ever wonder why there is so much division and chaos in this world? We can see the good and the bad playing out all around us but can't see where the influence is coming from.

Who are the real enemies against mankind and where did they come from? These enemies have been trying to discredit us before God as bad actors. And the bad guy in charge of them is Satan.

Find out who these enemies are, what their leader's goal is, and why! It can revolutionize your life! His entities are the real bullies producing chaos and discord from behind the scenes of life. They can only accomplish any part of their agenda through the minds of people who accept their thoughts knowingly or unknowingly as their own. They twist the meaning of truth into a lie and call lies the truth. They are the real culprits that cause division between us all, through their deception and influence.

God's presence has always been here all throughout history. He has given us his wisdom, his principles and promises through his written script, so that we can apply them to our own lives. When we diligently practice these truths, they can impart freedom, good health, success, and prosperity. All of heaven works together with us to make sure God's word and will, his plan, is accomplished. You can't possibly believe that God isn't here after you read all about him in my lessons. The truth is, God has not only been here from the beginning, he has given us a star performer who has already secured our future and redeem us all, if we accept him.

A brief look into the following scientific subject matters of life itself can help us to understand some of the biblical writings that have been divinely reserved throughout all of time. They are: (a) the different levels of consciousness, (b) facts regarding the body, the blood and DNA (c) atoms, (d) the light spectrum, (e) the seasons of seed time and harvest time, and lastly (f) the survival of our own bodily and spiritual existence.

The bible tells us how God works behind the scenes on our behalf. It gives us history lessons on how others broke through barriers, defeated invisible enemies, and accomplished great things in their own lives and the lives of their loved ones because of their relationship with God! When we learn what God has done for others, we have a better tendency to believe in him for ourselves. It makes it easier to accept and believe in him as we familiarize ourselves with his words, feelings, and desires.

There are numerous stories in the bible that help us to understand who God is, why he did a lot of the things that he did, and what he has planned for the future. These lessons cover some of the stories.

We can learn so much about our wonderful creator, when we look at how he treated others. We can learn of his love when we see how he interacted with: Angels, Adam and his sons, Enoch, Noah, Job, Abraham, Isaac, Jacob, Joseph, Moses, David, Elisha, Peter and Paul the apostles, and the rest of the church. Not to mention his chosen women like: Eve, Sarah, Rebekah, Rachel and Leah, Tamar, Mary the mother of Jesus and Mary Magdalene. Every one of God's stories are written so that we can believe in him.

We all need someone who has got our backs no matter what is going on in our lives, bad or good. We don't have to face our difficulties alone! God does not want any one of us to perish. But the reality is that we have our own free will and there are some who choose to reject him.

We have access to all good things: love, Joy, peace, freedom, forgiveness, healing, and miracles. Hebrew 11:1 says, "Faith is the substance of things hoped for, and the evidence of things not seen." Faith is the substance that brings together all the components needed to manifest God's good will for us, when we believe and act on our God given right. We need to know what that right is!

I would not be here today, if it wasn't for God. I know what it is like to be a victim of anxiety, depression, and fear because it almost destroyed my life.

I tell my story of how I was set free from unseen enemy forces tormenting my thought life. These forces kept me from living my best life with their mind-altering assaults of defeat. I had to learn how to disregard and stop the lies of the enemy forces from becoming a reality in my life by submitting my life to Jesus Christ and following his lead. I received back-up in resisting the bullying thoughts of enemy forces through the Holy Spirit, for he is here to help us.

Jesus, the Son of God, healed the sick, cast out devils, raised the dead and more! He said that he came to give us a more abundant life! It is not a coincidence that he was born of God, died during Passover, rose from the dead on the day of Firstfruits, and the promise of the Holy Spirit was sent on the day of Pentecost. Jesus was sent to dealt with the curse that came about through Adam.

He himself was the first to receive a glorified eternal body and he will never die again! He is the proof that there is life now and after death. He died and rose again, so that he could lead us into eternal glory to be with him, where there are no bullies, no pain, no sickness, no loneliness, no poverty and no more death!

There is no more curse for all who are in Christ Jesus. This means that we have access to the Kingdom of God and his blessings right here and now. God's script says so! All good things are possible for us through God's own Son, Jesus Christ!

God loves us and has got our backs if we let him!

FREEDOM TO DREAM GREATER DREAMS

LESSON 1

As children, we should have the freedom to dream big dreams for the future. As a child, I envisioned myself becoming a teacher and an artist. I also had a desire to see the world. I also dreamed of growing up and meeting my prince charming, my knight in shining armor, the one person who would sweep me off my feet. He would whisk me away to be with him and we would live happily ever after. We all want to live happily ever after.

We all need unconditional and complete love from someone we esteem higher than ourselves who can catch us if we fall. One who is always available when we need them for encouragement, love, attention, and protection. We need a love that is much deeper than what we can get from our parents, our spouses, our children, and our friends.

There are so many of us that have come from broken homes as children. Even some of our own parents have come out of some kind of difficulty in their own childhood. One's trust (confidence, faith, and hope) can be crushed through unforgettable and traumatic events.

Jesus will never let us down! He is the answer to our completeness! The truth is, Jesus is the real prince of peace that expresses and reveals the love that we need. He loves us unconditionally no matter who we are, or what we have done in our lives. Jesus is this prince charming of my childhood dreams!

Sometimes I wonder why I was ever born, and what I am supposed to be doing with my own life. Is there a purpose for my existence? I want to get it right, don't you?

We don't immediately go to be with Jesus when we accept him, but he does come to us. He wants to love us and others through us. He wants us all to know that he loves us even though we are not perfect.

We all make mistakes and wrong choices in our journey through life. I make a lot of mistakes myself that affect others, as well as sabotage my own life. Then I wonder, what in the world am I doing to myself and others that I love so deeply? There have been times throughout my life when I would think back to the mistakes I had made and wished that I would have done things differently. There are times when the more I try to do my best in a situation, the harder it becomes. I am very thankful that God is a loving and forgiving God and he does not give up on any one of us. He wants us to go forward and create new and better life events as we learn from our past mistakes. There are scriptures that relate to exactly how it feels to make wrongful choices. Even some of the characters in the bible came up against roadblocks which hindered them from becoming the best that they could. But God got them through them all.

Paul, who was noted as a great leader in Christianity after Jesus had ascended up into heaven became the author of various books in the New Testament. In his books, which were actual letters written to different churches, he talked about having the same spiritual battles that we face every day. These battles are between good and evil. There is something and/or someone that gets in the way to hinder us from our best efforts. Here is what Paul wrote in a letter to the church in Rome.

Romans 7:15 (NKJV), "For what I am doing, I do not understand. For what I will to do, that I do not practice; but what I hate, that I do."

This scripture is quoted from the "New King James Version" (NKJV) of the bible. It is a little hard to follow what he is saying. There are so many other versions of the bible online. If you have a hard time understanding what something means in one version, you have the option of reading it from another. It might help to understand what is being said by reading the different versions.

The New Living Translation, which is another version of the bible, reads it this way. It says in (NLT), **"I don't understand myself, for I want to do what is right, but I don't do it. Instead, I do what I hate."**

Why do we do some things without thinking them through first? Or, we may have thought it through to the best of our knowledge before taking action, and things still did not turn out right. Where does this come from and why do we struggle with it?

Sometimes having more of the right information about a situation can help us make better decisions. We have to learn from our mistakes and use them to do better the next time.

The reason that we struggle with tough decisions and wrong thinking is because of what Adam and Eve did in the beginning of mankind's existence, so let's start there. God had told Adam that he could eat the fruit from all the trees that he created in the Garden of Eden, except from the tree of knowledge. It was a tree pertaining to "good and evil" and if he took from it, he would die. Then God made a woman for Adam and Adam called her name Eve. They both ate the forbidden fruit which leads to death and now death has been passed down throughout all generations. Since then, all of mankind has been constantly struggling with thoughts of good and evil, with sickness and disease, and ultimately facing death at some point.

In the book of Romans, where Paul said, **"I don't understand myself, for I want to do what is right, but I don't do it. Instead, I do what I hate"**, he was admitting that he did not always win the battle of doing the right thing. He had the desire to do the right thing, but still struggled with something that was working against his own will to do good.

Romans 7:19 (NKJV), "For the <u>good that I will to do</u>, I do not do; but <u>the evil I will not to do</u>, that I <u>practice</u>."

Romans 7:20 (NKJV), "Now if I do what I will not to do, it is no longer I who does it, but <u>sin that dwells in me</u>."

Paul is a Christian! Why would he say, **"it is no longer I who does it, but it is sin that dwells in me"**, if he is a Christian"?

It sounds like he blames his weakness on something bad or sinful that is in him, but not his actual self. He had recently been converted from the belief system of the Old Testament laws to the new laws of Christianity. He had always desired to please God in everything he did, but he also faced battles that were going on, in his mind. I don't know exactly what he was referring to that he thought was so sinful in these verses, but whatever it was, he recognized that it was not part of his new Christ-like nature. It was a thought, deed or hindrance that he did not approve of. Instead of accepting it as a part of his new nature, he condemned it, not himself. He describes it as though it was a separate entity that he called sin. He did not let it overtake his feelings and put him under condemnation.

Before Paul (formerly called Saul) had become a believer in Jesus Christ, he had been a persecutor of the Christian church movement. He did believe in God, and thought it was in God's best interest to stop this movement. He thought it was a cult so he went from town to town trying to stop them.

Acts 8:3 (NKJV), "As for Saul, he made havoc of the church, entering every house, and dragging off men and women, committing them to prison."

Saul (who became Paul after his conversion) thought he was doing the right thing by protecting his religious beliefs about God, until the following happened that changed his life forever.

Acts 9:3-5 (NKJV), "As he journeyed, he came near Damascus, and suddenly a light shone around him from heaven. Then he fell to the ground, and heard a voice saying to him, 'Saul, Saul, why are you persecuting me?' And he said, 'Who are you, Lord?' Then the Lord said, 'I am Jesus, whom you are persecuting....'"

In this verse, Jesus himself confronted Saul and told him that the people he was persecuting were his people. From this experience, Saul asked for forgiveness and became a true believer in Jesus Christ. He dedicated the rest of his life to transforming others to the new Christ-like nature. He wanted to share his newfound experience with others. He was forgiven for all and any sins he had ever committed by accepting Jesus, the Son of God as his savior. He wanted others to know about Jesus and how they could be redeemed from their own sins too.

Romans 8:1-2 (NKJV), Paul said, **"There is therefore now no condemnation to them which are in Christ Jesus, who walk not after the flesh, but after the Spirit. For the law of the Spirit of life in Christ Jesus hath made me free from the law of sin and death."**

After Saul was renamed Paul, he developed a strong faith. But he still had struggles, and so do we. Paul says to "walk not after the flesh" which means to not give into the corruptible nature and desires caused by mankind's fall. Paul knows by experience that it can be hard to do so continuously, without making mistakes. We are not our own god. We did not make our own bodies or the world that we live in. As long as we live here on earth in our bodies, we are limited by our bodies. Like Paul, we should strive to do the best we can, even though we don't always do.

It is not necessarily a bad thing that we are limited by our own bodies. We can't see and hear everything going on around us with our eyes and ears. For example, we can't see sound waves or some light rays, but we know that they exist.

There are spiritual forces that we can't see or hear directly that are good and bad. We are somewhat protected by our bodies from being exposed to full-fledged evil that lurks in the spirit world. We can't normally see them with our natural eyes. There are also angels sent by God who work behind the scenes in the spirit realm for the benefit of mankind. The bible says they battle for us against evil forces.

On our own, we are not experienced enough to take on these forces that can hurt us. On the other hand, we have a God in charge of it all. He is experienced in dealing with the bad and the good in this world and everywhere else. These spiritual forces that we can't normally or physically see and hear can affect us through our thoughts.

Bad thoughts can come from spiritual forces at work that are separate from our own thoughts. The main character in charge of it all is called the devil. This enemy can pick a fight with us (through our thought life) in an attempt to stir up the wrong feelings. His spiritual influence can cause us to become stressed out, confused and unsure of our own ability to resist bad desires and thoughts. He wants us to except his thoughts as our own. For example, temptation is a real strong weapon of the enemy. Temptation can cause us to make bad decisions instead of doing the right thing. The enemy tries to use our minds as his battlefield, and if we don't resist his persuasive thoughts, they can cause chaos in our lives.

The enemy has been around since before Adam and Eve, and he has had plenty of experience preying on human weakness. He knows our weakness can be manipulated through the five senses. For example, a bad habit can become a stronghold when doing it obsessively in order to satisfy selfish motives and desires. If we focus on something enough, it can become a habit. It may satisfy temporarily and then leave us wanting more. In some cases, it actually causes chemical reactions in the brain. It affects the whole body by giving withdrawal symptoms.

We were made by God to have desire toward him, and to have a loving relationship with him. Before the fall of Adam and Eve, the bible says that the Lord God came down to where they were and visited with them daily (Genesis 3:8). Things were perfect between them all. Their desire was all good toward each other, and they probably never question anything before. They had just assumed and trusted God about everything.

The devil, who worked through the serpent appealed to their five senses, in order to trick them into wanting something they thought they didn't already have. He even twisted the truth about what God said into a lie. He told them that they would not die. He persuaded them to question and disregard what God had said. He caused them to sin (give offense) against God by feeding them thoughts that appealed to their senses. They listened, they saw, they touched and may have even smelled the fruit, and then they tasted. If the enemy would have never given them the suggestion, they would have not even thought about eating from the forbidden fruit tree.

When we do things that we think we shouldn't, we then have feelings of condemnation. Then these feelings affect our future decisions. They cause us to think about or focus on thoughts like, "I messed up. Why did I do such a stupid thing? I am worthless. I did it again. etc." Paul even said, **"Oh wretched man that I am! Who will deliver me from this body of death?" in Romans 7:24-25 (NKJV).**

He realized that we are far from perfect. If we dwell on negative things that we have done or that we do, we start to think that it is how we are. We accept it as our nature and identity. This in turn, keeps us stuck in that state of mind, and it affects our decisions the next time.

Throughout this study, we will find that we can be overcomers through what Jesus did for us all. When we study the man Jesus and how he gave his life, we find freedom from condemnation and unbelief. Once we learn and get it into our heads that we are loved by God, and are made righteous in his sight through Jesus Christ, our state of mind starts to change for the better.

We have to realize that there are spiritual forces that send thoughts our way. All thoughts do not necessarily originate from our own thoughts. Once we get this revelation, we have access to a new spiritual weapon of warfare through the armor of God. We can resist it instead of claiming it as our own.

The laws that the enemy uses against us to take us down are called the laws of Moses. They are also referred to as the laws of sin and death. It doesn't matter if we know these laws for ourselves. The enemy keeps a record of all failures against God's laws and tries to bring them to our attention. He first tempts us to do the wrong thing. Then he tries to give us self-condemning thoughts that we are a failure in the eyes of God. As we try to get it right the next time, he knocks us down by tempting us to do it all over again. His goal is to keep us practicing the wrong thing. He does not play the game fairly. He wants us to be stuck under his influence, and then he can control our thoughts to live a life of condemnation and defeat. If he can keep our focus on blaming ourselves, he can keep us from moving forward to do better things.

Once we realize that accepting Christ as our redeemer wipes out any penalty against us, we gain the upper hand. Satan has no ground to accuse us anymore, and his power over our lives is no longer in force.

If you don't know your rights, how can you defend yourself? If you are in Christ, you are not under the law of sin and death, but under the law of grace, and grace is all good. You are living in freedom from unbelief and can create better dreams for the rest of your life.

Let's say you have been practicing a bad habit, and then let's turn that around and focus on learning a good habit. For example, if you want to become good at a sport like football or basketball, then you have to practice. If you never teach yourself what works for you, how can you get good enough to score. You may get lucky now and then, but not all the time. You work on getting your body and mind in alignment to be able to hit the target. You work on were to stand, the force that you have to propel the ball, and the position of how to hold the ball before you throw or kick it. You practice until you get it figured out. You are teaching and changing your mind and body coordination. You don't stop there. You continue to practice.

There is nothing wrong with the word "habit" itself, which also means addiction. These words have gotten a bad rap. A definition of addiction is being dependent on a particular substance, thing, or activity. Ideas or suggestions can come from a good source or a bad source. Some of the other words for the word addiction are craving, compulsion, repetition, want, need, requirement or obsession. These words all affect and connect with feelings. Addiction can be anything you love to do or hate to do, but still do it. It depends on what you are addicted to. Is it good for you or is it bad for you? Does the addiction produce good or bad results? Does it pertain to life or death?

In this same chapter of the book of Romans 7:4-5, Paul talked about two kinds of fruitfulness. One was the (good) fruit of God and the other was the (evil) fruit that leads to death. How do we habitually or continually produce the good fruit or good life events? This fruitfulness Paul writes about can be described as the results we expect to achieve by our actions.

The book of Galatians tells us what good fruit is.

Galatians 5:22-23 (NKJV), "...The fruit of the Spirit is love, joy, peace, longsuffering (being tolerant of others), **kindness, goodness, faithfulness, gentleness, self-control."**

Paul says, **"Against such there is no law!"**

The good fruit always produces an abundant harvest. Just as farmers inspect their crops to separate the good from the bad, their focus is on the food they want to produce. This is what Paul did with the good and the bad. He remembered that he was not under the law of condemnation, but under the new law of grace. In this way, he could continue to focus on the good and move forward.

After his conversion, he went through so much in his ministry. He was shipwrecked, robbed, imprisoned, bitten by a poisonous snake and many times without food and shelter. The bible tells us that when he was bitten by a poisonous snake, he just shook it off and had no harm. God saw him through it all.

Romans 8:10 (NIV), "But if Christ is in you, then even though your body is subject to death because of sin, the Spirit gives life because of righteousness.

In **Romans 7:24 (NKJV)**, when Paul had said, **"Oh wretched man that I am! Who will deliver me from this body of death?"**, he goes on to say in the next verse that he knows what to do about this inferior feeling of worthlessness. He said, "**I thank God-through Jesus Christ our Lord!**" He got his focus right back on who Jesus had made him to be, which is in the righteousness of God.

Paul the apostle of Jesus Christ was determined to do his best to do the right thing. He would not let earthly passions and difficulties imposed on him by others keep him from finishing his course. He was obsessed with pushing through toward his goal. He was addicted to completing his cause.

He speaks about his determination in the book of Acts.

Acts 20:24 (NKJV), "But none of these things move me; nor do I count my life dear to myself, so that I may finish my race with joy, and the ministry which I received from the Lord Jesus."

Paul had many miracles under his ministry, and he loved his work. To him, all the bad things that happened did not compare to the joy he felt in helping others. God used him to perform marvelous miracles for people who were suffering in one way or another. He healed people of crippling diseases and unclean spirits. And, he raised the dead! He won thousands to accepting Jesus as their savior. He had a purpose for his existence. He expressed God's love to others by all the things he did for them.

One time, he and his traveling companion Silas were put in chains and imprisoned. They began to pray and sing songs of praise to God. As they were singing, the earth began to shake and their chains fell off, as well as the chains of all the other prisoners. It was a mighty demonstration of the power of God to set the captives free.

We have one chance to live this life. I want it to be the best that I could possibly have. My life is far from perfect, and I have made a lot of mistakes and still will. But I am not giving up and want to press through like Paul says in Philippians 3:13.

Philippians 3:13 (NKJV), "One thing I do, forgetting those things which are behind and reaching forward to those things which are ahead."

There was a reason that Paul was determined and excited about reaching his goal. There was a prize at the end of his race. Don't let your life be in vain. God has something in store for everyone who excepts his Son, Jesus.

You could think of this new lifestyle or way of living in Christ as being comparable to a sporting event of football or basketball. The idea is to cross the goal line or score points when throwing the ball into the target area. We have a star player and his name is Jesus.

Paul was determined to reach his goal and accumulate points (or victories) with as many souls as he could. Even in sports, mistakes are made. But you learn from them, you let them go, and move on. The whole point is to win. You will not loose with Jesus as your front-runner, your coach and your leader. The end of the bible tells us that he won the race already for us.

In Philippians 3:14 (NKJV) Paul said, **"I press toward the goal for the prize of the upward call of God in Christ Jesus."**

Someday, we will have perfect unflawed bodies. We will know and live in the perfect love, joy and peace as children of God forever. 1 John 3:2 says we shall be just like Jesus is right now. He is surrounded in the love of the Father and so will we. The prize at the end of our race is a life of peace, love and joy. It is accomplished by the nature and purpose of Jesus Christ, the perfect Son of God. So, run your race with your head held high!

TRUE IDENTITY

---◆---

LESSON 2

In studying about God, I have come to realize something about the whole ordeal of why we struggle with life. It has made me down-right angry that we were made from a pure and loving God and yet have to fight our way through life to stay afloat. As a young adult I used to feel like I had been short changed and that the world owed me. I felt that life should have been better than it was for me at that time.

We learn that nothing in this world is free, not even water. I hope we never come to the place that we will have to pay for clean air to breath. That is the only thing left that is still free. It all cost something.

It's a system that works in this world for most. We give to each other to get something in return. But, if we don't have money or something else to give, then we can't get some of our basic necessities needed to survive, like it is with the homeless. Everything comes with a cost in this world.

I have also come to realize that it's not the world that has cheated us out of having a 100% blessed life. It owes us nothing. It is because of Satan, the thief who has been trying to destroy us by stealing our true identity. We were originally created in God's likeness. We should be healthy, strong, fearless, wise, happy and at peace. We should be confident in the world around us and be able to live awesome lives. This is how we were made to live in the first place.

I sometimes get angry with myself for the mistakes I make. I then lose my self-confidence and like Paul had said, "I hate what I did". Don't let condemnation reign (or control) you're thinking. Don't let it become part of your identity. Get to know who you were meant to be. We all have a purpose in God's eyes. Jesus paid the price to give us abundant life and he did not die in vain. It cost him his life in order to give us a better one.

Romans 8:1 (NKJV), "There is therefore now no condemnation to those who are in Christ Jesus

Paul had mentioned the law of sin that dwelt in his body, but he also mentioned the Spirit of God, by Christ who dwelt in him too (Romans 7:17-25). Christ gives life to our whole being which includes our mortal bodies. We become children of God and even as children we get into trouble. Thank goodness God loves us as his children and does not condemn us for our shortcomings. Paul himself knew he was not perfect and did not always get it right, so he put his trust in Christ.

People had so much faith in the miracles of Paul that they were healed just by touching a piece of his garment that he had worn while ministering to others. Paul had opportunity to boast about all the miracles that were done in his ministry, but he knew that the glory belonged to God. God was the one who was really behind all the miracles. He used Paul as a vessel to bring healing to all those who asked.

Paul talks about a thorn in the flesh or messenger of Satan to "buffet" him, "lest he be exalted above measure" in 2 Corinthians 12:7-10. He asked God to totally take care of the harassment once and for all. But God said, "My grace is sufficient for you, for my strength (or power) is made perfect in weakness."

In verse ten Paul said, "for when I am weak, then I am strong." What he meant was that his strength and ability to overcome evil as it came against him was from God. Even though he was beaten, shipwrecked, bitten by a viper and faced many other dangers to his life, he made it through them all. He knew the credit belonged to God. When he was faced with a situation that he could do nothing about, he counted on God to show himself stronger than the situation at hand.

Paul had a servant attitude. His intentions were always good, and he tried to serve all who came to him. In **Philippians 2:3** he said, **"Let each esteem others better than themselves."** He did not boast in himself, but in Christ. In **John 15:5** Jesus had said, **"...without me you can do nothing."** Paul was trying to be an example of love to others in doing the works of Christ for them.

 Paul kept in remembrance what God had said, **"My grace is sufficient for you, for my strength (my power) is made perfect in weakness."** The way to resist the enemy and anything he may bring against us is to surrender to God and let him take over as needed. His grace is sufficient to get us through our trials. We don't lose! Even when we die, Satan does not win because God has that area covered too! Surrendering to God is the most important thing we can do in our lives no matter what happens in this world.

Romans 8:14 (NIV), "For those who are led by the Spirit of God, they are the children of God.

We belonged to God from the beginning. God has confronted the thief who scammed us out of our true identity and got it back for us. He then does even better by making us his sons and daughters, not just his creation. He takes our old identity and give us a new one as his children. We are his children under the name of Jesus, and the enemy is afraid of that name because it belongs to God.

HIS IMAGE

---◆---

LESSON 3

God must think it is very important for us to learn as much as we can about him because of what he says in the book of Hosea. In **Hosea 4:6 (KJV)** He had said, **"My people are destroyed for lack of knowledge."**

The bible tells us that there is life after death. Do you ever question what will happen to you or where you would go once you die? Do you think that you will just cease to exist? Depending on what you do with your life now determines what will happen to you forever.

The big question is, have you lived good enough that you can truly say you are going to a happier place when you die? Have you lived your life without ever doing anything wrong? Do you have the ability to save yourself from whatever is out there on the other side?

The sure way of knowing the answers to all these questions is in learning about the man called Jesus. The bible tells us that he redeems people from the lifelong effects of sin. So how is it possible for another individual (Jesus, who lived so long ago) free us from the effects of sin and secure our future?

Let's begin to explore who the Father and the Son are, and how they relate to God our creator. Jesus himself had said in the book of **John 14:9 (NKJV), "He who has seen me has seen the Father."**

"Like father, like son" is a popular phrase. It means that a son's character or behavior can be expected to resemble that of his father. Jesus was the first and only true Son of God Himself born through the womb of a virgin woman named Mary. He was born to reveal his own Father to the world.

While Jesus was living on the earth, he and his Father were characterized as two separate entities according to recorded history in the book of Matthew. On a couple of occasions, his own Father actually spoke from Heaven, while Jesus was standing on the ground. In **Matthew 3:17** and **Matthew 17:5 (NKJV),** a voice from heaven said, **"This is my beloved Son in whom I am well pleased."** This tells us that the heavenly Father and the Son were two separate beings of existence.

The book of Colossians was written after Jesus died, rose from the dead, and then ascended into the heavens. It was written by Paul to a church in the ancient city of Colossae.

In Colossians 1:12-14, Paul talks about giving thanks to the "Father" for He has delivered us from the power of darkness. He has also translated us into his "Son's" kingdom, and we have redemption through his "Son's" blood, and the forgiveness of sins. Paul is telling us what the Father has done for us through Jesus, his Son.

In the next verse below, Paul explains who the "Son" is.

Colossians 1:15 (NKJV) says, **"He is the image of the invisible God, the firstborn over all creation."**

The next few verses are where it starts to get a little harder to understand who Paul is referring to.

Colossians 1:16-17 (NKJV), "For by HIM all things were created that are in heaven and that are on earth, visible and invisible, whether thrones or dominions or principalities or powers. All things were created through HIM and for HIM. And he is before all things, and in HIM all things consist."

Who was the one who had a hand in creating the heavens and the earth? When these verses mention the word "HIM", who is Paul referring to? You could put "the Father" in place of the word "HIM" and it would seem to make more sense, except for the fact that in the previous verse (verse fifteen), the Father was not the firstborn over all creation. He was not born; however, his Son was.

If you were to put the word "God" in place of the word "HIM" it makes perfect sense. God is our creator. After all, in Genesis 2:7 it says that God formed Adam from the dust of the ground and breathed into his nostrils the breath of life.

So, let's see how it reads when we replace "HIM" with the word "GOD".

Colossians 1:16-17 (NKJV), "For by GOD all things were created that are in heaven and that are on earth, visible and invisible, whether thrones or dominions or principalities or powers. All things were created through GOD and for GOD. And He is before all things, and in GOD all things consist."

This is true! God is the creator! Now, if we go to the very next verse in Colossians and put it all together, we see that Paul is actually referring to Jesus, the Son of God because he is the firstborn human from the dead.

Colossians 1:18-19 (NKJV), "He is the <u>head of the body, the church, who is the beginning</u>, the firstborn from the dead, that in all things he may have the preeminence. For <u>God was pleased to have all his fullness dwell in him</u>…"

What is God's fullness? **Colossians 2:9 says, for in him (Christ) dwelleth all the <u>fullness of the Godhead bodily</u>.** What is the Godhead? The Father, the Son and the Holy Spirit are the Godhead. The body and man called Jesus housed the Godhead! Jesus, himself said, "Before Abraham was, I am" (John 8:57-58).

In Colossians 1:15 where it says, <u>he is the image of the invisible God, the firstborn over all creation</u>, Paul had to be saying that Jesus was the earthly or bodily image and presence of the invisible God. We can relate to God through Jesus. He has existed as the image of the invisible God from the beginning and He was also referred to as the Word of God.

John 1:1, 14 (KJV) states, "In the beginning was the Word, and the Word was with God, and the <u>Word was God</u>. (Verse 14) And <u>the Word was made flesh</u> (human) <u>and dwelt among us</u>, and we beheld his glory, the glory as of <u>the only begotten of the Father</u>, full of grace and truth."

We could say that the Godhead which is the Father, Son and Holy Spirit dwelt in the body of Jesus. God came to us in the body of Jesus which proves Jesus as our God. I could use "THEM" to replace "HIM" and it would still be right.

Colossians 1:16-17 (NKJV), "For by THEM all things were created that are in heaven and that are on earth, visible and invisible, whether thrones or dominions or principalities or powers. All things were created through THEM and for THEM. And THEY are before all things, and in THEM all things consist."

The Father, the Son and the Holy Spirit are one as God with different functions. They are referred to as the "Trinity".

I don't totally understand God, but I do know that he was pleased to dwell in a human body and acknowledged Jesus (a human being) as his own Son. If you accept his Sonship as your own, then

God will be pleased to dwell in you as he did with Jesus. This idea of Sonship is what I want to explore in more detail as we get deeper in this study.

In the book of Genesis, where it speaks about the beginning of mankind, the scriptures tell us that God had talked to someone while he was about to create mankind.

Genesis 1:26 (KJV), "Then God said, 'Let US make man in OUR image, after OUR likeness.'"

God was talking to someone when he said, "Let us make man in our image." Why did he use the word "our"? Who was the other entity or entities that God was talking to when he refers to us? There are angels and other such creatures that God created long before he created us. God may have been talking about their assistance in some way, I don't really know! But if he created the whole universe himself, then I don't think he needed their help in creating mankind. I figured he probably created mankind in the same manner that he had created everything else which was by his Spirit and his Word. In the first chapter of Genesis, it says that the "Spirit of God" moved upon the waters while the world was being created. There was at least seven times that the chapter repeated the phrase "and God said", as he spoke things into existence through "his Word".

When Adam was created, the bible only lists God as the one who made him. So, I don't really know for sure if the "us" and the "our" is referring to any other beings. However, the writer of the book of Genesis is recognizing more than one entity as unified in some way.

Genesis 1:26 (KJV), "Then God said, 'Let US make man in OUR image, after OUR likeness.'"

Genesis 1:27, "God created man in his own image..."

Who is his own image? The Son is the image of the invisible God. Who is the firstborn over all creation? The Son is the firstborn over all creation.

Even though these scriptures in the book of Genesis do not tell us that the image of God was God's Son, Paul tells us that he was. The word image is a form, reflection or representation of someone or something. In the beginning, Jesus was not born yet here on earth or named. He was kept secret and has now been revealed to the world as the man Jesus (Romans 16:25-26).

We were created after God's likeness. Maybe we are a little like him in personality. The bible shows that God can get angry. He can be compassionate and show other emotions like we do. Maybe we are like him in appearance or shape too. The bible does say that God made man in his image and his likeness.

But now we are not just born from a created being (Adam) that fell from grace. Through Christ Jesus we are a new creation born directly from his Spirit. We are sons and daughters of the most-high God.

SEEING GOD

———◆———

LESSON 4

Even though God is Spirit, he revealed himself to people of the earth from time to time throughout the Old Testament. There are many mentions of the particular phrase, "angel of the Lord" when God communicated with humans. Sometimes it was an angel who would bring a message or to complete a task as a representative of "the Lord". Other times it was the Lord.

For example, in Genesis 18:1-14, there was one occasion where the Lord and two men appeared to the man Abraham. The scripture says that Abraham saw three men. So the Lord must have somehow looked like the other two men.

A little later in the story, the two other men (who were really angels), were sent to a place called Sodom. They were sent to destroy the city with fire and brimstone because of the great wickedness of the people. Abraham had a nephew named Lot who happened to be living in that city. The Lord told Abraham that he was going to have the city destroyed. So, Abraham pleaded with the Lord not to destroy everyone in the city. He was concerned for his nephew, Lot and his family. At the request of Abraham, the angels brought Lot and his family out of the city before destroying it. Genesis 19:1,15 and 16 uses the term angels and men interchangeably to describe the two angels.

Wherever the phrase "angel of the Lord" was mentioned appearing before people, it was either the Lord himself or a representative sent on his behalf. People could literally see or hear him when he chose to let them.

There was another time when the "angel of the Lord" appeared to Moses in flames of fire burning within a bush (Exodus 3:1-4). It happened in a place called Horeb, or the mountain of God (which is also Mt. Sinai). Moses had noticed the burning bush because it was not being consumed by the fire. When he tried to get closer to see it, <u>God</u> called out to him from the midst of the burning bush and told him not to come any closer for he was now standing on holy ground.

There are scriptures that talk about God's appearance. His bodily form is mentioned in many places of the bible. There are stories that show he has hands and feet, a back side, eyes and a face. But God is different in that he is holy and supernatural.

Way before the birth of Jesus and in the book of Exodus, the Lord God's appearance is mentioned. Moses, the man who had talked to God in the burning bush became a leader to God's people, the Israelites. Throughout his life, he had a lot of conversations with God regarding what he was supposed to do to lead the people. Moses wanted to know more about this God who was giving him an important assignment, so he asked God to show him his **"glory"** (magnificence or radiance). God showed Moses a part of what he looked like. In this story, God had a body!

The Lord God said in **Exodus 33: 20-23 (NKJV), "You cannot see my <u>face</u>; <u>for no man shall see me, and live</u>.' And the LORD said, 'Here is a place by me, and you shall stand on the rock. It shall**

be, while my glory passes by, that I will put you in the cleft of the rock and will cover you with my <u>hand</u> while I pass by. Then I will take away my <u>hand</u>, and you shall see my <u>back</u>; but my <u>face</u> shall not be seen.'"

There are other scriptures found in other parts of the bible that I think are important to note. In the book of Exodus 24:1-2, 9-10, it says that Aaron (the High Priest who is also the brother of Moses), Aaron's sons and seventy elders (or leaders) saw God. But only at a vast distance! God had told them they could only "worship from afar". Moses was the only one able to get close enough to God in all his glory and holiness, and he was limited to seeing God's backside.

Here is what Aaron and the others saw of God.

Exodus 24:10 (NKJV) says, **"…and they saw the God of Israel. And there was under his <u>feet</u> as it were a <u>paved work of sapphire stone, and it was like the very heavens</u> in its clarity."**

God allowed them to see him from afar.

This manifestation of God that they saw was similar to another story that happened many, many years later. A prophet named Ezekiel had a vision of God up in the heavens. He saw living creatures in heaven, and over their heads he saw a throne and what God looked like.

In **Ezekiel 1:26-28 (NIV)** he saw, **"…what looked like a throne of lapis lazuli** (sapphire), **and high above on the throne was a <u>figure like that of a man</u>. I saw that from what appeared to be his waist up he looked like glowing metal, as if full of fire, and that from there down he looked like fire; and brilliant light surrounded him. Like the appearance of a rainbow in the clouds on a rainy day, so was the radiance around him. This was the appearance of the likeness of the glory of the LORD. When I saw it, I fell facedown, and I heard the voice of one speaking."**

These few scriptures describing the appearance of God had happened way before the birth of Jesus on earth. They are found in the Old Testament of the bible.

There is also another description found in the book of Daniel, also way before the birth of Jesus. It is a very moving story about three men that would not worship the golden image (or idol) that King Nebuchadnezzar of Babylon commanded all the people to do. These men were faithful followers of the real God. They were to be put to death by being cast into a large fiery furnace on the kings' order. The king got so angry with them that he ordered the fire to be heated seven times hotter. The flame was so hot that it killed the soldiers who were putting them into the furnace. When the king looked into the ferocious furnace, he got a surprise of his lifetime.

In **Daniel 3:25 NKJV)**, the king said, **"I see <u>four men</u> loose, <u>walking</u> in the midst of the fire; and they are not hurt, and the <u>form of the fourth is like the Son of God</u>."**

I believe the king did not know who the one true God was. He did not know who the Son of God was either, Jesus had not yet been born. He may have been told about the God of Daniel but did not accept him. The king was a worshipper of pagan gods. Pagan worshippers believed that their gods had offspring. He was acknowledging that he saw some sort of being (able to resist the fire) keeping the other three men from being burned. He knew there was a higher power than his own pagan gods at work here. In **Daniel 3:29** the king acknowledged the power of their God and said, **"There is no other God who can deliver like this!"** From this experience, the king called the God of these three men, "THE HIGHEST GOD".

In the book of Daniel there is another account of God. Daniel had a vision and he said he saw the "Ancient of Days" sitting on a throne (which was a fiery flame). His garment was white as snow and his hair was like pure wool. God may be invisible, but he presents himself with a form or shape.

The Old Testament books that were written long before Jesus was born, show that God had a bodily form, but he was definitely a different substance than us. His substance was so powerful that he said no man could see his glory up close and live. That all changed later in history.

DWELLING PLACE AMONG HIS PEOPLE

$$\sim\!\!\diamond\!\!\sim$$

LESSON 5

During the time that God had given Moses the ten commandments, the Israelites told Moses that they were deeply afraid of God's omnipotent presence. So, God had them build a portable earthly dwelling place (or tent) where he could communicate and be among them.

The ten commandments and other laws were presented to the people to show them what to do and not to do. There were over six hundred laws. This covenant was a conditional agreement between God and them. They were required to obey all God's commands, and in return, he would be their God. He would protect them from all evil, give them victory over all their enemies and bless them richly.

If they disobeyed any of the law, they were required to bring an animal as a sacrifice upon the alter for their crime. Instead of them being punished for their transgression of the law, they could transfer the sin sentencing (or consequence) to an animal, and the animal would be put to death instead. If they didn't follow through, then the consequence for what they did fell on themselves.

If they obeyed the laws, then they were blessed. If they disobeyed the laws, they would be cursed. The bulk of the blessings and curses are listed in Deuteronomy chapter twenty-eight.

This covenant between God and the Israelites using the ten commandments, other laws and animal sacrifices was to be a temporary solution for any sinful acts. The sinful person was dealt with for the good of all. It kept them all from total destruction. The sin nature has expressed itself in many horrific ways throughout history and we are affected by decisions of good and evil, blessings and curses all the time.

The old covenant laws that were set in place to deal with sin are similar to our laws of today. We make some laws based on an individual or group of individuals that cause a problem for themselves or others. For example, if you rob a bank and get caught, you will be judged and punished. You will most likely lose your freedom. The law shows you that it is wrong to rob a bank. The law also shows that if you speed and get caught, you can get a ticket (pay a penalty) or serve jail time. The law of speeding was put in to place because the act of speeding can cause a devastating car accident. The law protects us from danger and needed to be in place. Most of our laws were made for the lawless.

When we die, these laws that we live by now do not affect us anymore, and they certainly do nothing for us while in the grave. They can't save us from eternal death. Most of these laws punish for wrongdoing. They can take away freedom. They give evil for evil. You do bad, it does bad.

As I had said earlier, under the Israelites old covenant laws, the person who committed a crime would make amends by bringing an animal to be killed as a substitute. The animal would pay the price for them. Back then, animals were their livelihood, their food and their income.

Nowadays we pay with money to keep our freedom. Some crimes cost a lot of money. Some crimes can cause you to be enslaved in prison for years. You become a slave to the evil that you do. This is kind of like how the old covenant worked for the Israelites. They paid a price or in some cases they were put to death.

God's ultimate plan was to give all of mankind a better covenant and a better life. He had started this process over 400 years before the old covenant or the laws of Moses were even established. God said that he would bless the nations of the world through the seed (or offspring) of a man named Abram.

The old covenant was to be a temporary solution until God could bring about (through his people) a king and a savior that would permanently fix everything. This savior would be born through the Israelites and live under the old covenant that was between them and God. He would be the only one who could obey all of the old covenant laws and bring the sin penalty to its end for his own life.

Jesus was born the Son of God and the son of man. He was the earthly vessel and dwelling place that God himself housed. Mankind could interface with God Almighty without fear of his presence through an earthly man instead of a tent.

A PROMISE FROM GOD

LESSON 6

God had made a previous covenant with a man named Abram long before the time of Moses and the ten commandments. Abram had greatly honored God and was referred to as the friend of God. The Israelites that lived in the times of Moses were descendants of Abram.

This previous covenant with God and Abram was one that was to affect the whole world throughout time.

In **Genesis 12:2-3 (NKJV)** God said, **"I will make you a great nation; I will bless you and make your name great; and you shall be a blessing. I will bless those who bless you, and I will curse him who curses you; and in you <u>all</u> the families of the earth shall be blessed."**

In Genesis 15:1-5, God had promised Abram and his wife, Sarai, that they would have a son together, which they did years later in their old age. His name was Isaac. But years before Isaac was born, Abram had another son through Hagar, Sarai's maidservant (Genesis 16:1-16). He was named Ishmael. The promise that God had made was to come through the son named Isaac who was to be born from Abram and Sarai. God said that he would make all families of the earth be blessed through Isaac's descendants.

In **Genesis 15:5 NKJV)**, God said, **"Look now toward heaven, and count the stars if you are able to number them.' And he said to him, 'So shall your descendants be.'"**

The whole chapter of Genesis chapter seventeen is about God establishing his covenant with Abram. God changed Abram's name to Abraham and his wife Sarai to Sarah. Abraham was to have all the males of his clan to be circumcised as a sign of his part of the covenant. This circumcision included anyone who joined into Abrahams family like in-laws, servants and friends.

Things didn't get too complicated until later, when God had to make another covenant with Abraham's descendants. He gave them the ten commandments with all the detailed don'ts and dos. The over 600 commandments did not exist until the time of Moses. The Abrahamic covenant between Abraham and God was a much simpler covenant than all the strict rules that were pretty much almost impossible to keep that had to come later.

God tested Abraham's faith and obedience when his son Isaac grew into a young boy. God told Abraham to take his son Isaac to a particular place and offer him as a sacrifice. Even though he loved his son dearly, Abraham was willing to trust God at his word. He trusted that God would fulfill his promise to bless all the families of the earth through his son Isaac. He didn't know how God was going to keep his promise, but he trusted God with his own son.

That test had to be almost unbearable for Abraham to even think about doing. Don't worry, it had a good ending.

Genesis chapter twenty-two has the bulk of this part of the story.

Abraham did not have to follow through with the sacrifice of his son. <u>God gave him an animal substitute to sacrifice instead.</u> This animal substitute sacrifice became very important to the Israelite descendants during the time of Moses. It is also important to note God's own Son would become a sacrifice for the sins of humanity. Abraham was willing to do as God said even though he didn't have to, so God confirmed his covenant with him again.

Genesis 22:15-18 (NKJV), "Then the angel of the LORD called to Abraham a second time out of heaven, and said: 'By myself I have sworn, says the LORD, because you have done this thing, and have not withheld your son, your only son— blessing I will bless you, and multiplying I will multiply your descendants as the stars of the heaven and as the sand which is on the seashore; and your descendants shall possess the gate of their enemies. In your <u>seed</u> all the nations of the earth shall be blessed, because you have obeyed my voice.'"

God had tested Abraham and Abraham passed the test. Many, many years later, God gave us his only Son, Jesus through the bloodline of Abrahams descendants. Jesus was the seed God was talking about. He was a descendent of Abraham. Throughout history up until the time of Jesus, God was working behind the scenes to accomplish his promise to Abraham.

Abraham's own son Isaac grew up and had his own family. Isaac had a son named Jacob who God renamed Israel. Jesus would come through this lineage of Abraham, Isaac and Jacob. Jacob's children became known as the Israelites.

There is so much history in the bible regarding the Israelites and God. He had his work cut out for him in making things happen in his promise to Abraham.

In Genesis chapter thirty-seven and then again in chapter forty-five, it tells a story of a young man named Joseph. He was the eleventh son of Jacob (Israel). Joseph was a great grandson of Abraham. Joseph had one brother, ten half-brothers and one sister. He and his brothers eventually became known as the twelve tribes of Israel.

The story of Joseph is a very interesting and heartfelt story. When Joseph was a young teenager, he had two prophetic dreams and shared them with his brothers and his father. In one dream, him and his brothers were binding bundles of grain stalks in the field. He described the dream as if each bundle represented his life and his brothers. He tells them that all their bundles (called sheaves) gathered around his bundle and honored it with great reverence. He then had a second dream with the sun, moon and eleven stars all bowing down to him. His brothers hated him for his dreams, and thought it was ridiculous that he believed he would reign over them. Joseph's dream of reigning over them eventually did come to pass (Genesis chapters 37, 39-45).

Long story short, his brothers had sold him to be a slave and he ended up in Egypt. They had told their father that he was killed by a wild animal. While a slave in Egypt, he went through a few traumatic events. The worst thing that happened to him was that he was put into a prison for a crime he did not commit. While in prison, he was asked to interpret a disturbing dream that the Pharaoh of Egypt had dreamed. He told the Pharaoh that there would be seven good prosperous years of food and then seven years of famine. Joseph also gave the Pharaoh the solution to the problem. He told the Pharaoh to store up food from the seven good years for the seven bad years. Pharaoh was so impressed that he put Joseph in charge as second in command under himself. Joseph went from being a slave to becoming the right-hand man for the ruler of Egypt.

During the famine of the last seven years, Josephs' brothers came to Egypt to buy food for all of their own people. Joseph showed them kindness as he always did to others. He loved them despite what they did to him. His own family was very well taken care of throughout the famine. There would not have been any food, if Joseph had not been taken to Egypt, been given the interpretation of the dream from God, and given the wisdom on what to do about it. Joseph explained to his brothers that God had a hand in saving them all from the famine. Joseph's own dream regarding the bundled stalks that he had told his brothers years before the famine triggered the whole event.

Genesis 50:18-20 (NIV), His brothers then came and threw themselves down before him. "We are your slaves," they said. But Joseph said to them, **"Don't be afraid. Am I in the place of God? You intended to harm me, but God intended it for good to accomplish what is now being done, the saving of many lives."**

Joseph went from being a slave in Egypt, to being put into prison for a crime he did not commit, to becoming second in command over all of Egypt. He was a godly man with a good personality and had favor with God. God used the evil intentions of his brothers and made it all good. God was keeping his promise to Abraham about saving the nations of the world. We will see later how God implemented his plan to keep his promise.

JUST THE RIGHT FIT

—◆—

LESSON 7

Jesus was a descendant of Abraham. He was and is the promised savior and king who is to rule the world. His kingdom is growing with followers every day.

I believe God was patiently putting together the right mix of human characteristics that he liked from all the different descendants. He saw how men that made a positive impact on others conducted themselves. He was researching human qualities he wanted to instill or impart in his Son to be. This man needed to be faithful, obedient and courageous. He also needed to be just like God himself, full of purity and wisdom.

Some of the people and stories of the Old Testament are somewhat comparable with the nature that God wanted to give us in his Son. For example, in the story of Joseph, he was sent to Egypt to save God's people.

There is a saying that says, "If you want something done right you sometimes have to do it yourself!" God, who owns everything that exists, developed the perfect plan. He had to somehow come down to earth and become one of us in order to help us. He, himself, was too big and powerful for us as he was.

Let's imagine that God had a special robe. It represented his magnificence. It was very costly, kingly, beautiful and glorious, and it fits him exactly. It represents his majestic authority and power.

Psalms 93:1 (NKJV), "The Lord reigns, He is clothed with majesty; The Lord is clothed, He has girded himself with strength."

God the Father wants to hand his robe down to his soon to be earthly Son. But the robe will be too big for him because he will be in a human body. He would have to size it down to fit, in order for it to be useful. God provided enough of his Spirit (just the right fit) in the human seed to be born as Jesus. God wanted his Son to be clothed with his majestic strength, power and wisdom. Jesus was part of royalty and had access to all authority because he was sent from God above.

He, God's Spirit came to live with mankind through the human body of Jesus. Jesus was the Son of God and the son of man at the same time.

If God was his Father, then some of Gods features were passed down to him. Artificial fertilization technology was not around back in the time of Jesus. But it is today! We now know that it is possible to implant what is needed from the father into the mother to create an embryo without the sexual experience. If his Father was God, then he was born with some of the characteristics of his Father.

As for having the unique qualities given by his Father, (making him a descendent of God), he had supernatural creative powers and abilities. The human side of Jesus from his mother, Mary (a descendent of Adam) was able to have access to those supernatural creative powers and abilities, because he was of both God and human.

JESUS, THE DWELLING PLACE OF GOD

❖

LESSON 8

When Jesus was alive, he taught the people under the old covenant law that they understood and lived by. If we were to go live in another country, their laws might be different than what we are used to. We would need to learn what they are and how they work. Jesus knew how their law worked very well. He was born under the old covenant laws. He communicated with his heavenly Father continually, as well as studied the scriptures. Some of the teachings that Jesus taught were hard lessons and showed that it was almost humanly impossible to keep all the laws.

Jesus appealed to the emotions of his listeners. He pointed out the dangers, as well as the blessings and benefits regarding the old covenant laws. He demonstrated what the blessings were. He performed miracles, healed people from diseases and delivered people from issues beyond their own control. He helped people who could not help themselves. He called himself the great physician. He drew the attention of multitudes, and he became very popular and liked by many.

Jesus said to his disciples in **John 14:6 (NKJV), "I am the way, the truth, and the life. No one comes to the Father except through me."**

Jesus tried to explain to one of his disciples further what he meant.

John 14:10 (NKJV), "<u>The words that I speak to you, I do not speak on my own authority; but the Father who dwells in me does the works.</u>"

Jesus says here in this scripture that his words of authority are from his Father. Jesus was referred to as the "<u>Word</u> of God" in John 1:1. He was the <u>voice of God</u> in a human body, and he claimed that the Father dwelled in him.

Instead of the temporary dwelling place (or tent) in the old days of Moses that God used to be among his people, God created his own dwelling place in a body like us. He had an earthly Son and called him Jesus. This dwelling place was not made by the hands of men who made the tent. God the Father made his own dwelling place by creating his Son, Jesus.

You may say, how is that possible if God is a Spirit being. Well, if God can create a physical earth with trees, water, land and air and then the man called Adam in his creation, then why can't he create a seed or sperm to house his own genetics.

God is the creator who can create anything. He gave himself <u>his own dwelling place</u>, his own body, the body of Jesus his Son. The people in the times of Jesus could actually be in God's presence and live. They did not have to be afraid like they were in the times of Moses. Remember that they could not see the front side of his own glorious body, or they would die. They could now access God through the man Jesus instead of through the man Moses. They could see his face, hear him and touch him. He was Jesus! Jesus was the representative of an invisible God. He became one of us! This is the way we can relate to our creator. God put his own Spirit in his Son.

John 1:14 (NKJV), "And the <u>Word</u> became flesh (or a human being named Jesus Christ) **and dwelt among us and we beheld his glory, the glory as of the only begotten of the Father, full of grace and truth."**

After baby Jesus grew up into a man, he showed God's incredible character of love and goodwill to everyone he came in contact with. He did the works of his own Father. Through learning about Jesus, we get to know our creator at a more personable level. There are many stories of where he healed and delivered and performed miracles. He taught by giving examples, parables and he gave expert advice. These great stories have been passed down throughout history.

2 Timothy 3:16-17 (NKJV), "<u>All scripture is given by inspiration of God</u>, and <u>is profitable</u> for doctrine, for reproof, for correction, for instruction in righteousness, that the man of God may be complete, thoroughly equipped for every good work."

All scripture is powerful and supernaturally inspired by God. The Word is alive! He is backed by all of heaven and by his authority. The Word reveals the love that God has for us through his earthly Son.

THE VOICE OF GOD

―――――❖―――――

LESSON 9

Why are the scriptures so important?

Hebrews 4:12-13 (NKJV), "For the <u>Word of God</u> is <u>living and powerful</u>, and sharper than any two-edged sword, piercing even to the <u>division of soul and spirit</u>, and of joints and marrow, and is a discerner of the thoughts and intents (attitudes) **of the heart."**

I have experienced the Word of God, ministering or teaching me while reading the bible. He reveals and impresses thoughts into my thoughts as I concentrate or meditate. Sometimes, things just seem to jump off the page to grab my attention as I read. Sometimes he reveals helpful life-giving spiritual truths to me, and sometimes I don't get it. That is when I have to study it out, and every time I do, I find something spectacular about him that helps me in my own life. Jesus is the voice of God that spiritually talks to us through his written word. He speaks to us from within as we read or hear, to reveal a thought or message that can enhance our lives.

Speaking God's written words from our own lips to our ears is a good way to imprint his life-giving positive thoughts and promises into our minds. God's words of life can then penetrate deep within the heart of our being.

Romans 10:17 (KJV), "… faith comes by hearing, and hearing by the word of God."

Faith is defined as a strong belief and complete trust or confidence in someone or something. Studying the scriptures is good for the soul. It is good for the spirit, mind and body. It is just like learning a new skill or studying for a test at school. We study it over and over until it gets engrained within us, and we know we can handle the job or pass that test. His word gives us hope (confidence), and in some instances, it gives us courage to face challenging situations. It gives us a better awareness of our creator who is out for our best interest. It builds our relationship with him and as we get to know him, we learn to trust him and feel his love.

Emotions like anger, sadness, and the stress of dealing with pain and heartache all have a negative impact on our bodies. They can drain our mental energy. Negative thinking from stress causes chemical reactions. It elevates the stress hormone called cortisol and reduces the levels of dopamine, which can lead to depression or other mental health issues. It can cause high blood pressure, digestive problems and can wear out our immune system. Negative thoughts can keep us from living a long and happy life.

In Luke 4:18 (NKJV), Jesus said, "The Spirit of the LORD is upon me, because he has anointed me to preach the gospel to the poor; he has sent me to heal the brokenhearted, to proclaim liberty to the captives and recovery of sight to the blind, to set at liberty those who are oppressed; to proclaim the acceptable year of the LORD."

Jesus has been commissioned and sent to heal. We can receive healing by learning about him. The bible has the voice of God hidden within the words and stories. The Father and his Son Jesus tells us to listen to his word for it gives us life.

SNEAK PREVIEW

⎯⎯⎯◆⎯⎯⎯

LESSON 10

Jesus was born under the old covenant. The new covenant did not come in to effect until he was sentenced to death, died and rose again. In modern terms, all the things that Jesus did while he was alive was to give the world a sneak preview of what was to come. He was marketing (advertising or announcing) the exciting news of a new creation that was about to be unveiled. He was proving that it works. He had witnesses that told stories of what this powerful invention (or creation) did for them. People were healed, set free from harmful spirit forces, while others had their family members raised back to life, even after being put in the grave.

The good news was being spread abroad. The marketing technique was a success. Some people thought that he was saying a lot of weird stuff with his teaching technique and stories. They did not understand because he spoke mysteries by using parables. But, they were interested!

They didn't understand some of the things that Jesus said until this new covenant that he was marketing was put into place. The old covenant that punishes for sin that they understood was between God and the Israelites (in the time of Moses). Jesus was a descendant of the Israelites, and he kept the laws of the old covenant till his death.

I mentioned that many years before the old covenant, God had made the covenant with Abraham. God promised he would save the world through one of Abraham's descendants, and that descendant was Jesus.

So technically, the new Abrahamic covenant that Jesus was marketing was planned long before the covenant of Moses. God's promise that he had made to Abraham was starting to come to pass. The new covenant that Jesus brought is one of forgiveness and eternal life, and it would eventually affect everyone in the world in some way or another. Anyone could become a beneficiary of it. God had said that all nations shall be blessed through his promise to Abraham.

Only after the resurrection of Jesus, did the people start to understand the things Jesus was referring to. Through one man, Adam, came a curse because of sin. Through one man, Jesus, came redemption from that curse, and it is available to all who ask.

Jesus had pleased God with the way he lived his life. God condemned sin on the cross, not the man who hung on the cross. Jesus had no sin and God knew it. God made a way that wiped out the decrees that punish the guilty, if they were to ask for forgiveness. Even though we were not under the old covenant, the whole world was affected by the decision of Adam and Eve. Now the whole world is affected by the decision of Jesus.

Jesus said he was the good shepherd that laid down his life for the sheep in John 10:1-18. In John 10:17 (NKJV) Jesus said, **"Therefore my Father loves me because I lay down my life that I may take it again."** He came, he suffered and died on the cross, and then he rose again for our sake.

In Luke 23:34 as Jesus was dying on the cross, he said, **"Father, forgive them for they know not what they do."** This was the plea of the blameless man called Jesus, asking his Father to do something not for himself, but for us. He was full of compassion! He had always done and spoke only what his Father wanted him to. The people that were present at his death heard his words. And those words have been passed down throughout history. He spoke them for our benefit! It was to let us know the heart of both the Father and the Son. It was to let us know the heart of the living God!

He knew that if he asked the Father's forgiveness for us all, it would break the curse spoken of in the old covenant, and the death sentence that passed down from Adam and Eve. He paid the price with his own death to lift the curse from all who ask. This was all in God's plan.

Colossians 2:14-15 (NKJV), "…(God) having wiped out the handwriting of requirements (the don'ts and dos of the old covenant laws**) that was against us, which was contrary to us. And he has taken it out of the way, having nailed it to the cross."**

God forgives us through his Son's sacrifice once and for all.

Hebrews 9:12 (NKJV), "Not with the blood of goats and calves (animal sacrifices)**, but with his own blood** (the blood of Jesus) **he entered the most holy place ONCE for all, having obtained eternal redemption."**

He went as the chosen descendant of Abraham to bring the promise of God to the nations of the world. He entered the Holy of Holies in Heaven and is our high priest. He presented his own innocent blood as atonement or compensation for our sins. He has passed over into new life, and death has no power over him ever again.

Forgiveness is not automatic for everyone. You have to ask for forgiveness. You have to accept the death sentence that sent Jesus to the cross, as compensation for the corruptible nature residing in your body. It was not fair that all the human race was caught up in the evil plot of Satan to get God to condemn us. It wasn't fair that Jesus had to die. His life was cut short in his early thirties. Under the old covenant he should have had a right to live a full life and to be blessed while living here on earth because he never sinned.

Satan's plan to accuse Jesus before God failed! God found no fault in the life that Jesus lived.

Jesus was put to death because of who he said he was, the Son of God. Some of the Jews, as well as the religious leaders did not believe he was the begotten Son of God. They wanted to kill him because he said God was his Father, making himself equal with God. By the law of Moses, he was accused, convicted and killed. They accused him of breaking one of the commandments. But he was telling the truth when he said he was the Son of God. Unbelief of the people is what killed him.

According to the old covenant, God had promised blessings to anyone who obeyed his commands. God would be a liar if he didn't keep his promise to bless the innocent man, Jesus. So, the law owed him his life back. He was raised from the dead because he never let sin come alive in his being. Only the sin nature of Adam itself died and decomposed to nothing. The law could not raise Jesus back up from death. It had no power to do so, but God did! The first man's sin (from Adam) was nailed to the cross through the body of Jesus.

Jesus has been made the new Adam without the sin nature. Through God all things are possible. The new nature is blameless before God. Through Jesus we are forgiven and cleansed. The old nature needs to come to an end. We die to the old nature of the first Adam daily and live to the new nature of Christ forever. We are the righteousness of Christ! We just have to get our mind and body to believe it.

Jesus had trusted his Father with his very own soul, even while facing death on the cross. He knew God would not leave him in the grave. He knew that God would keep his promise.

Psalms16:10-11 (NKJV), "…you will not leave my soul in Sheol, nor will you allow your Holy one to see corruption. You will show me the path of life; In your presence is fullness of joy; At your right hand are pleasures forevermore."

The life that Jesus lived while here on earth made his Father very happy! He represented his Father's will and love to us perfectly. He wears the Father's robe as our gracious king and priest very well, and he has established his new kingdom. When we accept the new covenant for ourselves, we then become a part of his kingdom, his family, now in this life, as well as eternity.

By faith in the Lord Christ Jesus, we can know that we are loved unconditionally. He came and died for us to make our lives better. We can be healed, forgiven, or find it easier to forgive another. We can be made justified in the sight of God because of what he did. We can be redeemed and set free from depression and a sin conscience mindset. We are promised a wonderful tomorrow with new beginnings. We can live forever with joy in his presence and in his kingdom.

THE ACCUSER

LESSON 11

Colossians 1:13-14 (NIV), "For he (God) **has rescued us from the dominion of darkness and brought us** (transferred our citizenship) **into the kingdom of the Son he loves** (Jesus), **in whom we have redemption, the forgiveness of sins."**

The scripture above says we are delivered or rescued from the power of darkness. The enemy who hates us is called the devil, Satan, thief, father of lies, accuser of the brethren, as well as many other nicknames. He is a spirit being and works on affecting the thinking of as many as he can, in a very bad way.

Jesus said in **John 10:10 (NIV), "The thief comes only to steal, and kill, and destroy..."**

Satan has tried to convince God to condemn and destroy us. There are many stories of his horrible character. In the Old Testament, in the book of Job, he stood before God and caused a lot of grief for a wealthy man named Job.

God and Satan were having a conversation. In the book of Job chapter one, God pointed out to Satan that Job was a perfect and upright man, who shunned evil. God asked Satan, if he considered or thought carefully about the goodness of Job before passing any judgement, or making an evil assessment, or accusation against him. But Satan with all his hatred for mankind retaliated with his own questions and comments. Here is their conversation found in Job 1:9-12. Job said, **"Does Job fear God for nothing? Have you not put a hedge around him and his household, and everything he has? You have blessed the work of his hands, so that his flocks and herds are spread throughout the land. But now stretch out your hand and strike everything he has, and he will surely curse you to your face."** Then the Lord said to Satan, **"Very well then, everything he has is in your power. But on the man, himself, do not lay a finger"** (Job 1:9-12).

This incident was the first time Satan (the enemy) came against Job by killing his loved ones and stripping him of everything he had. If this wasn't bad enough, he tried a second time with Job's own health in chapter two. **Job 2:7 (NIV), So Satan went out from the presence of the Lord and afflicted Job with painful sores from the soles of his feet to the crown of his head.** Satan was not allowed to kill him, but he did make him wish he was dead.

Even though Satan caused disaster and heartbreak, as well as afflicting him with a horrible disease, Job stayed faithful to God. Satan was trying to get Job to curse God. Satan wanted to make his life so miserable, that he would get angry and blame God, and in return, God would retaliate and curse Job. Satan, himself was behind this horrific incident of testing Job and God.

Sometimes I wonder if this was one of those times when God was working on his strategy to stop Satan's accusations against his creation of man. He was looking and studying the mind of Satan to see how an evil mind works. God had no evil in him. One of the best war strategies is to learn how your enemy thinks so you can take actions to defeat him.

In the story of Job, his friends tried to comfort him throughout his suffering by being there for him. Their comfort lasted a little while. But just when Job thought it could not get any worse, it did. His own friends began to rationalize the situation. They decided that God must be allowing him to suffer because he had done something wrong to deserve punishment. They made Job, a man already hurting and at his lowest, feel even worse. They just added to his grief. They had gone too far! There so-called comfort caused him to wonder if God had abandoned him.

Just because a person is suffering, it doesn"t mean that they did something to deserve it. In the beginning of the book of Job, God was well pleased with him. Throughout the whole ordeal, Job stayed faithful and never got mad at God for his situation. He never turned his back on God. He did start questioning his own conscience, wondering if he had done something so bad to deserve a horrible tragedy.

Finally, God had had enough. In the last chapter, He shows his disappointment to the friends of Job for saying that he (God) was angry and caused the suffering. They should have encouraged and prayed with Job for as long as needed, but they didn't.

They had been coerced into causing division between Job and God. They played right into the hands of Satan and didn't even know it. The devil was behind the suffering and he wanted God to get the blame for it.

Job 42:7 (NIV) God said to one of Job's friends, **"I am angry with you and your two friends, because you have not spoken the truth about me, as my servant Job has."**

God wasn't angry with Job, but he did get angry with Job's friends. He told them to bring a burnt offering (of an animal sacrifice) to Job, and then have Job pray for them, so that he would not destroy them. Job may have not been perfect before God, but he was loyal and faithful. Job had a quality that God admired.

When Job obeyed God and prayed for his friends, God forgave them. The curse over Job's own life was also broken. **"The act of forgiveness broke the curse."**

Satan was the accuser that was behind the curse. He had tried to destroy Job by testing his faithfulness. In the end of the book of Job (Job 42:10), God blessed Job with twice as much as he had lost in family and prosperity. The rest of Jobs life was blessed even better than what it was before Satan interfered with his life.

Jesus, like Job, was faithful and loyal to God, too. He had to go as far as being put to death and still trust God with his life. As he was dying, he did as Job did. He prayed for God to forgive those men who were condemning and killing him. Both Job and Jesus prayed for others to be forgiven and the curse was broken in each situation. Job was restored with double. Jesus was restored to his rightful place with his Father and has been crowned as our King and savior. Because of the sacrifice given for forgiveness, the curse has been broken.

Job had always prayed for his children (Job 1:5). I believe that Job is now with all those children. He is with those he lost from Satan's actions against him, and he is with his children he had after the whole event. Because of Jesus, there is life after death. Through the actions of both men, others were affected by their decision. **Forgiveness breaks the curse.** Stay faithful and pray for those you love.

JESUS DEFEATS TEMPTATION

Have you ever went fishing? If you have, then you would know that you have to bait your hook with something that will attract the fish. You can catch the fish for food and/or entertainment. Maybe you fish in a competitive way to see who can catch the best and biggest fish. I for one used to love to go fishing. It was relaxing and exciting at the same time. Especially when I caught something big, even though I did not like to eat fish. Fishing is a good thing. In fact, Jesus recruited fishermen and said they would become fishers of men. They would use their skills to bring men and women to his Father. He said he would make them fishers of men (Matthew 4:19).

Fishing is also a way that the enemy of God works to catch men and women to destroy their lives. He uses bait to catch his prey. He uses the things that appeal to his victims. He is referred to as a deceiver, seducer, and tempter. Satan wants to take us out of the sea of life to suffocate and die without God. He wants to hurt God by hurting us.

Satan's plot is to convince us that we are unworthy of the benefits of a good life, or that God is not listening, or that God is not even a live being. His biggest trick is to convince us that we don't need God. But God is alive, and he does hear our prayers!

God is in charge of our final destination if we let him be, not Satan! God the Father gave his Son Jesus full authority, power and dominion over every creature and created thing that exist including the devil after he rose from the dead. Jesus can never die again and his final destination and supremacy came from the Father, not Satan!

Power and authority are the very things recorded in the bible that the devil used (as bait) to tempt Jesus early in his ministry. Matthew 4:1 and Luke 4:1 both talk about Jesus being led by the Spirit of God into the wilderness after he was baptized in the river. He stayed in the wilderness fasting and praying for forty days. At the end of his fast, Satan, the tempter came to test him regarding his identity as the Son of God and to offer him a proposition. He was baiting a trap for Jesus!

There were three specific temptations listed that Jesus faced. They are written in the book of Matthew 4:1-11 and again in the book of Luke 4:1-13. The temptations are not written in the same order in each book, so I will use Luke as a reference. We will explore more important details regarding temptation in the bible throughout the rest of this study.

It is important to see how Jesus with all his wisdom overcame Satan's temptations. It helps us to recognize the enemy, so that we can overcome his evil plots against us. It also helps us with our own faith in trusting Jesus, since he has already faced the devil and won.

Here is a quick summary of the three temptations that Jesus had to face before he went out to the surrounding areas to minister to others.

The first temptation begins with Jesus feeling very hungry from his fast. Satan used the opportunity to tempt him. He said to Jesus, "If you are the Son of God, why don't you turn these stones to bread for food." Jesus responded back to Satan using the ancient scripture stated in Deuteronomy 8:3 as his defense.

In **Luke 4:4 (NKJV)** Jesus answered Satan and said, **"It is written, man shall not live by bread alone, but by every word of God."**

Jesus was determined to trust God and not take any advice from the tempter. He knew how the tempter worked his evil from the past stories written in scripture. He used them to his advantage and knew what to do.

In this temptation, Jesus was referring to a story found in Deuteronomy chapter eight. It was a time when God led the Israelites through the wilderness for forty years. God had appointed Moses to be their leader, and this was the words of Moses to the people.

Deuteronomy 8:1-5 (NKJV), "Every commandment which I command you today you must be careful to observe, that you may live and multiply, and go in and possess the land of which the LORD swore to your fathers. And you shall remember that the LORD your God led you all the way these forty years in the wilderness, to humble you and test you, to know what was in your heart, whether you would keep his commandments or not. So, he humbled you, allowed you to hunger, and fed you with manna which you did not know nor did your fathers know, that he might make you know that <u>man shall not live by bread alone; but man lives by every word that proceeds from the mouth of the LORD</u>. Your garments did not wear out on you, nor did your foot swell these forty years."

Jesus knew that no matter what the devil threw his way, he had to obey God. We are going to see why Jesus knew what to say to Satan. He took the stories of the Old Testament as a learning tool of the don'ts and dos. We may face similar circumstances and can learn from the mistakes and victories of others in the bible.

The second temptation - Satan took Jesus up to a very high mountain top and tempted him with power and authority over all the kingdoms of the world. Satan said that he would put Jesus in charge of it all, if he (Jesus) would worship him. In **Luke 4:8 (NKJV)**, Jesus answered and said to him, **"Get behind me, Satan! For it is written, 'You shall worship the LORD your God, and him only you shall serve.'"**

In **Exodus 20:3 (NKJV)** God had said, **"You shall have no other gods before me."** This was one of the ten commandments. We will see what the bible says about idol worship and how it is still a problem today for us. This subject will be discussed in detail as we read along. It is very important in understanding the reality of what goes on behind the scenes outside of our own realm.

The third temptation - Satan took Jesus to the top of the pinnacle of a temple. He told him to prove himself as the Son of God by jumping. If he was the Son of God, then God would deliver him according to the scriptures. Satan used scripture himself to try and trip Jesus up. He quoted from the book of **Psalms 91:11-12 (NKJV)** which says, **"<u>For he shall give his angels charge over you, to keep you in all your ways. In their hands they shall bear you up, lest you dash your foot against a stone</u>."**

In this temptation, Jesus again responds with scripture. He said in **Luke 4:12 (NKJV), "<u>You shall not tempt the LORD your God</u>."** He was referring to the scripture Deuteronomy 6:16.

In this temptation from Satan, Satan wanted Jesus to prove his deity as the Son of God. He was testing the faith of Jesus. He wanted to see if Jesus trusted God enough to catch him if he jumped.

If he would have talked Jesus into jumping, he would have tricked Jesus into tempting God. Would God save him or just let him die? Would God have angels come to save him if he obeyed the devils command to jump? This is how Satan works. He works through negatively influencing our emotions, so we will make bad decisions. Satan is the one who causes contention between us and others around us. In this temptation, Satan wanted to create contention between God and Jesus.

Satan was trying to get Jesus to do what he himself said to do. God did not tell him to jump, the devil did!

The scripture that Jesus was referring to about tempting God was written under the old covenant scriptures. It was given by Moses to the Israelites. Jesus used commandments from God to defeat the devil. He used words, not physical violence.

In **Deuteronomy 6:16 (NKJV)** Moses had said, **"You shall not tempt the Lord your God as you tempted him in Massah."**

This verse tells us that the Israelites had tempted God in a place that Moses called Massah. The full story is in the book of Exodus, chapter seventeen.

Jesus had read all about the Israelites forty-year journey and their wilderness experience with God. There was a lot of things that happened through their journey that we will explore later on. While the Israelites were being led by God through the wilderness, we will see that they tempted him over and over again.

Satan, who is a corrupt spirit is behind all evil temptation. Just as God has angels as messengers and mighty warriors that fight against evil, Satan has his wicked army of spirits that do his bidding for him.

Jesus took the information he learned from the Israelites wilderness experience of mistakes and victories to heart. He knew what to do and not do. While he, himself was led by the Spirit of God into the wilderness for forty days, he did not give in to temptation or test God.

THE ENEMY'S FEAR REVEALED

Let's begin to piece together the puzzle that reveals Gods plan for mankind and how our enemy is trying to stop it from happening. Let's get into the story that triggered the Israelites forty-year long journey. Sometimes it is hard to figure out the whole picture of the puzzle until we start putting all the different pieces together. It all leads to understanding God's plan for our own lives.

We will start with the events that happened just before the journey of the Israelites while they were still in Egypt. Earlier I had said that Joseph (the grandson of Abraham) was sold into slavery, brought to Egypt, put in prison, interpreted the dreams for the Pharaoh and then became second in command in Egypt. Under the direction of Gods' plan, Jospeph saved the people from starvation. His own extended family was welcomed into Egypt and fed very well through the seven years of famine.

After Joseph and his family had settled in Egyptian territory during and after the famine, they multiplied and were very blessed. They were blessed more than all the other people in Egypt.

When Joseph and his generation became old and died, the Egyptian king who Joseph knew had also passed on. There was a new king who did not like the Israelites. He did not like that they were more and mightier than his own people. He started making their lives miserable and inflicting hard labor on them. He even tried to stop them from raising any newborn sons. **The Israelites became slaves because of the king's fear of them getting too strong for him to handle. I believe this is the fear of Satan regarding God's people.** I believe the tempter was behind the actions of the new king. The things that the new king had done to them is found in Exodus 1:7-22.

Exodus 1:9 (NKJV), "And he (the new king) **said to his people, 'Look, the people of the children of Israel are more and mightier than we; come, let us deal shrewdly with them, lest they multiply, and it happen, in the event of war, that they also join our enemies and fight against us, and so go up out of the land.'"**

I believe that Satan's own fear is revealed in what the new king said in Exodus 1:9 regarding God's people back then, and even today. The thoughts of the king were the thoughts of Satan. The decision of the king soon caused his great army to fall. Satan's own thoughts will cause his own great and evil army to fall someday in the future.

In Exodus, chapter two, it shows the Israelites crying out to God to deliver them from their slavery under the Egyptians.

Exodus 2:23-24 (NKJV), "Then the children of Israel groaned because of the bondage, and they cried out; and their cry came up to God because of the bondage. So, <u>God heard their groaning, and God remembered his covenant with Abraham, with Isaac, and with Jacob.</u>"

In chapters seven through fourteen, the Israelites had their prayers answered. They witnessed miracles that God performed to make the stubborn Egyptian king release them.

God appointed Moses to lead his people out of bondage and used Moses as his messenger to communicate with the Egyptian king. In the story, God had to send ten plagues, one right after another upon the Egyptians because of the stubbornness of the king who refused to let them go.

God told Moses to use a rod that he had in his hand as a tool to release his (God's) power against the Egyptians. When Moses and Aaron (his brother) struck the waters of the river with the rod of God, all the sources of water in Egypt were turned into blood. This was the first plague. Next, God sent hordes of frogs as the second plague. There were so many that the Egyptians gathered the dead frogs in giant piles. Then God turned the dust of the earth around them into lice and gnats. This was the third plague. When none of that worked, God then sent hordes of flies as the fourth plague. A fifth plague killed a lot of their livestock, and a sixth plague was on the Egyptians themselves. They developed horrible boils and sores all over their bodies. The seventh plague was a massive storm mixed with hail and fire that destroyed most of their crops. The eighth plague was a massive amount of locust which began devouring all their food sources. There were so many locusts that the bible said the whole land was darkened. The ninth plague was a thick darkness that lasted for three days. When the king of Egypt still did not let them go, all their firstborn children and livestock died. This was the last and final plague before the king let them go.

None of these plagues affected any of the Israelites, which leads to one of the biggest revelations ever. We will explore the reason why, a little later in great detail.

Shortly after the Israelites were released and starting their journey into the wilderness, the king of Egypt changed his mind. He and his army started to pursue them. His army was catching up and closing in behind the Israelites and this caused them to be overtaken by fear.

The Israelites had been living a blessed life in Egypt up until the new king came to power and treated them badly. This escape from Egypt was a new experience for them. They were in uncharted territory. They had more fear in the enemy pursuing them, than faith in God who was delivering them.

They began to lash out at their leader Moses who had been following the direction of God.

Exodus 14:12-14 (NKJV), The Israelites said, **"For it would have been better for us to serve the Egyptians than that we should die in the wilderness." And Moses said to the people, 'Do not be afraid. Stand still and see the salvation of the LORD, which he will accomplish for you today. For the Egyptians whom you see today, you shall see again no more forever. The LORD will fight for you, and you shall hold your peace.'"**

God had already told Moses what would happen regarding the Egyptian pursuit and that he would take care of it (Exodus 14:4,). Moses, as their leader, let them know that their God had a plan to save them. God purposely hardened the heart of the Pharaoh so that he and his army would come after them. God wanted the Israelites to see their enemy defeated (Exodus 14:8).

When they got to the Red Sea, God parted the waters so that the Israelites could pass over to the other side onto dry land. After they crossed over, God released the waters on top of the Egyptian army who were pursuing them, killing all of them. He showed the people that they did not have to be in fear of their enemy anymore. **"The LORD will fight for you!"**

VALLEY OF DECISION

———————— ❧ ————————

LESSON 14

The Israelites had a lot of things that happened on their journey out of Egypt and through the wilderness. Most of them never learned to trust God. They made some poor decisions that affected them for the rest of their lives.

On their journey, one of the first things that they did was to accuse God and Moses of bringing them out of Egypt to let them die of thirst. This was one of the many times the people came to Moses with complaints, distrust and accusations while in the wilderness. They were actually being downright rude, almost to the point that Moses was concerned that they were going to stone him to death.

Exodus 17:3 (NKJV), "And the people thirsted there for water, and the people <u>complained</u> against Moses, and said, 'Why is it you have brought us up out of Egypt, to kill us and our children and our livestock with thirst?'"

This took place at a place called the rock of Horeb. It happened to be the same area that the angel of the Lord had first talked with Moses from the burning bush years before. This was the place that God had first given Moses the assignment to deliver his people out of Egypt.

In this particular incident, when Moses had told God about their grumbling, God gave him instructions on how to give them water to drink. Moses was told to strike the rock with the same staff that he used to strike the Nile River at the crossing of the Red Sea. God stood before Moses on that rock and when Moses struck it, fresh drinking water began to flow out from it.

From the people's bitter complaint regarding the water, Moses ended up calling the place Massah (meaning temptation) and Meribah (meaning bitter waters) because of the people's contentious attitude. They were questioning God's motives and bringing accusations against them both.

Exodus 17:7 (NKJV), "So he (Moses) called the name of the place <u>Massah</u> and Meribah, because of the <u>contention</u> of the children of Israel, and because <u>they tempted the LORD</u>, saying, '<u>Is the LORD among us or not?</u>'"

When the ten commandments were given to Moses to give to the people a little later in time, **"You shall not tempt the LORD your God,"** became part of the commandments. It is mentioned in Deuteronomy 6:16.

The truth was that God had delivered them out of the hand of their enemy and was leading them to the land of Canaan. Their own forefathers, Abraham, Isaac and Jacob had been buried there near Jerusalem. God was planning on using the Israelites to drive out the evil idol worshipping people that lived there, so he could give them the rich and beautiful land.

Later on, Jesus himself quoted this phrase from the ten commandments (in Deuteronomy 6:16) to Satan himself, while being tested in the wilderness temptations. He knew the scriptures very well. He used this phrase, this law, as a weapon to push back against Satan, who was trying to be a god over him. Jesus was able to stand his ground by speaking from the scriptures, for he knew that they were the inspired written words and laws of God.

The Israelites in the wilderness experience had disregarded and disrespected God by showing a faithless attitude. They did not take him at his word. They did not believe him to get them to their destination. They needed to learn to listen to God and his commands in order to survive the desert, and make it to the promised land, but they did not.

God was physically trying to lead them on their journey. He led them by a cloud in the daytime, and a fire at night. In Deuteronomy chapter six, Moses told the Israelites what God had planned for their future.

Deuteronomy 6:10-19 (NKJV), "So it shall be, when the LORD your God brings you into the land of which he swore to your fathers, to Abraham, Isaac, and Jacob, to give you large and beautiful cities which you did not build, houses full of all good things, which you did not fill, hewn-out wells which you did not dig, vineyards and olive trees which you did not plant—when you have eaten and are full, then beware, lest you forget the LORD who brought you out of the land of Egypt, from the house of bondage. You shall fear the LORD your God and serve him and shall take oaths in his name. <u>You shall not go after other gods</u>, the gods of the peoples who are all around you (for the LORD your God is a jealous God among you), lest the anger of the LORD your God be aroused against you and destroy you from the face of the earth."

"<u>You shall not tempt the LORD your God as you tempted him in Massah</u>. You shall diligently keep the commandments of the LORD your God, his testimonies, and his statutes which he has commanded you. And you shall do what is right and good in the sight of the LORD, that it may be well with you, and that you may go in and possess the good land of which the LORD swore to your fathers, to cast out all your enemies from before you, as the LORD has spoken."

This "tempting God" became part of the "do nots" in the commandments under the old covenant of their day.

It was a hard journey for the Israelites at times, and they would remember back to their captivity where they had gotten comfortable. Even though they had been slaves, they had food, water and shelter. They had forgotten that things were so bad, they had cried out to God to deliver them. They had forgotten that they had no freedom!

Even though they were now free physically, they were imprisoned in their minds by their enemy. Just like a drug fix or other addition of today, they were being drawn or tempted to go back into captivity because they were accustomed to that lifestyle.

Egypt had met their basic need for food and water to survive. How could the Israelite people have had the strength to do their duty that was imposed on them, if their captor had not taken care of their physical needs. They had become co-dependents of the Egyptians.

God had delivered them from their physical enslavement under the Egyptian king. And now they were still feeling the effects of spiritual bondage, oppression and fear that their enemy caused them to feel. This is how Satan works to keep a person in bondage. The Israelites had a bad experience and it now continued to haunt them. Their trust level was not very good. It kept them from realizing their freedom. They let the enemy continue to rule their feelings. They let their feelings rule and dictate their destiny.

They were now in-between the enslavement behind them, and a promised land they could call their own in front of them. They were in the valley of decision to trust God to be among them or not.

God could have gotten angry enough for their spiteful attitudes to either abandon or destroy them. Which is exactly what I believe Satan himself would have loved to see. He does not want God's plan to succeed because the end result is his doom. God could have abandoned them, but he didn't!

As long as the Israelites kept going forward, God would equip them to be the ones that would drive out the idol worshipping people that lived in the land of Canaan. They were not to mingle with or practice the evil ways from the people of that area.

God is going to accomplish his plan to wipe out all evil in the world. It is a work in progress.

Deuteronomy 9:3-4 (NKJV), "He (God) **will destroy them and bring them down before you; so, you shall drive them out and destroy them quickly, as the LORD has said to you. Do not think in your heart, after the LORD your God has cast them out before you, saying, 'Because of my righteousness the LORD has brought me in to possess this land', but <u>it is because of the wickedness of these nations that the LORD is driving them out from before you."</u>**

The whole point of God's plan is and was to undo what Satan did to mankind in the beginning. He wants the world to be a place of peace and prosperity. God will take down the evil in the world. He really doesn't want to destroy people, but if the people reject him, and turn to the ways of the devil and the worship of idols, they will get destroyed along with it.

Evil is kind of like a toxic gas in the air. If you get to close and breath in the toxic gas, it can hurt or even kill you. You may not have even known it was there or that you breathed it in. The gas is toxic, not you. God has to rid the air of the toxic gas.

What about a deadly and contagious virus, how is it stopped? To keep it from spreading to all people, the victim of the virus has to be quarantined or separated from the others. Some die from it. If they don't receive an antidote for it, or stay away from it, then they may die. The overall remedy is to terminate the disease as to keep it from spreading to everyone else.

The toxic gas or the deadly disease is the same analogy of what evil does to people. God has to rid the world of evil because evil kills! He has to keep it from spreading to everyone else. We should strive to be part of the solution and not a part of the problem, it is our choice.

CROSSING THE BORDER?

———— ❖ ————

LESSON 15

Did all the Israelites that were in the desert wilderness ever cross the border into the promised land? The answer is that some did and some didn't. Deuteronomy chapter nine sums up the bitter attitudes that most of the people had while in the desert, and how Moses had to interceded for them. God was ready to give up on most of them and raise up others to fulfill his plan. He decided to give the opportunity to their own children and two other faithful men.

Satan wants to see us enslaved by our past. He also wants us to give up on God and his plan for our lives. We need to trust God even when going through the wilderness makes life uncomfortable.

Eventually most of the older Israelites did not enter the beautiful and rich land of Canaan. They had no faith in God to get it for them. Their mind was still enslaved by feelings of fear. They did not believe God could give them victory over the people that lived there.

He had brought them to the border of the land of Canaan. God was ready to conquer the land and give it to them. My goodness, he had listened to their complaints and demands the whole time. He proved himself over and over again by miracles. Why couldn't they trust him now?

They let their past experience affect their future. Most of the people kept going and trusting God up till the end of their journey and then would not go in.

Numbers 14:4 (NKJV), "So they said to one another, Let us select a leader and return to Egypt."

Some even tried to overthrow Moses and his brother Aaron and make themselves the leaders. They ended up being swallowed alive by a giant sinkhole (Numbers 16:32).

The only ones who ended up making it into the promise land were all the children under twenty years old, two men named Joshua and Caleb and their families.

Joshua had been the young assistant to Moses throughout the journey. Moses would meet with God in a special tent to hear what God wanted him to know. When he would finish his meetings, Joshua was known to stay behind in the meeting place, even after Moses would return to the rest of the camp. Joshua became the successor of Moses when Moses had died later. Joshua and another man named Caleb had great faith in God. They were ready and willing to go into the promised land and claim it. In fact, they were ready to go immediately.

Numbers 13:30 (NKJV), Caleb said, **"Let us go up at once and take possession, for we are well able to overcome it."**

The sad news was that they and all the children who were under twenty years old had to wait forty years until the majority of the other Israelites passed away who did not believe. Because of sin and unbelief, a lot of the people missed out on the promise while others had to wait.

The secret to crossing over the border into the promises of God is trusting him to get you there. These people were tested in the wilderness and most of them failed. Even after everything God had got them through, they still did not believe in him.

The whole time in the wilderness, God was showing them that he was their source for protection from scorpions and serpents. He was their supplier of food and water that was not naturally there. He made water come from the rock, and he gave them the quail and manna from heaven to eat. They would not have survived without him. He tried to teach them to be obedient and trust him. He was trying to train them to follow his leadership and to <u>depend on him</u>, so that when they faced the giants that were in the land, they would have no fear. They would know their <u>God was among them</u>.

God had given them physical evidence that he was with them. He had them make a tabernacle (a tent) as his own dwelling place among them. As they traveled in the wilderness, he guided them on their journey with the pillar of cloud in the daytime, and the pillar of fire at night to light their way. The pillar of cloud or fire hovered over Gods earthly tabernacle that they had made for him.

Throughout their journey from Egypt, and when things got a little tuff, they complained to Moses saying, **"Is the LORD among us or not?"** They tested God and his patients over and over again. He was taking care of their basic needs. His dwelling place was in a tent among them! The Lord was with them!

Years and years later, when God was about to give his Son to be born into the world, he sent the angel Gabriel to a virgin named Mary. He told her she would have a son and call him Jesus (Luke 1:26-35). Joseph, a man about to take Mary as his wife was also visited by an angel in a dream (Matthew 1:19-23).

Matthew 1:23 (NKJV) the angel said, **"Behold, the virgin shall be with child, and bare a Son, and they shall call his name Immanuel, which is translated, <u>God with us</u>."**

God was with mankind in a tent and then he made his own dwelling place, his own body, the body of Jesus! He first dwelt in a tent while the Israelites wondered in the wilderness for forty years and then in Jesus who was tempted in the wilderness for forty days.

I can see how these two stories of the Israelites in the wilderness, and Jesus in the wilderness are related. The difference was that Jesus came out of his wilderness experience and into the power of the Spirit, while the unbelieving Israelites stayed stuck in their wilderness experience by their own decision.

Satan tried to provoke Jesus to go against the Father's will in the wilderness temptations. If Jesus would have listened to and obeyed Satan, he would not have been following the plan of his own Father. Jesus had fasted and prayed for forty days and never even complained about food or water. He resisted the devil in all three temptations and won the battle for the time being. But Satan would be back to tempt him again later.

The three wilderness temptations were just a trial run for the big event on the cross, where Jesus was about to cross the border of life. He had to trust the Father, no matter what fear Satan would bring against him. He had to trust the Father to get him to his promised land.

THE PERFECT MAN

LESSON 16

Even as a young boy, Jesus dedicated his life to learning about the business of his Father. He was very familiar with the ancient scriptures. There was one time when his parents could not find him for about three days. When they finally found him, they found him in the temple listening to the teachers and asking questions.

Was the Son of God actually there in the stories of the Old Testament somehow, since he was with God from the very beginning (John 1:1-14)? According to **John 10:30** Jesus said, **"I and my Father are one."** In John 14:9-10 he said that the Father lives within him. In John 12:44-50 he said that he only spoke what the Father gave him to say. And, in John 12:44-49 Jesus explained his connection to God as his Father.

In **John 12:49 (NKJV)** he said, **"For I have not spoken on my own authority; but the Father who sent me gave me command, what I should say and what I should speak."** His heavenly Father that he had said lived within him, was the same God who was with the Israelites on their journey through the wilderness. God knows everything that happened throughout history and the beginning of time. He was now existing in the body of his Son Jesus, and he directed his Son what to say and do based on his own experience throughout time and from his magnificent wisdom.

I believe that all the events that happened throughout the Old Testament were used by God to crack the code of DNA to make the perfect man. I am going to call it JDNA (the DNA of Jesus). God had seen both the determination and the limits of the human race he created. Throughout time, God was looking for the human qualities that he wanted in his Son that was to be born to save the world.

He was also gathering information on how and what Satan did to influence mankind for the worst. God had put all the data together. He wanted his Son to be ready for his assignment, turn out perfect, and with the right temperament. Through the seed of Mary, he created a new living being, a warrior who had the skills to defeat our enemy and set us free. Satan had no idea what God was up to.

Adam and Eve were tempted by Satan and lost their position of authority. Satan knows that our minds can be vulnerable to his tricks, if we don't have a strong foundation to depend on and the protection needed through God himself. The Spirit of God has been with us watching and working his plan since the beginning of time. He knows all things and what to do. We must believe and trust the Spirit of God with our lives to keep the enemy out.

As the Son of God, Jesus proved who he was to the devil in the wilderness temptation. As a mortal man, he trusted God to bring him out of the wilderness experience triumphantly. Now God was able to use him to go forward in setting up his own kingdom here on earth. He was to lead others in tearing down Satan's false religions of fear-based tactics.

Jesus knew what Satan had done to Adam and Eve, to Job and to others. He had learned the scriptures that were written in the past. He was familiar with Satan's tricks already. He knew perfectly, how to interpret the scriptures because of his God ordained wisdom. He was challenged with temptations like Adam and Eve and the rest of us, and he won! He made up for Adam and Eve's mistake. He makes up for ours too!

After his victory over the tempter in the wilderness, he was able to go in the power of God's Spirit. He had passed the test. **Luke 4:14 (NKJV) says, "Then Jesus returned in the power of the Spirit."** He was ready for his ministry to help and deliver others, which he did up until his death and is still doing today through his followers.

Acts 10: 38 (NKJV), "…God anointed Jesus of Nazareth with the Holy Spirit and with power, who went about doing good and healing all who were oppressed by the devil, for <u>God was with him</u>."

Jesus the perfect man said he came to bless our lives, not to destroy it.

John 10:10 (NKJV) Jesus said, "The thief (Satan) does not come except to steal, and to kill, and to destroy. I have come that they may have life, and that they may have it more abundantly."

I like what God had said in the book of Jeremiah.

Jeremiah 29:11 (NKJV), "For I know the thoughts that I think toward you, says the LORD, thoughts of peace and not of evil, to give you a future and a hope."

Jesus is the perfect man who can lead us. He was sent to help us! Through him God is with us.

FINAL TEMPTATION ON THE CROSS

LESSON 17

At the end of Jesus's life, Satan tested his willingness in trusting God even in the face of death. He couldn't temp Jesus to jump to his death in the temptations, so he inspired others to put him to death.

In **John 19:7 (NKJV),** just before the decision to kill Jesus was made, the religious leaders said, **"We have a law, and according to our law he ought to die, because he made himself the Son of God."**

Jesus had obeyed the laws of the old Mosaic covenant that was still in force back in his day. He never committed a crime, yet he was wrongfully judged and sentenced to death because of the unbelief of the religious leaders. They were deceived into thinking that Jesus was not the begotten Son of God, so they used the religious law to condemn him.

Satan also manipulated the thoughts of others to speak horrible things to Jesus while he was dying on the cross. Satan was back to tempt Jesus again one last time.

Matthew 27: 39-43 (NKJV), "And those who passed by blasphemed (or insulted) **him, wagging their heads and saying, 'You who destroy the temple and build it in three days, save yourself! If you are the Son of God, come down from the cross.'"**

"Likewise, the chief priests, also mocking with the scribes and elders said, 'He saved others; himself he cannot save. If he is the King of Israel, let him now come down from the cross, and we will believe him. He trusted in God; let him deliver him now if he will have him; for he said, I am the Son of God.'"

Jesus could have been intimidated (or tempted) by all the insults. He knew he could call on God and have angels rescue him. He had said so to his disciples earlier, just before the soldiers had captured him to be taken and sentenced. **Matthew 26:53-54 (NIV), "Do you think I cannot <u>call on my Father, and he will at once put at my disposal more than twelve legions of angels</u>? But how then would the scriptures be fulfilled that say it must happen in this way?"**

When the soldiers came to arrest Jesus just before he was sentenced to death, Simon Peter (one of his disciples) began to defend him and cut off the ear of one of the soldiers. But Jesus told Peter to put up his sword and let them take him. (Luke 22:45-51 also tells the story in detail.) It included Jesus instantly healing the soldier's ear. Jesus knew that he was supposed to die as part of God's overall plan for mankind.

I pointed out in a previous lesson that Jesus had already dealt with a similar situation at the beginning of his ministry. It was where he was tempted by Satan to jump off of the top of a building. Matthew 4:6 and Luke 4:11 says that Satan quoted scripture from Psalms 91:11 to tempt Jesus. **Psalms 91:11-12 (NKJV), "For he** (God, the Father) **shall give his angels charge over you, to keep you in all your ways. In their hands they shall bear you up..."**

Jesus knew already not to test God's words with Satan's twisted ideas. He already knew he was going to be put to death. He was not about to die at the command of Satan. His calling was to be put to death by and for mankind. He knew he was to die for their sins. But he also knew that he did not have to die. He knew the scripture that Satan had quoted to him. He knew he could have called on his Father for help at any time, even at the cross. It was his choice to become the sacrifice to be given by mankind and not Satan!

He did not deliberately put himself in harm's way just to test God. The people did. He knew the plan of God, and he knew what the future would be. Our destiny, and the destiny of the whole world was in his hands. He knew he was born to die for the human race. This was the only way he could save us! God had to make a way to redeem us from the clutches of an enemy who hates us.

Jesus had defeated Satan at his own game before. He did not give in to Satan speaking to him directly in the wilderness, nor did he give in to him while dying on the cross. He was facing the same temptation regarding calling on his Father that he had faced in the wilderness. But now it was not through Satan directly, but through the very people who were crucifying him.

Even though his accusers thought they were just mocking and belittling him, they were being used as pawns for Satan. They were tempting him to call on God. Satan was feeding them the things to say. Jesus recognized that Satan was behind the accusations and bullying because he had been down this road before.

Jesus technically and willingly gave his life on his own, even though he could have called for angels to rescue him. He did not do what Satan or the people said. He did what God said and he did it for us all.

Take note from all this, if Satan can't get to you by himself (like he tried with Jesus in the wilderness), he will try and use others around you to temp, accuse, harass and bully you, in hopes of defeating you. It may be the tempter behind their actions, and they may not even realize it.

The bible says that if the rulers, and Satan himself, would have understood the mystery plan of God, they would not have had Jesus crucified.

1 Corinthians 2:7-8 (NKJV), "But we speak the wisdom of God in a mystery, the hidden wisdom which God ordained before the ages for our glory, which none of the rulers of this age knew; <u>for had they known, they would not have crucified the Lord of glory</u>."

God knew Satan and what he would do. Satan did everything he could to kill Jesus. Satan did not know that he had played right into the hands of God. It was all in God's plan to have Jesus Christ die on the cross, for us to be forgiven, and to break the curse of the law.

FORGIVENESS BREAKS THE CURSE

⚜

LESSON 18

As Jesus was dying on the cross, he did the opposite of what the devil and all his accusers expected. He did what the man Job did in Job 42:7-10. Job prayed and asked God to forgive his inconsiderate friends, instead of destroying them. He did what God told him to do. Jesus did the same thing when he asked his Father to forgive those who were killing him.

Luke 23:34 (NKJV), "Then Jesus said, 'Father, forgive them, for they do not know what they do.'"

Jesus knew ahead of time he was going to be put to death. He did not choose for his Father to deliver him from off the cross. I believe he was able to go through with his death, because God had prepared him properly. Jesus had all the human and spiritual qualities that God composed from throughout history. God completed the perfect man to do and be who he was.

Jesus had conquered temptation in the wilderness experience, and all the way through till his death. He was prepared to die. He loved us enough to go through the horrible pangs of death. He was ready for the final hours of his life as the mortal son of man.

Jesus had a spectacular secret that the enemy did not know about. Jesus knew from the Mosaic laws that forgiveness can be achieved through the sacrificial death of an innocent animal (like the lamb). This ceremonial gesture established by God breaks the curse of death and brings forgiveness. Jesus as the sacrificial lamb put into motion a new and better covenant when he said, **"Father, forgive them, for they do not know what they do."**

Jesus was the only perfectly innocent man to have ever lived, who could die for all and break the curse. He is referred to as the lamb of God, who takes away the sin of the world (John 1:29).

How did the death of Jesus, the Son of God change history? Physical death by the law was only for those who could not keep the law. But no one could keep all the commandments that were written in the over 600 laws except for the one man, Jesus.

James 2:10 (NKJV), "… For whoever shall keep the whole law, and yet stumble in one point, he is guilty of all."

Jesus kept the whole law, and by that same law, his lifeless body and soul had a right to life. He had done nothing wrong.

They killed his human body, but they could not destroy his soul. The law that punishes, was overpowered by the man who kept it. He mastered the law when he FULFILLED it (Matthew 5:17). He satisfied the requirement of the law when he died, so it can't claim his life ever again. He brought it to a completeness as far as God was concerned. Jesus rose from the dead and lives forever.

The good news for us is that he brough about a new and better covenant for us to live by. He was tempted by Satan to break the most important laws of God and never gave in. The old covenant (law) involving punishment is now no longer a stumbling block. We are treated as children and not criminals. God's plan was to restore his creation to himself by making us his children. The new covenant that Jesus brings is one of restoration and rehabilitation.

The law of sin and death was finally overpowered by a descendant of Adam. Jesus is the one human who is like us, who will lead us into life eternal and the promises of God. He is the one who defeats the giants for us. He is bigger and more powerful than any struggles or problems we may have because he is also the "Son of God".

Isaiah 53:6 (NKJV), "The Lord laid on him (Jesus) **the iniquity of us all."**

The word "iniquity" can mean immoral efforts or behaviors. It does not follow the accepted values or ideas set by God. Have you ever experienced someone being stubborn, headstrong or self-willed against what you know to be right, and have you ever been there and done it yourself?

Jesus himself prayed to the Father, "not as I will, but as you will." Jesus who never committed any sin went to the cross for our self-destructive will and nature, or for our iniquity. He died so that we could be judged righteous in Gods eyes, even though our sins be many. He asked his Father to forgive us, and their combined forgiveness breaks the curse.

We are not sinless, he was! We can't die for our own sinfulness, and then redeem ourselves. But since Jesus had no sin, death could not keep him. He rose from the dead in his own human body. His body had a right to life, and he became the first immortal human being.

John 3:17 (NKJV), "For God did not send his Son into the world to condemn the world, but that the world through him might be saved."

Romans 8:1 (NKJV), "There is therefore now no condemnation to those who are in Christ."

Hebrews 2:14-15 (NKJV), "Inasmuch then as the children have partaken of flesh and blood, he himself likewise shared in the same, that through death he might destroy him who had the power of death, that is the devil, and release those who through fear of death were all their lifetime subject to bondage."

Colossians 1:19-20 (NKJV), "For it pleased the Father that in him (Jesus) **all the fullness should dwell, and by him to reconcile all things to himself, by him, whether things on earth or things in heaven, having made peace through the blood of his cross."**

We are redeemed from the curse of condemnation and death. His shed blood and forgiveness changed our destiny.

When I think and meditate on all this, I say "WOW"! His forgiveness already broke the curse! It is a done deal!

Galatians 3:13 (NKJV), "Christ has redeemed us from the curse of the law, having become a curse for us."

What a mighty and awesome Lord he is!

HE GAVE HIS BEST

---◆---

LESSON 19

Let's look back on the life of Jesus just before his death. Jesus and his disciples were all assembled together to celebrate and observe their deliverance from Egypt. This would be his last meal with them before he would be taken, judged and sentenced by the religious leaders. His new covenant was about to be set into motion by his death and resurrection.

At this meal, Jesus presented his new covenant to them all. What Jesus and his disciples did at his last meal has led to what we now call "communion". It is celebrated by eating a small piece of bread symbolizing his body that was broken for us, and drinking wine (or juice from fruit) symbolizing his blood that was shed on the cross. Jesus told them, "Do this in remembrance of me." The bread and wine represented forgiveness and new life.

God shows in Leviticus 17:11 that the life of all creatures on earth is in its blood. We know that blood carries energy, oxygen and nutrients to all the cells in our body. It also carries waste to lungs, kidneys and digestive system to be expelled. It also has antibodies to fight off diseases. It is crucial for survival.

When Jesus was nailed to the cross, his body could not repair itself, even though he was the offspring of the Spirit of God. He was made of flesh and blood. His body could not hold onto his life (his soul and spirit, his being) anymore in its present state.

Isaiah 53:5 (NKJV), foretells the pain and death of Jesus long before he was even born. It states, "He was **wounded** for **our transgressions**, he was **bruised** for **our iniquities**; The **chastisement** (significance, consequence, payment) for our peace was upon him, and by his **stripes** we are healed."

Jesus was put on the cross and wounded for our transgressions. His body was beaten and broken, and his blood was shed to blot out, eliminate or satisfy the ordinances (Colossians 2:13-14) that gives clear evidence (to convict us of our sins). Jesus gave his own life, thus sparing ours from judgement.

The bread and wine that Jesus had shared with his disciples at the last supper of his life represented his physical life, his body and his blood, that was to be sacrificed on the cross for us, so that we can live free from the curse.

Galatians 3:13 (NKJV), "Christ has redeemed us from the curse of the law, having become a curse for us."

Christians all over the world take part in celebrating communion by eating the bread and drinking the wine as a symbolic act honoring Jesus. It was to remember not only his death on the cross, but the new life he gave, when he rose from the dead. We are saved from the wrath of God that will eventually bring down Satan and all his destructive works.

Romans 5:9 (NKJV) says, "Much more then, having now been justified by his blood, we shall be saved from the wrath of God through him."

At his last supper, and before his death, Jesus established a new tradition using the bread and wine.

Matthew 26:26 (NKJV), "And as they were eating, Jesus took bread, blessed and broke it, and gave it to the disciples and said, 'Take, eat; this is my body.'"

In John 6:48 (NKJV), Jesus said, "<u>I am the bread of life.</u> Your fathers ate the manna in the wilderness and are dead. <u>This is the bread which comes down from heaven, that one may eat of it and not (never) die. I am the living bread which came down from heaven. If anyone eats of this bread, he will live forever</u>".

Matthew 26:27-28 (NKJV), "Then he took the cup of wine, and gave thanks, and gave it to them, saying, 'Drink from it, all of you. <u>For this is my blood of the new covenant</u>, which is <u>shed</u> for many <u>for the remission of sins</u>.'"

We symbolically remember his blood and body that was broken for us by taking part in communion. His own death saved us from the wrath of God and when we take part in the communion, we are saying thank you!

Hebrews 9:12 (NKJV) tells us, "...<u>with his own blood</u> he entered the most holy place once for all, <u>having obtained eternal redemption</u>."

This celebration of his life through the communion was and still is an important event. Instead of God seeing our sinfulness and imperfections, he sees his Son's Spirit, his life accepted in us. We are covered, concealing our flaws, and we are sealed with his promise of full redemption forever. We are made acceptable to God by his holy life, his blood and his body.

Let's read **Isaiah 53:5 again. It says, "He was <u>wounded for our transgressions</u>, h*e was* <u>bruised for our iniquities</u>; The chastisement (punishment) for our peace was upon him, and <u>by his stripes we are healed</u>."**

Because of the stripes that were put on the back of Jesus, when he was beaten and sentenced to death, we can have healing. He does not have to be physically standing right in front of us, like he did when he healed people in the bible.

Just before Jesus had died, he had asked the Father to forgive those causing his death (Luke 23:34). Not just those accusers at his death, but all people throughout time that need forgiveness and eternal life. For he was speaking on behalf of all of mankind. He had already had the authority to give people forgiveness, because he had said so himself earlier in his ministry. **He said, "... For which is easier, to say, 'Your sins are forgiven you, or to say, arise and walk? But that you may know that the <u>Son of man has power on earth to forgive sins</u>." (Matthew 9:5-6).**

There are so many stories of what Jesus had done to heal and forgive people, while he was still alive here on earth. He taught that forgiveness and healing go hand in hand.

Here is the full story of where Jesus healed and forgave a paralyzed man.

Matthew 9:2-8(NKJV), "Then behold, they brought to him a paralytic lying on a bed. When Jesus saw their faith, he said to the paralytic, 'Son, be of good cheer; your sins are forgiven you'. And at once some of the scribes said within themselves, 'This man blasphemes!' But Jesus, knowing their thoughts, said, 'Why do you think evil in your hearts? For which is easier, to say, 'Your sins are forgiven you, or to say, arise and walk? But that you may <u>know that the Son of man has power on earth to forgive sins</u>'—then he said to the paralytic, 'Arise, take up your bed, and go to your house.' And he arose and departed to his house."

Jesus had used this occasion as a teaching moment as he explained that forgiveness can also bring healing. Jesus told the man to get up and walk home. No one had to carry him around anymore. He was free from his disease. Jesus proved his authority to forgive sins and heal mankind.

He used every opportunity to demonstrate the power of God given to him, and to proclaim the wonderful things available, because of what he was about to do. His death, his blood, his body, his whole being was about to pay the price to give us forgiveness, healing and redemption. He paid for it all with his life! He entered the most holy place with his own blood to obtain eternal redemption from the curse of the law, for us all (Hebrews 9:12 and Galatians 3:13). And he has given us access to the blessings of God (Ephesians 1:3). He has given us his best!

A NEW BEGINNING

❖

LESSON 20

If we accept the death of Jesus in exchange for ours, then we also accept his life as ours. If God accepts his death in exchange for ours, then God accepts his life as ours.

Jesus had referred to physical death as being asleep (Matthew 9:24 and John 11:11-13). Jesus also referred to a place called Abraham's bosom, where past lives looking ahead for his resurrection went to rest when they died. This was before he became the first to rise from the dead with a glorified body. Because of Jesus, there is a new beginning. Now Jesus receives all those who trust in him to give them eternal life, when they die. Jesus takes their spirit and soul to be with him in full and blissful peace and happiness.

Paul said in 2 Corinthians 5:8 (NKJV), "…to be absent from the body is to be present with the Lord."

Psalms 16:11 (NKJV) says, "You will show me the path of life; In your presence is fullness of joy; at your right hand are pleasures evermore."

I have read stories of people who have died and then revived back to life. You can find some of these kinds of stories all over the internet. These people say that when they died, they themselves left their bodies. They claim that they felt more alive than they ever had before. They felt so happy that they really did not want to go back into their bodies. But Jesus would tell them that they needed to go back for some reason or another. These people had the opportunity to witness how wonderful it felt to be in the presence of the Lord. They all claim that their fear of death was gone.

John 3:16 (NKJV), "For God so loved the world that he gave his only begotten Son, that <u>whoever believes in him (Jesus) should not perish but have everlasting life.</u>"

Romans 10:13 (NKJV), "For whoever calls on the name of the LORD shall be saved."

Hebrews 4 :14-16 (NKJV), "Seeing then that <u>we have a great high priest who has passed through the heavens,</u> Jesus the Son of God, let us hold fast our confession. For we do not have a high priest who cannot sympathize with our weaknesses, but <u>was in all points tempted as we are, yet without sin. Let us therefore come boldly to the throne of grace, that we may obtain mercy and find grace to help in time of need.</u>"

We don't have to seek our maker at a distance like the people had to in the old covenant days of Moses. The Spirit of God is not just in a temporary tent or a dwelling place made with human hands.

When Jesus traveled to Jerusalem for the Passover of the Jews, he went into the temple and drove out all the people who were selling animals. He called the temple his Father's house.

Then, Jesus referred to himself (his body) as a temple. He said that he would raise it up again within three days after his death (John 2:19-21).

By our own decision, we can approach the throne of God in prayer because his invisible presence can now dwell within us (1 Corinthians 3:16). We can allow ourselves to become God's temple, body or dwelling place in the name of Jesus.

In Matthew 18:20 (KJV) Jesus said, "For where two or three are gathered together in my name, there am I in the midst of them."

Together as many members of his whole congregation, we are referred to as his church body of believers. Jesus is with us in Spirit, and he is the head (or leader) over all his different members (1 Corinthians 2:16). Just like with a human body, there is a head and other body parts that function together as a whole.

Romans 12:4-5 (NKJV), "For as we have many members in one body, but all the members do not have the same function, so we, being many, are one body in Christ, and individually members of one another."

Think of how a business works to be successful. You have a leader who is in charge of the operation of the company. You also have the employees that make the company a success by following the directions of their leader. Think of how churches conduct their business. They have a leader and all kinds of people who have different roles as part of the church. They all work together as one body of believers.

We all become one through his Holy Spirit. We become the temple of God and his dwelling place. The Holy Spirit is our intercessor and helper here on earth. He teaches us the things he hears from the Father, just as Jesus did. We all hear from the same Holy Spirit that Jesus did.

The Holy Spirit was involved in the affairs of mankind all throughout the bible. He was <u>involved</u> in the birth of Jesus (Matthew 1:18-19, Luke 1:35). When Jesus was baptized in the Jordan river, the Holy Spirit <u>descended upon him</u> like a dove (Matthew 3:16, Luke 3:21). After his baptism, Jesus was <u>led up by the Spirit into the wilderness</u> to be tempted (Matthew 4:1, Luke 4:1). After the temptations, <u>Jesus returned in the power of the Spirit</u> (Luke 4:14).

In Romans 8:11 (KJV) Paul says, "If the Spirit who raised Jesus from the dead dwells in you, he who raised Christ from the dead will also <u>give life to your mortal bodies through his Spirit who dwells in you</u>."

Paul says the same Spirit who raised Jesus from the dead gives eternal life to us. He now dwells in our bodies as we accept Jesus Christ as our savior.

We can have a conversation with him about anything and everything. He can relate to our feelings and desires. He also understands the tempter because he had been there himself in the wilderness temptations of Jesus. We can come boldly to the throne of grace with our prayers. And just like with our cell phones, we can't see the sound waves going back and forth, but they are. Our words can travel through space and time when we pray, if needed. He is our intercessor and emergency contact. We can have his name and number on speed dial because we have his connection from within.

We can all have a new beginning. We can let our creator and savior be as close to us as our own hearts by the Holy Spirit of God. We should learn to trust him. We are not invincible in our present state. He is the only way that we can have eternal life and protection, even now.

If only the whole world could comprehend the full reality of God's love, and what he did to redeem us. He calls us his children! He wants to be our Father, friend, healer and counselor. There will be a new day in time when all sorrow will be done away with. He promises!

Revelation, 21:4 (NKJV), "And God will wipe away every tear from their eyes; there shall be no more death, nor sorrow, nor crying. There shall be no more pain, for the former things have passed away."

This is what any loving father would do for his children, if he could. God can, and he will.

MIRACLES OF JESUS

LESSON 21

Jesus came to heal the hurting physically and emotionally. He came to bring us love, joy and peace (Galatians 5:22). There is coming a time when there will be no loneliness, poverty or bondage. There will be no fear of another doing us any harm. There will be no fear of dying because there will be no more sickness or death. We won't need any hospitals or prisons. There will be no devil to hinder us or affect our thinking in a bad way. We are a work in progress and there will come a time when we will have no thoughts of sin, sickness, disease or pain of any kind.

God has created us with the ability (or power) for healing. We see this when we break an arm or leg or get a cold. There is something inside of all of us that knows how to restore or repair that broken bone or fight off that cold. We are meant to be healthy. If it were not so, then we would not be able to be healed of anything.

Jesus is the healer of all types of sickness, diseases and infirmities. Years ago, I heard that God only heals if it is his will. Well, duh, it is his will! It is recorded all throughout the bible. He healed those who looked to him, and Jesus said that he came to do the will of his Father.

Jesus was so full of compassion! There are so many scriptures that show how he cared and healed people. Most of the people he didn't even personally know. He Just loved people!

Matthew 8: 16-17 (NKJV), "When evening had come, they brought to him many who were demon-possessed. And he <u>cast out the spirits with a word</u>, and <u>healed all who were sick</u>, that it might be fulfilled which was spoken by Isaiah the prophet, saying: 'He himself took (removed from us) our infirmities (physical or mental weakness) **and bore our sicknesses.'"**

Matthew 9:35-36 (NKJV) says that "Jesus went about all the cities and villages, <u>teaching</u> in their synagogues, and <u>preaching</u> the <u>gospel of the kingdom</u>, and <u>healing every sickness and every disease</u> among the people. But when he saw the multitudes, He was moved with compassion for them."

In Matthew 11:5 (KJV) Jesus said that the "… <u>blind receive their sight, and the lame walk, the lepers are cleansed, and the deaf hear, the dead are raised up, and the poor have the gospel preached to them.</u>"

Matthew 15:30-31 (NKJV), "Then <u>great multitudes came to Him</u>, having with them the lame, blind, mute, maimed, and many others; and they laid them down at Jesus' feet, and he healed them. The multitude marveled when they saw the mute speaking, the maimed made whole, the lame walking, and the blind seeing; and they glorified the God of Israel."

All the miracles and healings proved God was a good God and it was his will to help and bless people.

Acts 10:38 (NKJV), "…God anointed Jesus of Nazareth with the <u>Holy Spirit and with power</u>, who went about doing good and <u>healing all who were oppressed by the devil</u>, for <u>GOD WAS WITH HIM</u>."

There are so many individual stories in the bible where Jesus healed multitudes of people just by a word or a touch.

Jesus healed a woman who had been bowed over because of a spirit of infirmity. She had been that way for eighteen years. In the story, Jesus blamed the infirmity on Satan. Satan does bind people with physical and mental disabilities. The woman was instantly healed when he told her that she was "loosed from the infirmity", and, as he laid his hands on her for healing (Luke 13:10-17).

At another time, a woman who had a persistent bleeding condition for twelve years came up behind Jesus and touched the hem of his garment. She was healed instantly. Jesus told her that her own faith in him made her whole (Matthew 9:20-21 and Mark 5:25-34).

Jesus multiplied five loaves of bread and two fish to feed 5,000 men and their families. There were twelve baskets full of food leftover after they all ate (Matthew 14:15-21).

In another miracle, Jesus had told Peter to catch a fish and that he would find a coin in its mouth. It was enough to pay their taxes that they owed (Matthew 17:24-27).

All these stories and more are found in the first four books of the New Testament. Matthew, Mark, Luke and John were disciples of Jesus and they tell their version of what they remembered.

Jesus said he was the resurrection and the life. He had power to bring people back to life. One of the biggest miracles that he had performed was when he raised his friend Lazarus back to life. The man had been dead for four days and had already been put in a tomb. This was very important for people to witness. He was showing them that it was possible for a human to be raised up from the dead. He proved to his spectators that he had power to raise them from the dead when they do finally die. He wanted them to trust him to raise them up to an eternal life of peace and joy when the time comes. He was revealing the power of the resurrection.

In the story, when Jesus got to the family of Lazarus, he said **"I am the resurrection and the life. He who believes in me, though he may die, he shall live. And <u>whoever lives and believes in me shall never die</u>…" (John 11:25-26 (NKJV)**

Then when Jesus got to the tomb, he said a thank you prayer to the Father out loud, then he raised his friend from the dead.

John 11:43-44 (NKJV), "He cried with a loud voice, 'Lazarus, come forth!' And he who had died came out bound hand and foot with graveclothes, and his face was wrapped with a cloth. Jesus said to them, 'Loose him, and let him go.'"

All these miracles that were written about Jesus happened **after** he had returned (to Galilee) in the **power of the Spirit**. He taught in their synagogues and then moved on to Nazareth where he was brought up. On the Sabbath day, he went into the synagogue and began to speak from the book of Isaiah. In verse eighteen, he explains what the power of the Spirit is for (Luke 4:13-14,18).

He said, "The Spirit of the Lord is upon me, because he hath anointed me to preach the gospel to the poor; he hath sent me to heal the broken hearted, to preach deliverance to the captives, and recovering of sight to the blind, to set at liberty them that are bruised (oppressed)" (Isaiah 61:1).

Jesus was the one that the Spirit of the Lord God anointed to fulfill this prophecy that was written some 700 years earlier. He was anointed with "the power of the Spirit" to fulfill scripture.

He healed the broken hearted, crippled, blind, mute, deaf, those bound by Satan with disease, infirmities and oppression, and he raised the dead. Jesus had power over all the power of the enemy.

Throughout his life, he was proving his identity that had been hidden in the scriptures. He had power, that no man ever had! He spoke with boldness and authority! The scriptures were coming to life!

We have superheroes all around the world! We have military men and women who risk their lives for our country. We have firemen, policemen, and others devoted to serving the community in some heroic way. We have doctors and nurses who do their best to alleviate our pain and suffering. We also have advocates, counselors and ministers who help us individually when we need it. The stories in the bible that showed what Jesus did are so interesting! If you like a good biography or historical book, the bible is the book for you! If you like drama and adventure, it's the book for you! If you like superpowers and superheroes, it's the book for you! But, there is no other superhero like him!!

LOVE COVERS A MULTITUED OF SIN

LESSON 22

When Jesus was living here on earth, he was asked by one of his followers what was the greatest commandment.

Matthew 22:37-40 (NKJV), "Jesus said to him, 'You shall love the LORD your God with all your heart, with all your soul, and with all your mind. This is the first and great commandment. And the second is like it: You shall love your neighbor as yourself. On these two commandments hang all the Law and the Prophets.'"

It is easier to focus on doing good to each other than it is to focus on the old Mosaic commandment of "do nots". Jesus asks us to walk in love as he does. He was asked how many times a person should forgive another. In Matthew 18:21-22, Jesus said seventy times seven.

Luke 6:37 (NKJV), "Judge not, and you shall not be judged. Condemn not, and you shall not be condemned. Forgive, and you will be forgiven."

Why wouldn't we want to learn from him? He tells us to focus on the good we can do. He gives many examples on how to live.

For example, to forgive someone doesn't mean to let them walk all over you. You may even have to walk away from a dangerous situation or avoid that person at all cost. Don't let the tempter get the best of you through others.

Forgiving is an act of kindness rather you feel it or not. You release yourself from a bad feeling that can eat at you from the inside. Don't let the bad feelings rule. Take control and just do it by faith.

Keep yourself in an attitude of love and peace. Don't burn bridges that you might need to cross again someday.

Luke 17:3-4 (NIV), "If your brother or sister sins against you, rebuke them. Even if they sin against you seven times in a day and seven times come back to you saying 'I repent,' you must forgive them."

Boy, sometimes that seems to be hard to do when you don't feel the love. When you forgive, you are the stronger person and God sees the sacrificial love you are giving. It helps to break the stronghold over you, as well as the other person. Forgiveness can bring healing.

1 Peter 3:8-9 (NKJV), "Finally, all of you be of one mind, having compassion for one another; love as brothers, be tenderhearted, be courteous; not returning evil for evil or reviling (insult) for reviling, but on the contrary blessing, knowing that you were called to this, <u>that you may inherit a blessing.</u>"

1 Peter 4:8 (NKJV), "And above all things have fervent love for one another, for <u>LOVE WILL COVER A MULTITUED OF SIN.</u>"

Jesus covered a multitude of sin by his act of love.

The solution to redemption is through Jesus. Through him we see God's love, mercy and grace, not punishment. You don't have to get everything right first in your life before you come to him. God is a God of new beginnings. You can start over and over till you get it right. Remember that Jesus said for us to forgive each other as many times as it takes to make things right. He does the same for us. He forgives us as many times as it takes, as long as we come to him and ask. He does not give up on us. Don't give up on him.

Jesus said in Matthew 11:28-29 (NKJV), "Come to me, all you who labor and are heavy laden (burdened), and I will give you rest. Take my yoke upon you and learn from me, for I am gentle and lowly in heart, <u>and you will find rest for your souls.</u>"

Learning about Jesus can lead to finding peace of mind and rest for your soul. No matter what happens in your life, he has a beautiful ending for those who trust in him. Your ending can become your new beginning.

WE ARE HIS DWELLING PLACE

In review of previous lessons, Jesus was filled with the Holy Spirit after his baptism in the river Jordan. He was then led by the Spirit into the wilderness to be tested. After he finished being tempted, he returned in the <u>power of the Spirit</u> and was ready to minister to others.

At the beginning of the official ministry of Jesus, three things happened. The heavens were opened, the Holy Spirit descended to him, and the Father spoke from heaven.

Luke 3;21-23 (NKJV), "When all the people were baptized, it came to pass that <u>Jesus</u> also was baptized; and while he prayed, the heaven was opened. And the <u>Holy Spirit descended in bodily form</u> like a dove <u>upon him</u>, and a <u>voice came from heaven</u> which said, '"<u>You are my beloved Son</u>; <u>in you I am well pleased</u>.' Now <u>Jesus</u> himself <u>began his ministry</u> at about thirty years of age."

All throughout the bible, there are scriptures regarding three divine and distinct positions of authority and functions. They are one in Spirit, and they operate in conjunction with each other.

Colossians 2:9 (NKJV), "For in him (Jesus) dwells all the fullness of the Godhead bodily.

The Godhead refers to the three (the Father, the Son and the Holy Spirit) sharing the same substance.

Jesus carried out his side of the plan here on earth for his heavenly Father. He did it by the authority and the anointed power of the Holy Spirit that was given by the Father. The three are all referred to as the Trinity.

Jesus was given all he needed to deal with the troubles of the human race, sin and evil spirits. He was given the tools needed to heal, deliver and save others through the Holy Spirit. He was the Son of God and a son of mankind. He was the link between man and God.

He has established his kingdom here on earth. His kingdom is full of life-giving gifts such as miracles of deliverance, healing and prosperity. **In Matthew 6:33, Jesus said to seek first the kingdom of God, and his righteousness and all the things you need will be given to you.**

We become born-again as part of his family when we ask him to come into our lives. Since it is a spiritual thing, it is not limited by physical things that we can touch, see or hear.

We are made up of spirit, soul and body. We have different emotions, personalities and outside factors of life that affect us. And of course, we live in a mortal shell of a body. He comes to dwell with us by his Holy Spirit to help guide us and get us through life.

If we don't understand how the Holy Spirit can live within us, think about how our bodies and our automobiles are similar in purpose. The car is like the shell or body that we can occupy. When we get into our cars to travel somewhere, we must take control and operate it as the driver. It will take us wherever we want to go, if we activate its devices. We know how to use the car for our benefit, just like we know how to use our own bodies for our benefit.

If for some reason the car breaks down or stops working properly, the car can't fulfill our needs until the problem is fixed. There is no life to the car in itself and it can't fix itself. It has no spiritual life of its own, but we do! We are the life of the car, and it can't even drive itself without knowing what to do.

If the car problem can't be fixed, the driver has to abandon the car because he can't operate it anymore. Like the car, if we die in our body, what happens to us? We are spirit beings and will still exist! Life here is temporary, and one day we will have to leave our bodies (like the car).

While we are still in our cars, we can go about our business and get things done for ourselves and others. We live not only for ourselves, but for our kids, spouse and those who are important to us. Our family and friends can be a part of our caravan. What we do affects their lives too! It is natural to want everything to turn out right. God knows everything and I mean everything! God's Holy Spirit, who was in the body of Jesus with him can also fit in our bodies with us, like the car in the example for it has extra seats. He knows the best routes in life, and he knows the way to our eternal home when it is time. He has already been there! He wants to help us live our lives. He wants to be our counselor, our mentor, our guide and best friend. Sometimes we even need him to take over driving. We don't always know the way or what to do next in getting things done.

The apostle Paul said to be absent from the body is to be present with the Lord. When we die (or vacate our body), we will be fully in the presence of Jesus. He wants to help guide us on our journey to our final destination.

If the life (or Spirit) that had lived in the body of Jesus is in you, then his life story (his history of what happens at the end of his life) is also a part of your life story. The debt for your sin was paid for, when he died. His death is only a small fraction of his whole story. It continues on forever. If his story becomes our story, then we have a right to live forever.

MARRIAGE NOT MADE IN HEAVEN

—◆—

LESSON 24

There was a time in history that marital ties became a major issue. It was the bond between human women and what the bible calls the "sons of God" according to **Genesis 6:1-4. It says that the "sons of God" took the daughters of men for wives and had children with them.** Their children were known as giants. It was not made clear who the "sons of God" were in this particular chapter.

Luke 3:23-38 lists the family line of Jesus all the way back through Adam. Luke calls Adam the son of God because he was the first man created by God. Adam was not born out from the womb of woman. His body was created from the dust of the earth, and he became a living soul, when God breathed into his body the breath of life. We are considered son and daughter offspring of Adam, by being born into this world through his bloodline.

The story in Genesis 6:1-4 regarding the "sons of God" is referring to a catastrophe that almost destroyed our species all together. Genesis 6:1-4 doesn't tell us if they were human or some other type of being.

There are other types of beings besides our own human race. For one, we can read about angelic beings all throughout the bible. There are some that are good and some that are not so good, just like with us.

Jesus said that when we are eventually resurrected to new life, we will no longer die and we will be like the angels in heaven, who do not marry (Matthew 22:30 and Luke 20:34-36).

I believe that the "sons of God" and the daughters of men that are mentioned in Genesis 6:1-4 are two different types of entities somehow. If angels in heaven are not supposed to marry, then who were the "sons of God" who had children? Were they some other created beings that were not born from our same bloodline? Or, were the "sons of God" angels?

To understand if they could be some kind of angels, let's look at what angels have been known for. There are many stories of where they were involved with the affairs of mankind. In the bible, angels have been known to appear and disappear in front of people. They can eat human food, sleep and physically touch people.

They have different jobs that they do for God, and there are multitudes of angels that we hear of in the bible. There is Gabriel, who brings messages from God among other things. He is mentioned in the book of Daniel, chapters eight through twelve, and he is also mentioned in Luke chapter one. There is Michael, the archangel who wars against evil. He is also mentioned in the book of Daniel, in chapters ten through twelve, as well as, in Jude verse nine and in the book of Revelation chapter twelve. Angels are watching over our world, according to Zechariah chapter one.

The bible mentions seraphim (Isaiah 6), Cherubim (Genesis 3), and the host of heaven around God's throne (1 Kings 22). Jesus even said that there are angels in the presence of God that look out for little children (Matthew 18:10).

Jesus also said that he could have asked the Father to send legions of angels to deliver him down from the cross, but he didn't (Matthew 26). All these different references to angels tell me that they can protect and rescue people. They are supposed to be ministering spirits that look out for mankind (Hebrews 1:14).

Angels are curious about us (1 Peter1:12), and they help mankind through God's instructions. Genesis chapters 18 and 19 gives us an example of their help. In the story of Sodom and Gomorrah, that I had briefly mentioned in an earlier lesson, it tells us that God had placed judgement on two cities to be destroyed by fire and brimstone. When God had told Abraham what he was going to do, Abraham had asked the Lord to spare his nephew Lot and his family that lived there. So, two angels went into the city to Lot and his household, took them by the hand, and quickly lead them out of the city.

Angels can be seen as ordinary men according to Genesis 19:1, where they are called angels, and then in Genesis 19:15-16 these same angels are called men. So be careful how you treat people, it could be an angel in disguise.

In Hebrews 13:1-2 (KJV) Paul said, "Be not forgetful to entertain strangers: for thereby some have entertained angels unawares."

There was a time in our very early history, when some of the angels fell from grace and caused mass destruction for all mankind living on the earth.

Jude 1:6 (KJV) written by the apostle Jude says, **"The angels which kept not their first estate, but left their own habitation, he hath reserved in everlasting chains under darkness unto the judgement of the great day."**

2 Peter 2:4-5 (KJV) written by the apostle Peter says, "God spared not the angels that sinned, but cast them down to hell, and delivered them into chains of darkness, to be reserved unto judgement; and spared not the old world, but saved Noah the eighth person, a preacher of righteousness, bringing in the flood upon the world of the ungodly."

Jude 1:6 and 2 Peter 2:4-5 both say that there were angels who did not stay in their "proper domain" or realm. They left their "own environment to make our realm of existence, theirs. God now has them preserved in chains of darkness. They were cast into hell, and the bible tells us that hell is in the lowest depths of the earth (Isaiah 14:15, Ephesians 4:9 and Psalms 16:10). They have been reserved until the great day of judgement, because of the chaos that they caused here on earth that was supposed to be our own habitation.

Let's look into what they did.

There is a book that was not included in the original books of the bible called the "Book of Enoch". It was an ancient Jewish religious text attributed to a man named Enoch. He was from the line of Seth, who was Adam's third son. Enoch was the great-grandfather of Noah. From what is understood about him, he was a godly man, and that God took him up to heaven where he resided among the angels. He had never died. **Genesis 5:24 (NKJV), says that Enoch "...walked with God and was no longer, for God had taken him."** The book of Enoch is based on his encounters with the angels of God.

The book of Enoch goes into great detail telling a story about some fallen angels, their children and a flood. The story is parallel to the story about the "sons of God" mentioned in Genesis 6:1-7. Enoch refers to these beings as angels, watchers and children of heaven, while the author of Genesis refers to them as "sons of God". Both books say that they had taken the daughters of men as wives, had children through them, and then there was a flood.

Both books talk about the offspring becoming evil giants. If we put the two versions of the story together, we get more details that explain why they were so evil. Their fathers, the fallen angels, had taught and supplied them and their mothers with evil arts not familiar to mankind. The giants used these enchanted spells for their own selfish gain for power. God saw that the wickedness of man was great in the earth (Genesis 6:5).

If the angels of God in heaven do not marry, are these "sons of God" some of the angels that fell from grace, or are they some other beings? In the book of Enoch, Enoch says they are angels! Did these "sons of God" misuse a heavenly type of gift that was meant for mankind? For example, was it like the miracle of life that God had given to Abraham and Sarah to have a child? Did the fallen angels misuse gifts that belonged to God, just to father their own children?

The quotes that are found in Jude 1:6 and 2 Peter 2:4-5 of the bible about the fallen angels, where probably taken from the information found in the ancient history book of Enoch, since both books mention the doom of fallen angels. Both books say that God dealt with them by chains and imprisonment.

Another reason that I believe Jude 1:6 and 2 Peter 2:4-5 are related to text that is found in the book of Enoch is because Enoch himself is mentioned a few verses later in the book of Jude (Jude 1:14). Jude quotes Enoch as saying "Behold, the Lord cometh with 10,000's of his saints." I don't think it was a coincidence, that Enoch's name was mentioned in this only chapter in Jude, or the fact that Enoch gave a similar prophecy in the book of Enoch.

Genesis chapter six and some of the parts of the book of Enoch are in agreement about the things that happened in each story. So, I am assuming that they are both the same story told by different authors.

To summarize the story of Noah and the flood in Genesis 6:1-13, it says that when men began to multiply and have daughters, the "sons of God" took the beautiful daughters of these men for themselves. It says that when the "sons of God" had children with the women, that the children were the giants in the land. In verse six and seven, God saw the wickedness of mankind and was sorry that he had made them. He was so upset that he decided to cause a flood to destroy them. In the end of the story, the flood destroyed all of those who did evil, except for Noah and his family.

There has been a lot of speculation of who these "sons of God" were that lived before the flood. When I look through Genesis in the "KJV", this is the only place where I see the phrase "sons of God". There seems to be something different about them in particular. In the rest of the book of Genesis, the writer usually uses the word angels when referring to angels as God's helpers. Some believe that the "sons of God" were a different kind of being, that may have been created similar to us. Some believe they were just certain men possibly from the generational line of Seth. It does not say that they were sons of Satan, sons of Adam, sons of Seth, or sons of Cain. It says "sons of God", because they were referred to as being associated with or having their origin from God somehow.

In the story of Job, it gives another clue of where they may have come from.

Job 1:6, Now there was a day when the sons of God came to present themselves before the Lord, and Satan came also among them.

Job 2:1, Again there was a day when the sons of God came to present themselves before the Lord, and Satan came also among them to present himself before the Lord.

According to the book of Job, "sons of God" apparently presented themselves before the Lord in heaven. Was Satan himself considered or called a son of God like the others in these verses? They all had to be able to congregate in the heavens, so they had to be some kind of heavenly beings.

I believe that the "sons of God" in Genesis were fallen angelic beings. They had their own children, who were born from the two kinds of beings (human and angelic). It created an explosive and erratic body of people. It produced humans that could not handle their own abilities of supernatural power that was packed into their earthly bodies. Not only that, but they were associated with Adam's bloodline that had been affected by the sinful tendencies passed down from the beginning of our time. They were said to be very evil.

They did horrible and despicable acts that you can't even imagine would happen here on the earth, according to the book of Enoch. Some versions of the bible called these offspring of the "sons of God", Nephilim. Genesis 6:4 says they were mighty men of old, men of renown. The Living Bible translation said that the children became "giants of whom so many legends were told".

If the "sons of God" or fallen angels that had the offspring were eternal beings, they would most likely never die and have to leave their bodies like humans do. They already existed as a whole being (mind, body and spirit). For the horrible things that they did, they are now in chains waiting for their day of judgement.

Their eternal children who were part human would most likely have died and been forced to abandon their earthly bodies that drowned in the flood. Their fleshly body was not eternal. It came from the ground and returned to the ground from where it came from, when they died. They had corruptible bodies just like ours.

I was wondering what happened to them after they died, since they were born here on earth from fathers who were eternal beings. Are they still existing without a body since the body was destroyed? Could they be the disembodied angry spirits talked about in the days of Jesus? It could explain Matthew 12, Luke 4 and 8, Mark 5 and all the other verses throughout the four gospels where Jesus had to deliver people from wicked spirits.

Were they still around in a form that couldn't be seen, since they had no physical body of their own? Since they already learned secrets from heaven that their fathers had taught them, are they the same beings that torment humans here on earth with oppression, depression, sickness and disease? Do they cause infirmities? We can normally only see what is physically around us with our natural eyes. Do they still work to influence and hurt God's creation even though we can't see them?

These rebellious children of the "sons of God" had continued in the sins of their fathers till the day that their bodies died. They could not make their own bodies become incorruptible. They had not been given the authority or power to do so. Only Jesus Christ has the authority and power to do so. So, their spirits lived on without Christ. In the book of Enoch, they were called evil spirits.

When these offspring had been born and living in their own bodies, they were associated with a different type of existence than we were. Maybe, just like we are connected to Adam and Eve by DNA, the offspring of the "sons of God" were connected through DNA of their own eternal fathers and their earthly mothers combined.

Maybe, their soul and spirit were trapped by their sin here on earth. Maybe, the judgement of sin pronounced on their fathers was passed down to them and they will also face judgement for their own evil on judgement day.

Throughout time, Satan has tried to set up his kingdom here on earth using God's created beings. Satan and his evil friends don't go by the commands of God. They are out to overthrow God and his kingdom. So, they do the don'ts of the ten commandments, and they don't do the dos of the ten commandments, using humans that will let them.

In the beginning, and in the story of the garden of Eden, Adam and Eve had not eaten from the **tree of life that causes mankind to live forever** yet (Genesis 3:22). They were cast out of the garden before they had a chance to eat from it (Genesis 3:22). They might have been in the same boat as the offspring of the fallen angels, if they would have eaten from the tree of life. Maybe, they would have been stuck in their sin forever.

The ending results regarding the death of the evil giant children by a great flood, and the salvation of Enoch's grandson Noah and his family during the flood, became a new beginning for mankind. It became a baptism of saving grace for some and an eternal death for others.

If you think about it, Jesus had a Father that was eternal and a mother who was earthly. If the story about the "sons of God" were true, then Jesus as half eternal being of God himself, would also be alive. The "sons of God" lost their bodies and will be destroyed by God in judgement. Jesus was judged as righteous by God, and his body became immortal.

Thanks be to God that we have a savior. He is the real and only begotten Son of God, a man who died to pay the price for our sin. Jesus Christ is the "Holy One" that takes away or separates our sin from us before we become eternal. Revelation 2:7 tells us that whoever overcomes, will eat from the tree of life which is in the midst of paradise. We will have incorruptible bodies and live forever with Christ Jesus who is the true "Son of God".

GIANTS IN THE LAND

LESSON 25

Many, many years later after the flood, the bible says that giants were on the earth again. They are mentioned in Deuteronomy 3:11, 9:2, Numbers 13:32-33, 1 Chronicles 20:2, 4-8, 2 Samuel 21:18-22 to name a few. They were referred to as giants and people of great stature. They were called Nephilim, sons of Anak and other names. There is mention of a man of great stature with 6 fingers on each hand and 6 toes on each foot, who was a son of the giants (2 Samuel 21:20). The giants are mentioned many times after the great flood was over.

These giants may or may not have been the same giants born before the flood. They could have been just very large or tall men that were picked to be the top soldiers because of their strength and size, but I don't think so. Did some of the giants find a way to escape from the flood or, was some of Noah's family that survived the flood from a mixed race of these giants? The gene from the giants could have been mixed in with the family line leading up to Noah, his wife or from any of his three daughters-in-law. From there, it could have passed on through the children. I don't really know the answer for sure! But I do know that there were giants after the flood. Many years later, most of the Israelites did not go into the promised land because they were so terrified of them (Numbers 13:31-33).

The Israelites had already been affected mentally and emotionally by their past experience as slaves in Egypt. They were so afraid, that they would not go in and fight for the promised land that God had told them they could have.

In the book of Numbers, chapters thirteen and fourteen, it tells the story of Joshua, Caleb and ten other men who were sent to spy out the promised land of Canaan, just before the Israelites were supposed to go in and conquer it.

After 40 days, all twelve men came back to give a report of what they saw. Ten of the twelve gave a bad report. They first said that the land was very fruitful, but the men that lived there were strong and "of great stature".

In Numbers 13:32- 33 (KJV) they said, "...... all the people that we saw in it, are men of a great stature. And there we saw the giants, the sons of Anak, which come of the giants: and we were in our own sight as grasshoppers...."

This bad report had terrified the Israelites so much that they did not want to go forward. Joshua and Caleb were the only spies who were not alarmed by what they had seen. They knew in their heart that their God was much bigger. They were so eager to go get their promised land that they wanted to go at once, but they had to wait. None of the other adults were willing to trust God to help them conquer the land and they were already tired of the journey. They even said that they wanted to turn back to Egypt.

The whole trip should have taken them around 11 days to get there. Their disobedience and mistrust cost them dearly. The ten spies who had given the bad report all died of a plague. Most of the adult Israelites ended up wondering in the wilderness for 40 years until they all passed away (Numbers 26:65). Joshua and Caleb were the only ones who did get to go forward, but they had to wait for forty years instead of going right away.

So, after the 40 years, the only ones who were allowed to go into the promised land and take possession of some of the land, were Joshua, Caleb and the Israelite children, who were now adults themselves (Numbers 14:22-24, 30-32).

David and Goliath, the giant

There is another story in 1 Samuel chapter seventeen about a giant who was said to be 9 to 10 feet tall. His armor alone weighed 150 pounds. The story is in regards to David (a young teen who later became the famous king of Israel) and Goliath (the very tall giant and soldier of the Philistines).

In the story, the Philistine army came up against the Israelite people and had them terrified of their fearless champion warrior. Goliath taunted the Israelite soldiers with threats of how he was going to slaughter them. He teased them for forty days before he was to attack.

David was not part of the army of the Israelites since he was just a young boy. He had the job of tending his father's flock. Before the actual battle, David was sent from his father to the front lines to bring his three brothers, King Saul and the other Israelite soldiers some food.

While David was standing there among his brothers and other soldiers, he saw how Goliath was taunting the Israelite army and started asking questions. King Saul had David brought before him to find out what was going on.

David tells him that he will go and defeat the giant himself. In 1 Samuel 17:33, the king tries to explain to David that he is just an inexperienced young boy and that Goliath has been a warrior since his youth.

David was not intimidated by the enormous size of Goliath, nor what the king had told him. He explained to the king that he had killed a bear and a lion while doing his own job of protecting his father's flock. He claimed that the same God who protected him and helped him come against the lion and the bear, would do the same concerning the giant. He was not afraid!

The king approved him going and gave him his own armor to wear. The armor was made to fit a larger more muscular man fit for war. When I think of the story in my mind, I picture David trying on the king's armor. It had to be a funny sight to see because it didn't fit him right! He tried to walk around in it and couldn't! He told the king he could not fight with it and took it off.

David took his own staff, his slingshot and gathered five stones and put them in his shepherd's bag. These were the tools he was familiar with.

In 1 Samuel 17:45-47 David tells Goliath that the **battle is the Lords**, and that God **would** deliver his carcass into his hands. He spoke powerful words and God saw his faith! David had so much confidence in God that he expected it to happen. Even as a young boy, he had qualities that God was impressed with.

The Philistine army started advancing towards the Israelites to kill them, and in verse forty-eight David took off running towards the enemy, Goliath. He pulled out a stone from his bag and slung it at the giant, hitting him in his forehead, killing him instantly. The rest of the Philistine army ran for their lives, because their fearless champion was dead.

David was a mighty warrior because he knew he could go to battle in the strength of his God. He knew God was bigger than the obstacle in front of him. Later in years he ended up becoming a mighty king, after the death of King Saul.

Evidence of Giants

There is evidence still around today of gigantic ruins of the past. Some of these ruins were temples of worship and had pictures inscribed on them of strange looking creatures and very tall men, as well as normal sized humans. Some of the ruins could have been destroyed in the flood of Noah, while other ruins we see today could prove that these same types of beings existed even after the flood.

All throughout the bible there were stories of people who were rebellious against God. They had built altars, and performed sacrifices as part of their worship and dedication to a host of beings that they believed to exist. Some of the idol worshippers believed that they could influence the foreign gods (or devils) to get them what they wanted by powers of witchcraft and sorcery. The people were appealing to the images of these false gods and worshipping them.

These beings were called strange gods or devils in Deuteronomy 32:16-17. They are also referred to as demons and evil spirits. I believe that the giants who lost their bodies in the flood contributed to idol worship. How can people put their trust in beings that failed and corrupted the earth so long ago, instead of trusting God himself?

MARRIAGE MADE IN HEAVEN

------ ❖ ------

LESSON 26

When we accept Jesus Christ into our lives, our spirit is rebirthed from his Holy Spirit nature. The sinful desire is then considered dead (lifeless, unconscious, separated, severed or crucified) from our spirits. It's like getting out of a bad relationship or marriage and into a good one.

Romans 8:2 (NKJV), "For the law of the <u>Spirit of life in Christ Jesus has made me free</u> from the law of sin and death."

Galatians 5:22-23, But the <u>fruit of the Spirit</u> is love, joy, peace, longsuffering, gentleness, goodness, faith, meekness, temperance: <u>against such there is no law</u> (of sin and death).

In Romans 7:1-4, Paul compares a marriage agreement to a commitment with Jesus. In a marriage agreement, you sign papers and say your vows of commitment to each other. You are agreeing to become as one. You say or make a declaration that you are accepting him or her in your life.

Genesis 2:24 (NKJV), states, "Therefore a man shall leave his father and mother and be joined to his wife, and <u>they shall become one flesh</u>."

Jesus repeats this scripture in Matthews 19:5 and Mark 10:7 when he was questioned about divorce. Separation from one's spouse had become an option only when sin damaged the marriage relationship. Nowadays, a marriage ends when one of the parties die or through divorce for just about any reason.

The relationship is somewhat different in your commitment to Jesus. If you commit to him, the relationship does not end with the death of either party. It becomes forever. It only ends if you reject him. If you are going to accept Jesus, it has to be now in this life in order to remain permanent in the afterlife.

This is my take on becoming as one with him in comparison to a marriage. Jesus referred to himself as a bridegroom coming for his bride. The events leading up to and into the marriage has been and will be celebrated throughout time and eternity. He is so in love with his bride to be, that he takes her with all her faults and past failures. He doesn't care if she is broken. He takes her because he loves her and that is all that matters to him. He is obsessed with her and will do anything to get her for his bride. He redeems her from her past by giving his life for her. He gives her his name as he claims her as his bride.

Unlike a marriage between two people, the relationship does not die because he dies. He has risen from the dead and is alive forever more. He goes to prepare a place for his bride. The bride is his church or body of believers. In this marriage, they both become one as children of God.

John 14:1-3 (NKJV), "Let not your heart be troubled; you believe in God, believe also in me. In my Father's house are many mansions; if it were not so I would have told you. I go to prepare a place for you. And if I go and prepare a place for you, I will come again and receive you to myself; that where I am, there you may be also."

He does not leave his bride alone here on earth. He stays with her through his Spirit. They are still as one! After she finally grows old and it is time to go, he will still be there with her, ready to take her home with him to live forever.

GOD, WHY GIVE THE TEN COMMANDMENTS, IF THEY KILL?

—◆—

LESSON 27

I asked God, if death was the fate of Adam and Eve's disobedience, then why did he later set up the laws that include the ten commandments? The over 600 laws made it almost impossible to live out one's life without breaking any one of them. How is it all related?

I felt like God's answer to me was so that we could continue to live out our lives, even after sin. He made a way for forgiveness. He first made it possible for us to know what sin is. If you disobey a law, then there is a consequence. Someone gets hurt in the process. If you did not know it was wrong and hurtful, why would you even consider changing your actions? If you commit a sin and you know it is wrong, that sin is responsible for separating you through your own conscience from a holy God.

Adam and Eve hid from God after they sinned. No one likes to be condemned or found guilty, and then have to face the consequence for their actions. But, if you die hiding from God, evil has free reign over you. You can't hide your sin from God anyway!

The Father wants you to bring your sin to his Son for forgiveness instead of judgement. Let the Father look down from heaven to you, through the eyes of his Son. When we are one with Jesus, his death covers our sin, and his eternal life redeems us because we are in a relationship with him.

I believe that God gave the written laws to explain the one wrong act of Adam and Eve. It had spread and multiplied like a contagious disease down throughout their bloodline. God had to develop a cure that would stop it from spreading and wiping out the world. I believe that the laws in the time of Moses are all summed up or rooted in the sin of Adam and Eve.

Adam and Eve's disobedience was the sum of all sinful acts. It began to spread like a cancer into all kinds of evil acts against our own world and our creator. It destroys and devours! It separates us from or dissolves our relationship with our creator who is our life support. We can't exist without him.

In Exodus 20:1-20, God gave the people the ten commandments. They were to follow these warnings of do-nots among each other. They were told the things to not do. God even put a little feeling behind his warning with lightning, thunder, and smoke. He really wanted to get their attention and stress the importance of his commands. It is the same thing that a parent would do to warn their own children, so they don't get hurt. God wanted his people to fear him enough to heed his warning. These commands were based on the one sin that Adam and Eve committed against him. What Adam and Eve had done caused them to fear and draw away from God's presence. I believe that if Adam and Eve would have lived in the days of Moses and the ten commandments, they would have been guilty of breaking all ten.

Here are the Ten Commandments taken from the Old Testament in the book of Deuteronomy 5:7-21 (NKJV) that was given to the Israelites:

1) You shall have no other gods before me.

2) You shall not make for yourself a carved image—any likeness of anything that is in heaven above, or that is in the earth beneath, or that is in the water under the earth; you shall not bow down to them nor serve them. For I, the LORD your God, am a jealous God, visiting the iniquity of the fathers upon the children to the third and fourth generations of those who hate me, but showing mercy to thousands, to those who love me and keep my commandments.

3) You shall not take the name of the LORD your God in vain, for the LORD will not hold him guiltless who takes his name in vain.

4) Observe the sabbath day, to keep it holy, as the LORD your God commanded you. Six days you shall labor and do all your work, but the seventh day is the sabbath of the LORD your God. In it you shall do no work: you, nor your son, nor your daughter, nor your male servant, nor your female servant, nor your ox, nor your donkey, nor any of your cattle, nor your stranger who is within your gates, that your male servant and your female servant may rest as well as you.

5) Honor your father and your mother, as the LORD your God has commanded you, that your days may be long, and that it may be well with you in the land which the LORD your God is giving you.

6) You shall not murder.

7) You shall not commit adultery.

8) You shall not steal.

9) You shall not bear false witness against your neighbor.

10) You shall not covet your neighbor's wife; and you shall not desire your neighbor's house, his field, his male servant, his female servant, his ox, his donkey, or anything that is your neighbor's.

Adam and Eve broke all ten in one act of disobedience.

1) "You shall have no other gods before me." They chose to yield to the words of the serpent and against what God had said. They put Satan the serpent first. They did not stay loyal to God.

2) "You shall not make any graven image in the form of anything, nor bow down to or worship it." God is the only true God! Satan fell because he wanted God's position. He was trying to steal that position over mankind through Adam and Eve. Adam and Eve submitted to a false god, Satan, when they did what he said to do. By touching and eating the fruit, they had respect for the serpent (Satan) at his word and his idea, above the words spoken by God. They bowed to a different being. One made by God, not God himself.

> *Satan had found a loophole. If he could tempt them (or cause them) to want the fruit, by telling them it gives them special power, he catches their attention. He convinced them that God was holding out on them. God had told them not to eat it or they would die. Satan got them to mistrust God. He tricked them into turning their back on the real God and opening the door to a part of his world of false gods.*

They wanted to be like God, instead of who God made them to be. They opened themselves up to spiritual wickedness that they knew nothing about. This has led to idol worship and other false religions around the world.

Mankind was meant to have God as their leader, protector and provider. When people turn their back on God, the desire for something to believe in is still there. So, to fill the void, people find whatever they can to fill it. They want to be happy and satisfied. They look for it in all the wrong things and places.

3) "You shall not use the Lord's name in vain." They insulted or slandered God's name. They let the serpent (Satan) defame God by calling him a liar. Satan said to them, "You will not die!"

God is a good and holy God! Adam and Eve took his word as of no value. They did not believe or reverence God at his word. His name is above every name and should not be recognized as anything but holy and good. His name should not be spoken in vain or cursing. His word should not be taken lightly for it is the power that gives life or takes it away. His words matter!

4) "The Lord blessed the sabbath day as a holy day." It is a time of rest and fellowship with God. God had often visited Adam and Eve to enjoy fellowship with them. After they ate the forbidden fruit, they became afraid and hid from him. They tried to isolate or separate their presence from him.

5) "Honor your parents so you may have long life." Honor means great respect and high esteem. Parents are more experienced and most likely to look out for our best interest. Adam and Eve were created by God, and like a parent he was looking out for their best interest.

6) "Do not murder." They caused their own death, as well as, for everyone born after them because of their action. When they had their two sons, Cain and Abel, one killed the other over jealousy. Murder was born out of selfish or raging anger, which Cain acted from in killing his brother.

(It is different than defending yourself, your family or country. God wanted the Israelites to destroy the wicked people in the land to wipe out the evil. Sometimes, you have to defend your cause in order for it not to overtake you or the ones you love. Then it is not murder, it is self-defense. It is defending your loved ones or your own country!)

7) "Do not commit adultery." In Jesus's day, a woman that was caught in the act of adultery was brought before him by the teachers of the religious law and the Pharisees. This was found in John 8:1-11. They said that she should be stoned to death for her actions according to the law of Moses (or the ten Commandments). They asked him what he thought should happen to her. He told them that he who was without sin to go ahead and stone her. They all had to walk away one by one because they all had their own sin of some kind or another.

Adam and Eve had a special intimate relationship or connection with God, but they became unfaithful. It was not sexual as in the story of the woman caught in adultery, but they still became unfaithful to God. They gave their devotion to the serpent behind Gods back. According to the marriage law, adultery (which also means disloyalty or betrayal) damages the marriage or relationship.

8) "Do not steal." Satan convinced Adam and Eve to take of something that did not belong to them.

9) "Do not bear false witness." They allowed themselves to believe a lie contradictory to God's own words. They should have defended God's honor and words against the serpent. They should have guarded the tree that belonged to God. Jesus (the second Adam) defended God's honor to the devil in the wilderness of temptations.

10) "<u>Do not yearn to possess or take what belongs to your neighbor.</u>" They coveted the fruit of the forbidden tree so they could be like God. They became dissatisfied with what God had given them. They wanted more, so they took what belonged to someone else, God himself.

I don't believe it was Adam and Eves intention to overthrow God. I also believe God knew this. Adam and Eve just wanted to be more like him or as gods knowing good and evil.

When God said that they would die if they ate the fruit, he was trying to warn them of its danger. Satan lied and told them that they would not die, but that they would be more like God or a god themselves. Satan was calling God a liar!

The words that God had spoken to them regarding the tree has been proven to be true all throughout history. Humanity has been acting upon the good and evil power and influence of the tree's knowledge, and, we do die!

God wants us to (first of all) love and be loyal to him and (secondly) love one another. We fall into the devil's trap, when we knowingly put ourselves and our selfish needs above others, even if it hurts them in the process. Don't you think it hurts and offends God when we distrust him?

We can't all be chiefs or be our own gods, either! Just like the nature of Satan who wanted to be his own god, so goes the nature of mankind. This nature does not particularly like someone else ruling over or telling it what to do. Sometimes this nature wants to be in complete control without God's interference, until it gets into trouble.

God eventually gave mankind the knowledge of what is good and what is evil, through the written laws. Now we can know what this knowledge is, how it works, and how it affects our own lives. These laws would prove to be impossible for any human being to keep without breaking any one of them. Breaking just one without recompense could lead to death. These laws are associated with the blessing and the curse.

God does not lie, and his word accomplishes what he says it will. Even though he said, "you shall surely die" in Genesis 2:16-17, he accomplished a miracle. Satan had no idea of what God's Word could or would do. When I say word, I mean word with a big "W", because eventually it happened through Jesus, who is called the "Word of God" (John 1:1-14).

Here is my thought. Adam and Eve took (or gained possession and ownership of) some of the fruit that belonged to the tree, that belonged to God. What if the fruit was like some kind of fig? Would it not contain seeds that can produce more fruit like itself, and did you know that you eat the seeds that are within its fruit? I wonder, if whatever the fruit was, did its seeds take root within them somehow? Adam and Eve chose to eat the fruit because of their desire to know and be as gods. They got what they desired, but did not know what to do with it.

Seeds become fruit and are destined to multiply. This fruit became part of what is passed down to their children. They passed down the desire to be their own gods, in choosing to do good or to do evil. It would depend on the person's own desire to play God or not.

Satan has a plan. His strategy is to make himself a god over God's creation and do things his way. He has to be insane or seriously mentally ill! He used Adam and Eve to steal some authority and power from almighty God. It was God's personal tree. Satan would not have tried so hard to get access to it through mankind, if he didn't feel he could use it to overthrow God.

Satan wanted something from the tree, and now we have it, but don't know what to do with it. It has rooted itself in mankind. It is apparently dangerous and can destroy life. Maybe, that's why he wants it so bad.

Satan's agenda is to take over, but he can't. He wants to train unsuspecting people to be leaders under his rule. He wants these people to reject God. He wants to use them to take God's creation (here on earth) away from him and, he is willing to fight for it! In the future, there will be a great battle between good and evil and the bible tells us that good will win (Revelation 19:11-20).

God's army is growing every single day all over the world. It has multiplied into a humungous territorial army here on earth. His army includes those who have passed on into the spirit realm to be with Jesus and the rest of his heavenly armies.

God asks us to give reign over our lives back to him through accepting Christ Jesus. When we do, the desire of wanting to be our own god, that was handed down to us dies out. It dies because we reject it and choose a different choice. The new desire to let Christ be our leader, counselor, guide, helper, and our Lord, comes alive within us.

Even though the death process started through the bloodline of Adam and Eve, and we do die, we go to be with Christ in the spirit realm, and not the realm where the devil resides. We can get what we ask for! We are originally born in the "valley of decisions". God gives us the choice before we go into the eternal realm of existence. We have access now to the knowledge of evil and good. We have access to good through giving ourselves to Christ.

Satan tempted Adam and Eve, and they yielded to his suggestion. He does not have to use a mediator like the serpent to talk to humans anymore. He has gained access to an open door through their thoughts. He was able to access them from the spirit realm.

God had to take what Satan meant for evil and fix it. And over time, he did. We do literally die in our bodies, but we will also live forever. We die to sin and raise up in new life as God's little gods, (his children). God makes himself our Father when we take on his true Son's nature and name. The gift that God gives us now, came out of the hidden message that he said to Adam and Eve. We would know good and evil, die to sin, and become God's little gods. God turned the curse of death into a blessing by his Son.

Deuteronomy 30:19 (NIV), "This day, I call the heavens and the earth as witnesses against you that <u>I have set before you, life and death, blessing and curses. Now choose life, so that you and your children may live."</u>

HIS IMAGE VS IDOLS

LESSON 28

While Jesus was alive and teaching in the temple to the people, he addressed a lot of their questions. Someone asked him about the greatest commandment from God.

Matthew 22:37-40 (NKJV), "Jesus said to him, 'You shall love the LORD your God with all your heart, with all your soul, and with all your mind. This is the first and great commandment. And the second is like it: You shall love your neighbor as yourself. On these <u>two commandments</u> hang <u>all the law and the prophets</u>.'"

He was referring to the commandments stated in the Old Testament books of Deuteronomy and Exodus.

Deuteronomy 6:5 (NKJV), "You shall love the Lord your God with all your heart, with all your soul, and with all your strength."

The greatest commandment is to show our love to God and be true to him above all else. Then, and only then, do the second commandment, which is to love others and treat them as we would want to be treated ourselves. The ten commandments show how to be towards God and secondly towards each other. Jesus summed it all up in these two commands.

How do you love God? If you don't know him, it might be hard to feel any love towards him. Love is not just a feeling! It is an action, or something we continuously do to express our good will and faithfulness toward another. This is how love is developed. Getting to know God through the scriptures and through prayer, help us to have a better understanding that he truly loves us. If we start to comprehend his love, then it becomes easier to love him back.

If you hate someone, you show your hatred toward them by doing or saying hateful things or ignoring them completely. If you feel love for someone, you show your love by doing good things for or to them, and you give them your attention. Jesus said to do good rather you feel the emotion or not. First priority is God, then others.

In the Old Testament, God told his people that it was important that they teach his commands to their own children (Deuteronomy 6:7). These days, it is important to teach our children about Jesus, and how he came about. A lot of young people of today know nothing about the kingdom of God and God's Son, Jesus. They are left to be their own god trying to make good decisions for themselves. They need to know that there is a God who loves them and can be there for them, especially when all else fails.

Jesus gave a lot of life lessons on how we should treat each other.

In Romans 13:10 (NKJV) Paul himself said, "Love does no harm to a neighbor; therefore, love is the fulfillment of the law."

Throughout the history of the bible, God had to deal with his own people being drawn into the false religions of others who did not know him. They disobeyed the greatest commandment of putting God first. God knew it was important to pass his teaching down throughout the generations and as time went on, the newer generations grew colder towards God. They did not know the Lord God of their fathers well enough to keep themselves out of trouble.

In the Old Testament, after the death of Moses, the book of Judges shows the struggles of the Israelites in taking over the land that God had promised. The people of the promised land had their own images of worship and altars of sacrifice to false gods. They had been taken in by the idea and deception of Satan and his false religion of gods (or ungodly spirits).

God wanted the Israelites to go forth and take down these false idols and destroy the ungodly people. He promised them, that if they did, he would be with them in the fight and give them the victory.

He had good reason for destroying the people with their false religion. They were influencing his own people to stray away from him. Instead of destroying them, the Israelites accepted the idol worshippers as their friends, and were drawn into their lifestyle of false religions.

They did not destroy or drive them out of the land, and this angered God. It was similar to the action of Adam and Eve when they did not drive out the devil or defended God's honor in his own garden.

Why did it upset God so much that the Israelites did not drive them out of the land? Wasn't the second commandment to love your neighbor? It is because the Israelites broke the greatest and first commandment. God had said in Deuteronomy 5:7, "You shall have no other gods before me." He recaps it again in Deuteronomy 6:14, where he said not to go after other gods **at all**. In Exodus 23:13 he said for them not to even mention the names of the false gods.

Exodus 23:13 (NKJV), God said, "…make no mention of the name of other gods, nor let it be heard from your mouth."

The belief and evil done in the name of false gods was a big problem all throughout the history of the bible. God knew that mankind was a curious being and did not want them to be drawn into false beliefs and the devil's trap.

Idol Worship

Don't have anything to do with them because they can deceive you into believing a lie about yourself, and about God. Adam and Eve should not have listened to the devil and his lie, but they did. God is the real giver of all life.

He is the creator, not an image or an altar created by mankind.

In Deuteronomy, chapter four, Moses had talked to the people of God and warned them about idol worship. He reminded them of the first time they had experienced God's presence, where all they had seen was fire and heard a voice. They did not see any visible being made of earthly material nor anything else made by the hands of men. The invisible God himself had stepped down from heaven.

In Deuteronomy 4: 15-19 (NKJV) Moses said, "Take careful heed to yourselves, for <u>you saw no form</u> when the L<small>ORD</small> spoke to you at Horeb <u>out of the midst of the fire</u>, lest you <u>act corruptly and make</u> for yourselves <u>a carved image in the form of any figure</u>: the likeness of male or female, the likeness of any animal that is on the earth or the likeness of any winged bird that flies in the air, the likeness of anything that creeps on the ground, or the likeness of any fish that is in the water beneath the earth. And take heed, lest you lift your eyes to heaven, and when you see the <u>sun, the moon, and the stars</u>, all the host of heaven, you feel driven to <u>worship them and serve them</u>, which the L<small>ORD</small> your God has given to all the peoples under the whole heaven as a HERITAGE."

These are not something to be worshipped!

Everything is made up of atoms and molecules just like us, and it all came from God. He gives us tangible and touchable things as an inheritance, not as an idol to serve or worship. Anything made with human hands is not to be made our god. It should be made and recognized as tools we can use to enhance our welfare, and to make life easier and more profitable. It should be to do good. If it does not, then it needs to be tossed or made into something else that is helpful.

All throughout the book of Judges, the Israelites married into and gave their own children in marriage to those who were worshippers of the false religions. The problem with the marriages was that the Israelite would accept and join their spouses in the worship of these false gods. They turned their back on God and learned to do and live evil lives.

They got into all sorts of trouble and would then cry out to God to deliver them. When they did turn back to God, he raised up judges to lead, guide and deliver them. They would live in peace as long as the judge was alive. When a judge passed on, they went back to idol worship, and doing evil in the sight of God. They would cry out to him again, and he would raise up another judge.

They became lost and lead astray, when they did not have their own judge or leader to guide them. As long as there was a judge, they followed God.

In the beginning, we were created as part of his being, his thoughts, his decision that made us. Separation from our maker leaves us feeling like something is missing. There is a void, an emptiness. People without God try desperately to fill that void with anything they can, just to get a little temporary satisfaction or relief. But these things never satisfy in the long run. We were originally made to be a part of God's household.

God was someone you could not physically see. Idols made out of wood, stone, gold or silver were things that could be seen. But these false gods never did anything good for the Israelites, or even gave them deliverance from their impoverished life of bondage that they were experiencing. In fact, the lack of God's presence in their lives, exposed them to evil that took away their freedom, and their advantage over their enemies. They were finding that the false idols were empty, lifeless forms, just as God had said they were in Exodus 26:30. There was nothing good that came from them. These empty images opened the door for evil to take over their lives, because they were not mindful of God.

God had to show his people that if they didn't fight to keep their freedom from the enemy, the enemy would overtake them. They had to become warriors. God did not just jump in right away every single time to deliver them. He had to step back and wait for them to learn for themselves the consequences for their actions. They saw for themselves where their actions against their own God would lead them.

The only way that the Israelites could get free was to fight their way out. Most of the non-Israelite people of the land were not willing to join in their religious belief in the God of creation. They were not willing to give up their own gods, or their land. The Israelites had to learn to go to war against evil, not embrace it. Even if it meant destroying and driving out the people to get rid of the evil. They had to realize that they had the power to reject and defeat the enemy. They had this power through God. He wanted them to cleanse the land of evil and he would help them do it.

In this lesson, I had asked God why does he stress the importance to have "NO OTHER GODS BEFORE HIM". He communicates to me, "Don't you get it? It is for your sake, to keep you as my gods (my children), so Satan can't get you. I am trying to keep the enemy from destroying you and all my other children."

The Israelites were supposed to follow the plan of God for their own sakes. God ended up delivering them repeatedly. They had to learn who and what the enemy was. They had to learn to fight, in order to get the enemy out of their lives before it destroyed them all.

God is very experienced in seeing mankind make senseless mistakes over and over again. His word, the bible shows us that he is willing to forgive and help us, when we turn back to him. He has had plenty of practice with others throughout history. He also wants us to know, that there is a real enemy, and to keep our guard up.

If you are having trouble staying true to God like the Israelites did, or staying out of trouble, try God one more time. If need be, try again and again. Never give up on yourself or God. He does not give up on you!

PUTTING AWAY FOREIGN GODS

LESSON 29

Every time that the Israelites called out to God, he would deliver them. Remember that God wants to be on our side, just like he was for them. But God also wants us to learn to fight against the enemies of spiritual wickedness. He wants us to take down the false gods and everything that relates to them, instead of embracing them. If the Israelites would have willingly taken down all the foreign gods and their temples, the actual spirits would have no choice but to stop and leave, since they would have no followers. Eventually, all the false gods of deception will be annihilated, and there will be no more to try and influence and enslave God's people, like with the Israelites.

We sometimes have to fight an unseen enemy for the good of our homes, our jobs, and for the good of the land that we live in. We always need to be on guard because spiritual enemies can pop up out of nowhere to cause discord, poverty, disease and even death. James 4:7 says to submit to God, resist the real enemy, and he will flee from you.

People from our jobs and community are part of our extended family. If there is a problem, we should lift them up in prayer instead of letting them fall. When we do, we are spiritually fighting for them. We are putting them in the hands of God and letting him deal with them in his own way.

We are to love others by bringing them to our God and his Son, Christ Jesus. It should be our mission! We can show love towards others without accepting their false beliefs. God must always be first in our own lives no matter what!

Politics is becoming more like a religion in itself with its different beliefs in what is right or wrong. Each politician has their own ideas and no one can come to an agreement. When the White House is divided, so goes our country! Jesus said that a house divided against itself cannot stand. We cannot let Satan and his band of rebels destroy us with division. If God could be included in the decision making, there would be less chaos and confusion and more things getting done the right way.

Our leaders who have pledged to lead our country should be responsible for praying for our country, not just voicing their own opinion. They should be prayer warriors that come against unlawful and damaging spiritual principalities, powers and rulers of evil intent (Ephesians 6:12)! They need God in making the right choices, so our country will not fall to those who wish to take it down. God should be the one top-most leader and true head over our government, and our leaders should be those who confide in God for direction. We, ourselves are also responsible for praying for our country and for the leadership positions, without bias.

Ephesians 6:12 (NLT), For we are not fighting against flesh-and-blood enemies, but against evil rulers and authorities of the unseen world, and against mighty powers in this dark world, and against evil spirits in the heavenly places.

We don't always know the whole and truthful story when chaos breaks out regarding our government and leadership. We are influenced by words of truth or deception. We can watch a TV station to get the details of the story, and then go to their opposing TV station and get a totally different view of the same story.

People's biased opinions show up in their presentation of the story. They use dramatic, sarcastic and opinionated words to express their own feelings.

But God knows all truths, and he knows what is best for our country. He can and has used ungodly men and women to fulfill his purpose. We are his creation, and he does not want his world destroyed. His creation is his pride and joy. There is power in united prayer and we are to pray God's will be done.

Luke 11:2 (NIV) (Jesus said), **"This then, is how you should pray: Our Father in heaven, Hallowed be your name. Your kingdom come; your will be done on earth as it is in heaven.**

Jesus tells us to put God first and to love each other. He, himself dealt with all the hurtful (do not do) commands in the Old Testament when he died. The acts of love (or do's) are what Jesus said we are to preserve. Would we steal, kill or covet if we have love for one another? If we all love one another like we should, wouldn't that take care of the rest?

In some ways, our country is slowly drifting away from the one true God. Some (including leaders) have turned to other religions that have been slowly creeping in. As others move into America with their non-Christian cultures and religions, they introduce their beliefs to our land. Don't accept any other man-made idols, or get curious about their gods or belief systems, it always leads to bondage and disillusionment of the truth, and it can alienate you from the real god. If you don't believe me, then believe the history of the bible. Idol worship was recorded all throughout the bible.

In Deuteronomy 4: 15-19 (NKJV) Moses said, "Take careful heed to yourselves, for <u>you saw no form</u> when the L<small>ORD</small> <u>spoke to you</u> at Horeb <u>out of the midst of the fire</u>, lest you <u>act corruptly and make</u> for yourselves <u>a carved image in the form of any figure</u>: the likeness of male or female, the likeness of any animal that is on the earth or the likeness of any winged bird that flies in the air, the likeness of anything that creeps on the ground, or the likeness of any fish that is in the water beneath the earth. And take heed, lest you lift your eyes to heaven, and when you see the <u>sun, the moon, and the stars</u>, all the host of heaven, you feel driven to <u>worship them and serve them</u>, which <u>the L<small>ORD</small> your God has given to all the peoples under the whole heaven as a HERITAGE.</u>"

First commandment in Exodus 20:3, Deuteronomy 5:7 is, **"<u>You shall have no other gods before me.</u>"**

The book of Deuteronomy, Exodus and Numbers tell us that the Israelites did let strangers (or non-Israelites) become part of their people. The only way this could happen was if the stranger accepted God as their own and obeyed his commands. They had to put God first to be accepted.

As we can see through-out history, God is a jealous God. That is a good thing! It means that he cares and loves us, and that he does not want to lose us. I believe he is watching to see what we will do. It is a good thing to spread the news of Jesus Christ to others around the world. This is his will! He wants all to turn from their wicked ways and he promises he would heal the land.

2 Chronicles 7:14 (NKJV), "If my people who are called by my name will humble themselves, and pray and seek my face, and turn from their wicked ways, then I will hear from heaven, and will forgive their sin and heal their land."

There is one true image that we can look back on and know that he is from the one true God. It is the image of Christ, God's own Son on the cross. When we see an empty cross, we are looking into the image of the invisible God. When we see the empty cross, we are reminded that he is now living in and with us.

THE IMAGE ON THE CROSS

---◇---

LESSON 30

There is a tremendous story behind the history of the cross. When we see images of Jesus hanging on the cross, we are reminded of the price he paid for our sin. When we see images of an empty cross, we know he has risen from the dead.

The empty cross represents healing and salvation that has been provided for already. The cross of Jesus tells his story. Jesus is the only image of worship that we are to pay tribute to and look up to. He is our High Priest, our king and fearless leader.

Image of the serpent

There was a time in the days of Moses, when an image of a serpent was used to heal the Israelites.

In the book of Numbers chapter twenty-one, it mentions one of the times when the Israelites grew weary in their travels and grumbled against God and Moses. They complained about not having fresh water and said that they were tired of eating the manna that he had given them for food. But without it, they could have starved to death. They rudely questioned God's motive for bringing them out into the wilderness.

They actually accused him of bringing them out of Egypt and into the wilderness to let them die (Numbers 21:5). They were now snared by their own words against God and started getting exactly what they said. They started dying! They started getting bit by poisonous snakes (serpents) where they had not before. I thought, "Wait! What? Why would you do that, Lord? I thought you were trying to keep them alive and take them into the promised land! Why would you allow what they said to come to pass in there moment of weakness and rebellion?"

I believe this incident became a teaching moment for them about their God. They needed to learn to be more careful with the words that they were speaking about and to him. He was not their enemy! He had been trying to take care of them the whole time. I even wondered if they had realized that God had been protecting them from the poisonous creatures of the desert in the first place. Did their own words of complaint cause an even bigger problem for them now? Had they brought this misfortune upon themselves when they stopped believing and trusting God with what he originally said he would do for them?

Did they reject God's leading at this point in time with their complaining? And, as they turned their back on God, could the elements of what was in the desert overtake them without his provision and protection? They couldn't just gather up all the snakes and kill them. It was impossible! They were still in the desert and there were snakes everywhere. When they rejected God, did they curse themselves?

They realized that they needed God's help if they wanted to live and not die! What could they do to break the power of the curse that they caused for themselves?

They admitted that they had sinned against him by speaking wrongly and then begged for his help. Their fear of death from the serpents, caused them to stop their complaining to God, and truly focus on getting back into his good graces.

Numbers 21:8 (NKJV), "Then the LORD said to Moses, 'Make a fiery (poisonous) serpent (made out of bronze) and set it on a pole; and it shall be that everyone who is bitten, when he looks at it, shall live.'"

God made a way of escape from the serpents that were killing them. If and when they were bitten by a deadly snake, they would look upon the (bronze or brass) serpent that was hanging on the pole, and they would be healed. On the other hand, if they got bit and didn't believe God enough to look upon the image of a serpent hanging on the pole, then they would be overtaken by the venom. Proverbs 29:18 says, "Where there is no vision, the people perish." They had to do what God said to do! They had to **see** what God told them to see!

Why did God use a snake (serpent) as the image that they were to look upon? It was the very thing that was killing them, and why hanging upon a pole? How would doing so save their lives from death? And, why did God have Moses make an image of a serpent out of earthly material? God hated idol worship (Exodus 20:4 and Leviticus 26:1).

Most of the time in the bible serpents symbolized power. Their venom brought on the sting of death for anyone wounded by it. If you think back to the story of Adam and Eve, they had a bad experience with a serpent. Even Paul himself was bitten by a poisonous snake, but he just shook it off with no harm (Acts 28:3-5). Jesus had associated serpents and scorpions with the power of the enemy. Jesus himself had said that he gives us power to tread on serpents and scorpions, and over all the power of the enemy (Luke 10:19).

After the Israelites exodus from Egypt, Moses had told God's people to put evil away from among them (Deuteronomy 21:21-22). These Israelites had come out of an idol worshipping civilization, where the people looked up to false gods to obtain something they wanted or needed. There are historical pictures depicting snakes or serpents as accepted idol worship. The Israelites could relate to this kind of concept because man-made idols were things that related to the Egyptian gods. They had been delivered out of such an environment. So, were they committing a sin of idol worship at God's command, or were they putting the evil away from them?

They were in desperate need of deliverance from death. I believe that God worked with what was already buried deep within their subconscious mind from their past experiences. He devised a way that they could put the evil away from them.

The truth was that they needed healing, so God gave them a prescription to follow. It wasn't a "take two of these and call me in the morning prescription." It was an actual cure to kill off the venom itself that had infiltrated their bodies. It was like taking an antivenom.

The Lamb and the Serpent

Think about the night before the Israelites were delivered from their captivity in Egypt. They had to sacrifice a lamb, spread its blood on the door post and eat the body of the lamb, so they would not die. They were protected from the deadly plague because they did what God told them to do. Every year after, they celebrated with the lamb sacrifice to commemorate their freedom.

God had set into motion a spiritual process for them that led to Jesus shedding his blood for our protection. The lamb's blood that was spread on the doorpost in Egypt for protection was a temporary process. The blood of Jesus that spilled onto the cross was, and is, permanent.

I found it very interesting, that the devil is referred to as the serpent who causes the sting of death, whereas, Jesus is referred to as the lamb of God who takes away the sting of death. The blood of Jesus cleanses us from the sting of sin (1John 1:7).

Did you know that snake anti-venom in the US is derived from sheep? Anti-venom is an antitoxin that comes from the blood of certain animals like a horse or a sheep? It is created by injecting small amounts of venom into the animal, in order to bring about an immune system response. It becomes a purified, venom neutralizing, antibody product that can stop the venom from killing you.

The Israelites had to believe in what God had said enough to take his prescribed spiritual medicine! He gave them a bodily image of the very thing that was hurting their bodies. To be healed, it required them to respond to the visual aid that he set before them. If they looked at it, it meant they were giving him permission to cure them. He had to know that they were now repenting (or changing their mind) for rejecting him. He had to have their individual permission in order to give them the spiritual antidote.

This serpent wasn't even a real serpent! It was made by human hands and only to be looked upon as a focal point for healing from God, at GOD's command.

God proved to his people, that he had the power over their deadly enemy, not the enemy having any power within itself, but eventually, they forgot. You would think that they would probably never trust in the false gods associated with snakes ever again. But later on, the bible shows that the Israelites kept the brazen serpent and used it as an object of worship for some 900 years.

A good king who had done right in the sight of God, whose name was Hezekiah, began to reign in Jerusalem. He had to destroy the manmade serpent, so that it could not be worshipped any more (2 Kings 18:4 and 2 Chronicles 29:2-10).

God expects us to put away or destroy the idealism of idols. The thoughts can enter into our imaginations and distort our view of who he is. We can look to the cross where Jesus hung and know that he died to pay for our healing, himself. He is the only visual aid that we should look up to, since he is the image of the invisible God himself (Colossians 1:15).

Idol in the home

For us today, we should not take the subject of idol worship lightly. When I was a young adult living in my own apartment, I had purchased an eighteen-inch-high statue of a gold-colored Buddha sitting in the lotus position. It was pretty popular back in those days and I bought it as a table ornament for my living room. Soon after, I began to feel a strange presence in my home, and it wasn't good. A common belief of the Buddha statue was that it acted as a guide for his followers, after his own death. It was an idol! It was a statue representing a man other than Jesus Christ. Jesus was the only man who was anointed and appointed by God to be our savior, leader, shepherd and omnipotent king, not Buddha.

I had never thought about the statue being a religious item known to have any power. The bible tells us to destroy any false images that can lead us astray from him. If the item having a specific meaning behind its existence is left standing in sight, it still has the ability to stir up curiosity to the imagination of the beholder. It can cause confusion and wrongful worship. False gods are hungry for attention and worship. They can attach themselves to the idol and feed on the energy of the beholder that gets drawn to it. Maybe, you don't agree with me, but if you think about it, God was known to dwell in a tent among the people, where do you think the evil spirits can dwell?

I sought out the advice of a local minister at the time, and he told me that I needed to clean up my home of anything that was of a different spirit other than God. I went through all my books that I had read throughout the last few years, gathered the ones regarding spirituality or mysticism and burned them. I also broke the statue in pieces and disposed of it so that no one else could get ahold of it. Sometimes, we just have to do some housecleaning physically and mentally. What I did, I believe, made a statement! I was saying I renounce any other imagination that speaks against the knowledge of God (2 Corinthians 10:4-5).

For the weapons of our warfare are not carnal, but mighty through God to the pulling down of strong holds; casting down imaginations, and every high thing that exalts itself against the

knowledge of God and bringing into captivity every thought to the obedience of Christ (2 Corinthians 10:4-5).

In Jesus, we have the history that God wanted us to all see. He wanted us to physically see his Son and what he could do. We read throughout the New Testament that Jesus healed because he was (and still is) anointed to do so. We have his stories of healing and restoration to rewrite into our own imaginations.

His physical body was put to death on a cross (tree or pole) for us, in order to give us freedom from the venomous sin that kills. God can save or heal us from our own sinful bitterness and self-destruction that we cause for ourselves. We can look to the one who hung on the cross for healing.

God had considered the Israelites his own nation, and his laws show that there are consequences for bad behavior. He viewed every "sin of rebellion" as national insurrection or treason against him and his people. It was a crime worthy of death (Numbers 25:1-4). One of the ways that the Israelites were punished for a crime worthy of death was to be hanged on a tree (Deuteronomy 21:22-23).

With all the prophecies about a king and savior who was to come to save the world, God knew he would send his Son. His Son was to be a substitute and sacrifice, who would die for us on a cross (pole) in order to save us. God knew way before the law was even given to mankind, what he was going to do. Christ was made sin for us, so that we may be made free and healed from the effects of our sin.

If we as his people could just trust him to take care of the sin problem, then we would be more likely to be at peace and strive to do the right things. We would stop grumbling and complaining like the Israelites did in the wilderness. We would not react out of a spirit of rebellion, fear or desperation. The Israelites had to "look at the lifeless figure hanging on the pole (the tree) in order to live". They received a miracle of forgiveness and healing by finally listening to God and acting on his instruction. So should we in regards to Jesus and the cross. We would be a healthier and happier people! Matthew 8:16-17 says that Jesus fulfilled prophecy, when he himself <u>took</u> our infirmities and bare our sicknesses in his death on the cross.

Throughout his lifetime, Jesus was seen healing the sick and casting out evil spirits. People were looking to him already even before his death and resurrection, and lived (Matthew 18:1-17). He had taught that it was the same thing to be healed as it was to be forgiven (Matthew 9:5-6). They were healed and forgiven because they listened to him, saw what he did, and believed for themselves!

Anyone who has been bitten by sin (the thing that destroys their life), can <u>look upon the cross of Jesus Christ</u>, to receive physical, spiritual and emotional healing, as well as eternal life to live forever. 2 Corinthians 5:20-21 tells us to be reconciled to God for he has made Jesus, his Son "to be sin for us". 2 Peter 2:24 says <u>his own self</u> bare our sins <u>in his own body</u> on the cross, making us dead to sins and alive to righteousness. If we are forgiven for our sin, then we are in right standing with God. And, by his stripes (his punishment), we were healed. It is a done deal!

It had to be the hardest thing that God ever did, when he had to see his own Son hang and die on a tree for our own sinful rebellion. Jesus died for past, present and future sins. We need him in our lives forever, in order to survive forever! He is our source for new life! Because of God giving us his own image, the likeness of himself, to become one of us and be lifted up, we can look to him for forgiveness and healing every time we need to.

John 3:14 says as Moses lifted up the serpent in the wilderness, even so must the Son of man be lifted up.

Jesus, the Son of man and the Son of God is the real and genuine body and image of God himself. He hung on the cross to give us the antidote for sin. There is no other God!

God wants us to cast our care on him by way of his Son, who sacrificed his own life to give us life. We can bring our troubles to the cross, instead of them destroying us.

"It shall be that everyone who is bitten, when he <u>looks at it, shall live</u>" (Numbers 21:8). So, I repeat **Proverbs 29:18 that states, "Where there is no vision, the people perish."** And I say, "*Where there is vision of the cross, the people live.*"

So, when we see images of Jesus hanging on the cross, we are reminded of the price he paid for our sin. When we see images of an empty cross, we know he has risen from the dead.

KEEP YOUR EYES ON THE PRIZE

――――――⋆――――――

LESSON 31

In Mark 15:34, when Jesus was dying on the cross, he said, "My God, My God, why have you forsaken me?" I wondered, why did he call out to God as his God and not as his Father? And, why did God forsake (abandon) and leave him to die on the cross instead of rescuing him?

Even though God himself loved his Son, he made the decision to step back and let him suffer and die. You might think to yourself, "Why God would you let him suffer and die? He is your own son!" It is a hard thing to understand! But God gave his Son for the good of all. As the Father of Jesus, he understands heartbreak and the effects of death and separation.

What about your own children? How hard would it be to give up one son or daughter for the saving of the others, when you love them all? If your only choice was to give up one to save the others, which would you choose? Which one would you sacrifice, or give up to pay the price that would redeem the others?

As God, God had to let Jesus die for the sins of many. As his Father, God rescued him from the eternal everlasting power of death and the grave when he did die.

As a man, Jesus had to pass from death to life, in order to give us the Holy Spirit that secures our future and his. And God, the Father knew that if they both went through the hardest most excruciating thing anyone could ever endure, no one would have to be lost forever or abandoned, including his own Son.

Their story was the greatest story of sacrifice ever to be told! Father and Son gave their all for humanity. In order to accomplish what they did, they had to keep their eyes on the prize at the end of road.

This world is a "give to get" world that we live in. It cost us all something to survive in this world system. We give up things that we have, just to get something else that we don't have. It cost to have children, from the time that they are conceived, until the time that they are old enough to pay into the system themselves. Nothing is free!

Even if you own your own home and car, you still pay into the system just to keep them. You pay tax and license fees over and over again every year. You pay for lights, heat, food, water and so on. You have to have some kind of income (or way to pay the price) in order to survive and live at least a comfortable lifestyle.

When we get sick and need help, it can cost a lot of money for health insurance, tests, doctor fees and prescriptions. In some cases, we could even die, if we don't have a way to pay for the help that we need.

It is not free to live in this world!

Jesus paid the price for us to survive eternal life itself. If only we could just grasp the full concept of him also becoming our source of payment for the things that we need to survive, even here on earth. **He** said, "I am come that they might have life, and that they might have it more abundantly" (John 10:10).

This world is full of corruption, loneliness and poverty, as well as, prosperity, love and success. It is a world out of balance, and we are exposed to both good and evil.

When we decide to acknowledge Jesus, and profess that we accept him as our Lord, our faith (or readiness to trust him with our lives) links his Holy Spirit with our spirit. God-like faith comes alive in the heart of our being. We are vindicated (justified, made right and blameless) in God's eyes. When we agree to become a part of the family, God gives us a new life immediately.

We no longer have to pay the price from what the enemy did, to infect all of mankind with sin. He will pay the price for what he did, not us! We are made innocent because Jesus already paid the price with his own innocence for us.

In Romans 10:11-13 (NIV) Paul wrote, "As Scripture says, 'Anyone who believes in him will never be put to shame'. For there is no difference between Jew and Gentile—the same Lord is Lord of all and richly blesses all who call on him, for <u>everyone who calls on the name of the Lord will be saved</u>."

In the first part of my book, I had quoted some of the things that Paul had said about his journey through life. In Philippians 3:12-14, he compared his journey to a race. He had said that he did not dwell on things of the past. He pressed on toward the goal ahead of him, so he could obtain the prize at the end of his journey. Paul did not let any shortcomings of his past, distract or sidetrack him. In a race, if you stumble, you get right back up and keep going. The race of your life isn't over yet and the best is yet to come.

Philippians 3:20-21 (NKJV), "For our citizenship is in heaven, from which we also eagerly wait for the savior, the Lord Jesus Christ, who <u>will transform our lowly body</u> that it may be <u>conformed to his glorious body</u>."

If we accept Christ, we will have our own glorified body that will be made like his. It will last forever! So, why not enjoy being in the race all the way to the finish line that is set before us. Our membership and citizenship have already been approved and established just by applying for it.

In our journey or race, there are things that get in the way to distract and confuse us. These things can even cause us to lose self-confidence or be paralyzed with fear. They can become stumbling blocks.

God, as our Father, sees our struggle and determination to make it. He has proved over and over again in the bible, that he uses brute force, if necessary, to get the enemy out of our way. His own first Son finished the hardest course for us and has won the race. He received the prize already, and so will we, all because we are on the same team and of the same family.

Every single person that is born in this world is born to meet and get to know God as their Father. He is watching our race (or birthing process). He wants everyone to make it to the finish line to receive their award. He also wants us to enjoy the race while trying to get there.

The story of the Israelites when they were in Egyptian captivity is one example of God saying, "Don't mess with my family". Moses had told the Pharaoh to let God's people go, so they could freely worship him, and be led on a journey to a better place. The Pharaoh would not let them go, so God took drastic measures by sending the ten plagues. He then drowned the Pharaoh and his soldiers, who were pursuing his people, in the Red Sea.

God can put a stop to the enemy hindering us from freely moving forward, when we consider ourselves a part of his team and his family.

Always remember to keep your eyes on the prize like Paul said that he did (Philippians 3:13-14 and Hebrews 12:1-2). He also had said that if he does something that he knows he should not even want to do, and still does it, it is no longer him or his will that does it. He says that it is "sin" that dwells in the body (Romans 7:20-23, 8:1-3,6). My take on what Paul was trying to tell us is that sin tries to take control to stop us from finishing our race. Sin tells us that we are not worthy to even be in the race. Paul does not identify himself with it, and he does not let it keep him captive. I believe that Paul is telling us to just pick ourselves up, get back on track, and keep going forward for the prize.

Genesis 4:3-8 is the detailed story about Cain and Abel, the two sons of Adam and Eve. Both of them brought an offering from the resources produced in their job, as a gift to the Lord. Cain brought fruit from the ground that he farmed, and Abel brought the best of the flock that he shepherd. God only showed favor to Abel and his gift, so Cain became very angry.

God then spoke to Cain about his attitude.

Genesis 4:7 (NIV) God said, "If you do what is right, will you not be accepted? But if you do not do what is right, <u>sin is crouching at the door; IT desires to have you</u>, <u>BUT YOU MUST RULE OVER IT</u>."

Sin was at the door of his heart, and ready to pounce like a hungry wild beast. It has its own evil desire and wants to be in control. In this scripture, God said to Cain that "it desires to have you." He warned Cain that the anger needed to be restrained before it would cause him to do something he would regret, something out of his own control. He was to rule and take control over the wild beast of sin, and not even let it in the door. But instead, Cain let the thoughts of anger fester until they overpowered him.

Cain did not feel any remorse for what he would do to his brother. He coaxed his brother to go out with him into the field, and then he killed him. This was the first physical death of Adam's children that we know of. It happened because Cain accepted hateful thoughts, let them get in control, and then acted upon them.

A little later, God had come to him and questioned him about where his brother was. His response was, "I don't know! Am I my brother's keeper?"

He expressed no shame or guilt for what he had done, and he lied about it. He needed to know that it was wrong. He could not just go around and destroy another life, just because things didn't go his way.

God then told Cain that he heard the voice of his brother's blood crying out to him from the ground. Cain had robbed his brother of life, their parents of a son, and God of his joyful relationship with Abel. Cain had caused heartache and loss for all.

God then explained to Cain that he had changed the course of his own life. Now, he was cursed from the ground that received his brother's blood prematurely (Genesis 4:12). Any offering that he could have brought to God in the future would not be worthy of God's approval anymore. He could no longer try to bring his best before God, because it had been tainted or cursed by the evidence of his sin. The ground would no longer yield or thrive for him anymore and he was driven off of the property, all because he let evil thoughts into the door of his heart, and then the thoughts took control of his mind. He accepted them as his own and had to pay a great price for his sin.

Paul shows us in Romans chapter seven, that in order to overcome any kind of bad thought or feeling like anger and jealousy, we should treat it as if it is a real thing, a presence that is separate of ourselves. He wants us to know that it is sin, and that it is trying to infect us with its negative information.

Paul explains in the book of Romans that you have to want to not want it. You may know you want or desire to partake of a certain wrongful act like Cain did when he was tempted, but you don't want to want it. You may want to be free from wanting it.

Cain needed to think of the consequences of his actions first, so not to do it. I am pretty sure that the image of what Cain wanted to do to his brother, played over and over in his head. He was so jealous of the praise that his brother had gotten, that he ignored God's advice and yielded to the beast of anger that was crouching at his door (Genesis 4:7). He accepted the wild and murderous thoughts of sin. He ended up doing the opposite of what God said he should do. He did not think about the consequences and had no way to make amends for what he had done after he killed his brother. He did not take rule over it.

There were other options! He could have learned from the experience, pressed forward and brought his best gift the next time in the future. It would have been a better choice. Or, the next time, the brothers could have put their best offerings together as one spectacular offering, and then present it to the Lord. I believe God would have been very pleased with their combined gift. We don't always think things through first before we do them. It all boils down to choices of good and evil.

If you compare the story of Cain and Abel regarding sin at the door, with what Paul had said about sin, we find that Paul knew what to do. In Philippians 3:13-14 he said he forgets what already happened, and continues to press forward in trying to do the best that he could. He treated sin of past experience like a separate entity, and he would not let it rule over him. He learned from it and continued on in his journey. Paul had it figured out. He treated it for what it really was, his opponent.

Cain had to pay his own price for his sin. But now the price for sin has been paid for by Jesus. Paul was able to turn to Jesus for forgiveness and to get a fresh new start. It takes a repented heart for God to accept your offering of reconciliation.

If the enemy of your soul has distracted you and caused you to stumble and fall in your race, get back up and shake it off. Reject and kick him out, and then reinforce the door of your heart. Repent and then put it behind you. Let it go and continue to go forward in your race. There is a finish line, and you can make it! Don't let past failures stop you from winning your race!

PURGING YOUR CONSCIENCE

—◆—

LESSON 32

In the Old Testament, God taught his people to keep good habits to cleanse their conscience from evil. The Israelites were instructed to performed daily and yearly rituals and to pass them down to future generations. Some of these traditional ceremonies gave them time to reflect and refresh their commitment to God. They could make amends for their evil deeds by confession, repentance, and animal sacrifices, as well as, acknowledge and thank God for what he has already done for them, and for what he is still doing. Everything that God instructed them to do was for their own benefit, not just his.

They had a hard time believing that God was out for their best interest, and there were times when they had to learn some lessons the hard way. While they were in Egypt, they had to make a decision to either follow God's instructions to get out of Egypt or stay in their current situation of slavery.

They decided to follow his instructions and God kept them safe while he delivered them from their physical bondage. It took a desperate situation for them to turn to God for help (Exodus 12-14). The evening before God was to miraculously bring them out of bondage, they were instructed to kill a lamb, cook it and eat it. They were also instructed to spread its blood on the doorpost (sides and top) of their homes, and then stay inside.

God had said in Exodus 12:13 (KJV), "…and when I see the blood. I will <u>pass over</u> you and the plague shall not be upon you to destroy you, when I strike the land of Egypt."

Moses had said that the blood of the lamb that was spread on the doorpost, would be a sign of protection, as a deadly plague spread throughout Egypt to kill all the Egyptian firstborn sons and firstborn male animals. All the Israelites and what they owned including their animals were not touched by the plague.

Throughout the traditions of the Israelites, they had times of celebration for the good life events that God had given them. These festivities helped them to remember and identify with the character and love of God. Every year on a certain date, the Israelites celebrated the Passover. They remembered the lamb sacrifice that had kept them alive during the plague of Egypt. Every year they celebrated their freedom from bondage with a feast.

Even though Jesus died for our sins once and for all a long time ago, and we are forgiven, we still need to keep good habits for conscience's sake, just like they did with their celebrations.

Hebrews 9:14 (KJV and NIV) says that the blood of Christ (like the Passover lamb) **was offered through the eternal Spirit of God and "<u>purges the conscience</u>" from acts that lead to death.**

All throughout the (NIV) version of the Old Testament, the word purge was used to express purging out the evil and purging away sins. In the online Oxford dictionary, "purge" means to rid or free someone from an unwanted feeling, memory or condition.

Our conscience is that inner feeling or voice, acting as a guide to the rightness or wrongness of our behavior. Habits become embedded within the chemical structure of our minds, and in turn also affect the core of our being.

In the Old Testament times, God's people had times of reflection. They had to cleanse their own conscience by remembering the good that came out of a bad situation.

We need these times of renewal too! It keeps our minds healthy and moving forward on the right track. We have to occasionally purge our minds in order to achieve freedom and well-being. We have to consciously keep ourselves refilled with good memories, celebrations of our victories and remind ourselves who we are in Christ.

FOR CONSCIENCE'S SAKE

───────◆───────

LESSON 33

There are many reasons why some people have trouble going forward in their lives. They may feel like they are stuck in a rut and can't free themselves from where they are. If we look at the Israelites that came out of bondage, even though they were being led by God to a better place, their minds were still in a state of bondage. The Pharaoh's sinful actions scarred their lives. These people were on the receiving end of a very unpleasant and traumatic time in their lives. This is the case for some people even today.

I am not an expert in the field of the mind and how it works, but I know that there are therapists who use hypnosis to help their patients. They use verbal commands to help their patient in gaining control over unwanted behaviors, or to help them to overcome anxiety, phobias, and post-traumatic stress and in some cases real pain. Most of the time, therapy can help a person when they can't help themselves. Hypnosis can be dangerous in the wrong hands. The therapist must know what they are doing and striving for the good of their patient.

Recently I saw a game show on TV that I thought was a good example, in showing how powerful words of suggestion can be. On the game show, there were contestants that had to work together as a team to perform certain tasks given to them by the game show host. They could make up to $100,000 to split between them. The catch was that they had to allow themselves to be hypnotized by a hypnotist before they were allowed to perform each task. The hypnotist would give each person a simple command to do that would interfere (or hinder them) from carrying out their original instructions that would be given by the host. The commands were all different for each person. He told them that they were to carry out the command, when they would hear a trigger word, a sound like a buzzer or be gently touch on the shoulder. His words of instruction caused them to think and act out his command, while they were trying to follow the other instructions from the host.

It was shocking to see that these people would carry out the verbal command when told to. They were in full control in understanding and carrying out the instructions from the game show host and would accumulate points for their team. But when the trigger word, sound or touch was presented, they averted from their task as a team, to carrying out the command that had been given to them by the hypnotist.

The commands were not bad things. They were simple, harmless, and comical distractions. Their behavior was very funny to watch. The contestants really believed that they were in the character role presented to them. The suggestions they carried out interfered with their completing each task, and the game became very challenging for all of them. At the end of the game, the contestants were interviewed as they saw the video of themselves. They said that they remembered doing the silly things. But they were surprised to see themselves doing something that they did not normally do, or would have ever done.

Hypnosis is a state of consciousness where the individual being hypnotized is highly responsive to suggestions or directions. It is a deeper state of concentration and focus in that moment. Your mind accepts what it is given as long as you allow it.

The words conscious, conscience and subconscious have totally different meanings. The word <u>conscious</u> means that you are alert and aware of what is going on around you. Your <u>conscience</u> is the inner feeling or voice that acts as a guide. It analyzes everything it already knows, as well as the knowledge it has just been given. It gives recommendations, about the rightness or wrongness of a situation. It is based on your own belief system. The <u>subconscious</u> is the deeper part of the mind than the conscious mind. It simply accepts whatever it is told even if it is wrong or not true. It can influence all feelings and actions without one being fully aware.

The game show of contestants that were under hypnosis reminds me of a group of team players actively playing a game on the playing field. They play the game by whatever rules are given to them.

The people in the example of the game show decided to allow and trust the hypnotizer. They decided to let him access their subconscious part of the mind. In other words, they willfully gave him permission, and decided to accept what he had to say.

Your conscience (or your guide) will not let you carry out suggestions that go against values that you have already developed over time. It is important to develop good values and beliefs. But your conscience is not perfect and can be deceived into a bad decision. It puts data together for processing based on your belief system. Then it causes the mind to respond with different types of feelings like fear, love, excitement, or even anger, which then affect the body. These feelings can cause the body to react with high blood pressure, palpitations, sweating, headaches, stomach acid, stress, and sickness. Feelings can also cause good reactions in the body, like a burst of energy, a happy smile, and recovering health. You can feel so good that others can see it in your countenance. You can just have a glow about you! When you feel good about your life, it makes it easier to have a good attitude towards others.

Your bodily senses (eyes, ears, nose, mouth, and skin) are receivers of the things in the world. They receive good and bad information through seeing, hearing, smelling, tasting or by touch. The message that they relay to the mind causes an immediate positive or negative response, that is based on what you already have learned about life. The body is not in control of itself. It is flawed in the fact that it can accept instructions that cause it to self-destruct or act out wrongly. It all depends on the stuff that is stored in your short and long-term memories.

Our subconscious part of the mind accepts emotions, images and instructions, as if we ourselves gave them. All our life experiences are stored in our memory banks somewhere in a chemical form. Our thoughts can express themselves in weird ways that we don't always understand. They can even be expressed in our dreams. Life experiences can affect our overall behavior and emotions, even though we may not know why. They can make us feel, say or act a certain way.

What if, in your past you had been a victim of a violent crime? What if you were violated in some way by another? Maybe they abused and bullied you mentally, physically and/or sexually. They may have cheated on you, stole from you, or rejected you. These bad experiences could impact your feelings, thoughts and actions in a negative way, for very long time.

Being violated in some way causes us to question why it happened. After all, life should be full of good experiences. A bad experience confuses our conscience (our inner feeling or voice that guides us). And, it has an effect on future decisions. The bad event gets embedded in our memory banks. A part of us knows or feels that something about it isn't right but doesn't know what to do with the negative information. All it can do is use the resources it already has, put it all together and save it. What is stored in our memories is destined to be repeated.

Our mind tries to make sense of a situation, by examining the details that it has accumulated. For example, if you are a victim in a bad situation, you may ask yourself questions. Why did they do this to me? What did I do to deserve this? Am I a bad person? Why do they hate me? What is wrong with me? Why didn't I fight back or leave? Why did I retaliate or act that way? Why do I feel like I can't function without this person, drug, or addiction? There are plenty of self-condemning questions you might ask yourself. Whatever answer you choose may be right or wrong, but the decision you make about yourself, and/or others, gets embedded deep within your memories.

Being victimized can produce feelings of guilt, embarrassment, shame and low self-worth. You could be punishing yourself because you could not figure out how to get control over the situation.

As life goes on, and you face a similar situation, the similarity triggers or searches for comparable already stored memories of your mind. This thought mechanism is meant to help you in making a decision on what to do with the current situation. It decides based on your past experiences.

The memory of someone or something else taking control of your body or your mind through deception (and without your permission), signals to you that you are not the one in control of you. Some of your thoughts can become distorted and cause you to believe a lie about yourself. These thoughts can influence your conscience to make bad decisions.

Paul called it "the sin that dwells within" and he did not accept it as a part of his life. He focused on his goal and did great things.

In the bible story of Job, his friends tried to get him to question his own integrity, when Satan had come against him with poverty and disease. His friends took a bad situation and made it worse. They told him that he must have done something wrong to deserve the terrible things that happened to him, and this was his punishment. Sometimes it has nothing to do with what you did or did not do. It could be the fault of another. It could be the fault of our enemy.

In some cases, and for some reason, you may erroneously convince yourself that this is your lot in life and continue to accept it. You give up and give in to it, repeatedly. Thus, harboring guilt, shame and a sense of failure, from not being able to control or fix what is wrong.

The subconscious part of our mind that accepts information rather it is right or wrong, stores it in our memory banks. It judges it as okay to keep because it happened.

Stories in the bible of how God interacted with mankind help to guide us on our journey. When we read the stories and advice given from the bible, it gets stored in our memory banks. The ideas, stories and images that they create in our heads get labeled. We then can identify and bring them to the conscious level of the mind when needed to make decisions. The label is the trigger. It then helps us in creating our own life stories.

If you think about it, Adam named everything to identify it for himself. He named the woman Eve. He can think or say the word "Eve" and picture her in his mind. He made the word and the image connect. The trigger word was "Eve". He did the same thing for all the animals, he named them!

Commands that the hypnotist create in the subconscious minds of the contestants caused a condition to exist. He first spoke words that would spark their imagination to deeply focus on the scene he was creating in their minds. It was kind of like a dream state. He planted a hypnotic suggestion for them to act out as if they were a part of the dream that he had created in their minds. Then he labeled the suggestion with a particular word, sound, or touch. I like to call them triggers. The trigger for some of the contestants was the sound of a bell. Later, when the trigger was presented to them, they would carry out the command, even though they were not currently under hypnosis. All it took was the word, sound, or touch. It stimulated the thought that he had already planted in their memory, and they would carry out the command.

Another example would be in training a dog to sit on command. The animal would first need to understand what the word meant. Then he could carry out the command when presented to him. He would need a trigger like a word, gesture, sound, or visual thing, like a treat. The biggest part of training the dog would be in getting him to understand what is meant by the command to sit.

If the words from hypnosis can affect our thinking, then we can change our own thinking in a positive way ourselves. We can affect our lives for the better. As Christians, we can become more like the image of Jesus, who is perfect, as we partake of things involving him. But we first need to understand some of the ideas in scripture, in order to know how to apply them to our own lives.

Through the words and feelings that we feel from reading the stories, we can implant life changing revelations of God's love in our being. The trigger word is "Jesus". All throughout the New Testament we are told to use the name of Jesus. Even the followers who preached, healed, delivered and raised loved ones from the dead said, "In the name of Jesus" to activate the command of miracles and healings.

On a more individual level we have to educate ourselves. We have to keep reminding ourselves that we are in right standing with God because he loves us. If we want answers, we have to ask him questions about his word and his stories. He will always point us to Jesus as the answer. We are to renew or build new thoughts in our minds continuously.

It is not our responsibility or our right to punish ourselves for the abuse that happens in our lives. You, punishing yourself means nothing to God. The punishment of God's Son does. This is the truth that can set our minds at ease and turn our lives around for the good.

We should not let the punishment that Jesus went through be in vain. Jesus, God's Son does not condemn us, he saves us. He already paid the price. He came to save us from condemnation, and to give us rich and full lives. Any sin that we have done or has been done to us has been dealt with on the cross. We just have to prove it to ourselves.

Mark 5:25-34 is the story about the woman who had a blood issue for twelve years. She had spent all her money on physicians and was getting worse. She then heard about Jesus, and it changed her life forever. She came among a multitude of people who were trying to get to Jesus to ask for healing. She said within herself that if she could just touch the hem of his garment, she would be healed. She imagined it first in her head. She had her mind made up that when she TOUCHED him, she would be healed, and she was.

MY TESTAMONY

LESSON 34

John 1:1,14 (KJV) reads, "In the beginning was the Word, and the Word was with God, and the Word was God. And the Word was made flesh and dwelt among us."

According to this scripture in the book of John, God's Word has always existed with and as God. This scripture tells us that the Word of God came to live among us as Jesus, in a real flesh and blood body. Jesus spoke the things that God, his Father told him to speak. Jesus was given to us as a human representative that we can relate to.

God is seeking souls to save through his Word or his spokesperson, who was made flesh and blood like the rest of us. I may not have been here today, if it wasn't for God's sacrificial love called Jesus. He rescued me from depression, torment and death many years ago. He basically rescued me from my own self!

If I would not have taken a chance on trusting him with my life, I believe that it would have ended in disaster! One of my biggest fears was a fear of dying. I had a lot of questions and wanted to know the truth, but I was so afraid of dying, that I avoided the subject as much as possible. I didn't want to find out that I would possibly go to a place called Hell. The more I tried to avoid the subject, the more it pursued me. I began to fear the future and even wondered about my destiny here on earth. I might be okay one minute, and then something would happen to trigger my thinking about the subject again. Then all the feelings and thoughts would resurface to cause me to feel miserable. I had to find out the truth about death in order to be set free!

<u>MY TESTIMONY</u> –

As a little girl, I had a fairly normal family life and grew up in the church environment. My family and I had our ups and downs, and there were times when things got a little tuff for my parents. I was an only girl with younger brothers, and sometimes it felt kind of lonely. What I learned from being in the church environment helped me get through my loneliness. I believed in God to be my best friend and remembered talking to him about all kinds of things.

I was curious about how he made the heavens and what was beyond the ends of the heavens. Did whatever there was at the end of the heavens have an ending? What was beyond its end? What was at the end of everything? It seemed to me that it was impossible to have an ending point of all things.

I heard positive and negative things about God while attending church and did not understand what he was all about. Even though I did not know how to pray elegant prayers, I still prayed for him to helped me through any difficult times. I remember being told that there was a real scary place called Hell, and I knew that I did not want to go there. I was taught that the only way to avoid it, was to accept Jesus Christ, the Son of this big and powerful God. I had to face some fears about him and remember struggling with nightmares a lot, but at the same time, I felt comforted in the fact that he was all knowing, all caring and able to handle anything in regards to my life.

There were different events that helped to shape my life for what I am today. Some of it bad and some of it good.

My fears as a little child grew up with me and I took them into my adult life. I don't think I ever talked to my parents about the way I felt; I just thought it was normal to feel the way I was feeling about life.

When I was a pre-teenager, I began to leave God behind. I got involved with drugs and even ran away from home a few times. As I got a little older, I tried to fit in with others of my age or older. It worked for a while, but I still had this nagging feeling that something was missing. For years I tried desperately to figure out what was wrong in my life.

While I was a teenager, my parents got divorced and my mother moved to California with her new husband. I eventually went to live with her and ended up staying for a number of years.

Just before my eighteenth birthday I got pregnant and had a baby. Even though I was a little young to be responsible for a child, I loved her very much. I was looking forward to having my own family to love and get love back. Since then, and years later, I also had a son that I love just as much as my first child. They both are now grown and have their own lives. I believe that our children give us a wonderful reason to even be alive.

There came a time, when I started feeling that my life was empty, and I fell into a deep depression. Back when my first child was a toddler, I had shared an apartment with some friends. We would hang out together doing different activities, and sometimes we would hang out at our favorite night club. I thought life was fun! I thought I was happy and satisfied with my lifestyle. But then depression set in and I had no idea what was wrong, I just knew something wasn't right! I lost a lot of weight because I had no appetite. I developed ulcers and low blood sugar, and I couldn't sleep at night because of the constant nightmares. I just couldn't shake it off and I couldn't bare it anymore! One day, the depression hit me so hard that I knew I had to get some help.

I called my mother who came over right away. We went driving around town trying to find someone that would be willing to talk to me. It was a Saturday afternoon, so professional counseling places were not open as far as we knew. We had no idea where to start. We stopped at a phone booth on the side of the road (which by the way, shows about how old I am now). My mother started looking through the yellow pages of the phone book and tried to call a few churches. Some of the ministers that she was able to get in contact with said that they were too busy, or they said to wait till Sunday morning and bring me in to the church. I needed someone immediately! She kept calling different churches until she found someone willing to meet with us. He said that he would be glad to help. He told my mother to bring me to the church right away and that he would meet us there.

My mom drove us to the address that she found in the phone book. What was so amazing to me about this particular church was that it happened to be right across the street from the bar that I had been going to with friends. What a coincidence! We had been parking in the church parking lot at this address for months when there was no other place to park.

Anyway, when we got there, I told the minister about being fearful and depressed, and how things had built up against me so much that I could hardly bare it anymore. I also told him that I felt my life had no future and that my destiny was doomed.

At the time, the only thing that was helping me to hang on to life was my child that I loved. I could not, and would not, leave her alone in this world.

Throughout the earlier years of my life, way before my spiritual breakdown, I had been exposed to some weird and unusual experiences that should have never happened.

When I was a young child, one of my aunts who was dabbling in spiritualism gave me a "reading" from her tarot cards.

As a teenager in high school, I had a history teacher who assigned me and two other girls the religion of witchcraft. We were to study it and then give a report. My assignment was to explain how it worked.

Then as an adult, a friend and I went to see a tarot card reader to get our future read. Some of the things that the spiritualist had told me were not pleasant things to look forward to, and I worried what it meant, for years. (By the way, her shop burned down shortly after.)

I had also got interested in palm reading and other mystical practices. They were very popular and accepted everywhere.

Back then, I had no idea the dangers of it all. Needless to say, this all contributed to my depression. None of these experiences ever helped me to find answers that I needed. I felt my destiny was doomed. None of these things should have ever been acceptable and they were certainly not godly practices. If anything, I believe they exposed me to the dark side of spiritualism.

While me and my mother were at the church meeting with the minister, he prayed for me and then he had me pray a prayer of commitment to accept Jesus in my life.

The minister then told me to tell Satan that I now belonged to Jesus, not him. I remember that as I was getting ready to say the words that he told me to repeat, suddenly, a shocking thought came to me. It just popped into my mind out of nowhere! The thought was, "If you do, I will kill you!" I had no idea what was going on or where it came from. I didn't understand much about Satan and didn't even know I could order him to leave me alone.

At that moment, I <u>decided</u> I was going to trust and accept Jesus because he was my only hope. After I said the words that the minister told me to say to the devil, I felt a great relief. It was as if a heavy burden had lifted off from me.

Then a different thought came to me. It was "Hey, I said my commitment to Jesus and renounce the devil, and I am okay! Nothing bad is happening to me"! That frightening thought was a lie! I also realized that it didn't come from me! The minister knew who or what it was, and he showed me that day how to take my authority over it.

Whatever or wherever that frightening thought had come from, I now had a new revelation and realized that the threat was a lie. I began to understand that it was the enemy coming against me and he had been feeding me the thoughts the whole time to keep me in bondage and despair.

That day, I got my first revelation of how powerful the Spirit of God was. He impressed the thought to me that I did the right thing, and I was now going to be okay. Thoughts come from somewhere! We can either reject them or embrace them. They will affect our life decisions. I started feeling better, after accepting Jesus and realizing that I did not have to listen to (or take crap from) an enemy that I could not see.

James 4:7 (NIV), "Submit yourselves, then to God. Resist the devil and he will flee from you."

I struggled with some depression from time to time, but as I began to read the bible and learn about Jesus, my thoughts began to change. I was renewing my mind with good promises from God. I learned that Jesus healed, set people free and raised the dead. He did good things to anyone who asked him. He cared about people and loved everyone. I became excited about my newfound friend.

Romans 12:2 (NIV), "Do not conform to the pattern of this world but be transformed by the renewing of your mind. <u>Then you will be able to test and approve what God's will is, his good, pleasing and perfect will</u>."

For the record, I don't believe it was a coincidence that I was directed to this particular church, where I had parked my car for months and walked to the local bar. Also, we found out a little later, that the minister who prayed with me had just moved there to that town, in California, just a few months earlier. He had moved there from my hometown in Michigan. What another coincidence!

Since then, I have experienced times of refreshing from God and have felt great joy in his presence. I have even experienced healing in my body without even asking for it. There was a time when I had hurt my back and was in pain for months. On One particular day, I was sitting in a church service and while the preacher was preaching, I got this revelation that just popped in my head of how wonderful God was. From that thought, I realized that I really, really liked him! I liked everything I was learning about his character and love, and that he was a very good God! Then all of a sudden, I felt a warm and gentle electrical sensation go into my back. It was a wonderful feeling! Then I realized that my back did not hurt anymore. In fact, it felt pretty good! Then the preacher immediately stopped preaching long enough to announced that there was someone who was just healed in their back. It was me! I was surprised he even knew! So, this experience prompted me to learn more about Jesus and how he healed people. I read that he always healed whoever asked him. It was his will to heal, and he always did the will of his Heavenly Father. He was sent here by the Father to bring us all kinds of good tiding of great joy.

There are so many things that Jesus has done for me in my life. I have failed him so many times, but he still loves me. I am so thankful that he is forgiving, merciful and loving. This is why I wrote this book. I hope that someone who needs him will get to know him even better. There is so much we can learn from him.

You can say a prayer over a loved one (your child, your parent, or your friend) who you can't help. Maybe they live far away from you, and you can't get to them. Jesus can be there, and he can help them even when you can't. There is a peace in knowing him. There is also a peace knowing that no matter what happens in this life, our future is full of wonderful surprises.

1 Corinthians 2:9 (NLT), "…No eye has seen, no ear has heard, and no mind has imagined what God has prepared for those who love him."

OVERCOMING EVIL WITH GOOD

———◆———

LESSON 35

We briefly read a little bit about the story of Job in previous chapters. I still had a couple of questions about the whole ordeal that I would like to explore. When Satan the accuser came against Job to curse his life, Job did not tell Satan to leave him alone. Did he know it was Satan who caused his misery? And, I was also wondering, could he have told Satan to leave him alone? Could Job have been able to defend himself against the attack of Satan? Truth be told, Job was not in on the conversation between God and Satan. The actual conversation between the two took place in the heavens not on the earth (Job 1:6-8).

When Satan cursed the life of Job, Job stated that he wished that he would have never been born. Satan had made his life miserable! The only thing that Job knew to do was to stay faithful to God, even though he lost everything, except his life.

Throughout his life, up until this time, Job had kept a good relationship with God. God had even told Satan in their conversation that Job was an honest and just man. Job 1:1 says that Job feared God and avoided all evil. He even went as far as giving sin offerings to God on behalf of his children just in case they were to sin. In Job 1:10, Satan confronts God regarding a hedge of protection and blessing that he had surrounded Job's life with.

When Satan was allowed to cause destruction in Job's life, Job never cursed God or accused him of any wrongdoing. He had positive thoughts regarding God in the back of his memory. He knew in his heart that God was good. His trust in him was strong enough to help him hang in there in the toughest part of his life, even though he did not understand what and why it all happened. God saw his faithfulness!

God was moved by Job's complete faithfulness, even in the face of the worst thing that could ever possibly happen to anyone, other than actual death! If you read the story, you will find out that God was listening and watching Job deal with his problem the whole time. In the end, God stepped in and delivered Job from the whole situation. He healed him and restored to him double of everything he had lost. The rest of his life was blessed with more than what he had before Satan had caused him to lose everything.

Jesus had not been born yet to take care of the devil's accusations against Job and the rest of mankind. When Jesus came into our world, Satan also tested him regarding his faithfulness to God. Satan is trying to prove that mankind will curse God, if they don't get their way. He is trying to prove that mankind acts just like himself. Jesus knew all about Satan and his plan to discredit mankind, and he knew he had to put a stop to or terminate the devil's stronghold.

Paul writes in a letter to the saints in Ephesus to, **"Finally, be strong in the Lord and in his mighty power. Put on the full armor of God, so that you can take your stand against the devil's schemes. For <u>our struggle is not against flesh and blood</u> but against rulers, against the authorities,** against the powers of this dark world and <u>against the spiritual forces of evil in the heavenly realms</u>." (Ephesians 6:10-12 NIV).

Jesus knew about the schemes of the devil. He had prepared way ahead of time for the big battle that he was to go through himself, because of Satan. Even when he was a young teen, he told his earthly parents that he had to be about his heavenly Father's business. He studied until he knew the scriptures very well. He renewed his mind all the time. He had prayed and fasted, as he built on his relationship with his heavenly Father, in order to help the rest of us. He was a miracle worker. He was able to do great things and became the deliverer for mankind against Satan!

Jesus had power to do great things.

Jesus turned water into wine (John 2:1-10).

Jesus told Peter (one of his disciples) to go fishing and that he would find a coin in the mouth of the first fish that he was to catch. It was enough to cover their taxes that was owed (Matthew 17:27).

Jesus took five loaves of bread and two fishes, multiplied them, and distributed them out to his disciples to feed 5,000 men and their families (Matthew 14:15-21).

Jesus walked on water (Matthew 14:22-31).

Jesus healed diseased people (Matthew 14:35-36).

There are so many stories of where Jesus performed miracles, healed people and cast out evil spirits. He was the anointed one mentioned in the Old Testament book of Isaiah 61:1, that was to come in their future. He had said it himself when he quoted from the book of Isaiah, **"The Spirit of the Lord is upon me, because he hath anointed me..." (Luke 4:17- 21).** He was sent by God and had access to God's power by the Holy Spirit (Mark 1:10-11, Luke 3:21-22, John1 :32-34). Jesus knew secrets to the power of God because he was anointed. He knows secrets that we don't because he is God's Son.

In the temptation, Satan could not put any sickness or disease on Jesus like he had done with Job. I believe it would not have done any good because Jesus was given the greatest anointing and faith as a healer, and he had no sin. I believe the only way possible to kill Jesus was by binding him and inflicting wounds that would cause him to bleed to death. Like us, his blood carried his life force to keep his body alive. In Leviticus 17:11 God said that "the life of the flesh is in the blood." Without the life that was in his blood, the organs of his body couldn't survive anymore. Since Satan could not touch Jesus with sickness and disease, he tried in other ways. He tried to get Jesus to stumble in his belief by offering him riches, power and authority that had been handed over to him in the garden by Adam. Jesus would not give in to Satan's tricks of temptation and influence. So, Satan thought the only other option was to kill him through others. Even though Jesus was healthy all his life, it was possible for him to be put to death.

In the case of Jesus verses Job, God did not let Satan himself take Job's life, but God did allow Satan to influence others to take the life of Jesus. Jesus cooperated completely and willfully to become a martyr. He became a willing sacrificial victim. And, like Job's friends who had to offer up an animal sacrifice to receive forgiveness and let Job pray for them, we receive forgiveness by the sacrifice of Jesus and his prayer.

Satan killed the man Jesus through coaxing the religious leaders with thoughts. They were the same thoughts of jealousy and rage that Cain felt when he murdered his brother Abel. This shows the true nature of Satan and the influence he can have over people.

God used Satan's evil purpose to fulfill his own plan. When Satan caused the death of Jesus, what he really did was made it possible for the eternal Spirit that was in/with/upon Jesus to become available to the rest of us. **Satan had a hand in God's plan, and he didn't even know it**! God overcomes evil with good!

I want to bring to light a theory that I have given some thought to regarding spirit beings. There may be some of you who may not agree with me or feel the same way that I do. My idea is probably true enough to help us understand more about the difference between the word "spirit" and "Spirit", and the Holy Spirit verses evil spirits. I believe that there is some kind of similar existence between the "Son of God" verses the "children of the fallen angels". Both had fathers who were eternal spirit beings.

When Jesus had started his ministry, he was anointed and filled with the Spirit of God to do good works. The different between evil spirits and God's Spirit is that God's invisible Spirit is identified with his only true Son, Jesus Christ.

If the story in the book of Enoch is true, regarding the offspring of the fallen angel's becoming disembodied spirits when their bodies died, then it could make sense that the invisible Holy Spirit identified in Jesus (the offspring of God himself), was released into our atmosphere too, when his body died. The Holy Spirit had filled the body of Jesus with his presence while Jesus was alive, so that tells me that he can do the same to us. If evil spirits have been known to dwell in people, then so can the Holy Spirit.

If evil spirits can imbody people, then it would make sense that the Holy Spirit who is good for us can reside within us? Evil spirits have been known to oppress, depress and possess people. We still have our own bodies unlike them, and they want to use us to accomplish Satan's own evil trick to destroy us all. If evil spirits can actually oppress, depress or possess people to take them captive by their sick game, then we should understand that the Holy Spirit can imbody us to help in our fight against them. Devils tremble in the presence of God (Matthew 8:29-32 and James 2:19). Evil spirits oppress humans; The Holy Spirit oppresses evil spirits.

We have power through the Holy Spirit to overcome sin and evil with good. The problem is in not knowing that we do. That is why God had said his people perish because of a lack of knowledge (Hosea 4:6). Evil spirits oppress (distress, afflict, torment, discourage, agitate and upset). The synonyms for oppress regarding the Holy Spirit means he crushes, grinds, overcomes, overpowers, drowns and defeats. The antonym (or opposite) for oppress is invigorate, comfort, inspire, encourage and uplift.

The presence of the Holy Spirit in Jesus did wonderful things for people, before Jesus died. He had been the companion of Jesus. Jesus proved that this Spirit was the best thing that they could ever have. He wanted them to desire this Spirit enough that they would accept it, when it would finally become available.

Maybe Jesus did have some kind of possible access to the power of good and evil, just like the children of the fallen angels did, before he started his ministry, all because of being born of an eternal being himself. I don't really know for sure. Jesus could have done the same things as they did, when they were alive, if he wanted to. We do know that the power of good and evil was released into our world already in the beginning with Adam and Eve. After all, the stolen secrets that the fallen angels knew about were taught among their children and others.

The giants were influenced by their evil desire for power, and who does the bible say is the master over evil influence? Satan. He also tried to influence Jesus in the temptations. He tried to use Jesus to accomplish his own evil desire to rule the world, just as he compelled the children of the fallen angels to do.

In the Old Testament, when people began to seek out the false gods (or the spirits) to get what they wanted, they praised and worshipped them in hopes of getting their attention. Maybe, these people wanted the spirits (possibly of fallen angels) to use the "secret enchantments" that had been taught to them by their own fathers, when they had been alive. These enchantments did the evil spirits no good unless there was a body involved. Just maybe, these spirits could give the idol worshipping people what they wished for, but they would attach themselves to the request to cause it to happen. Did the idol worshippers open a door to the spirit's presence in their own life? Are these spirits acting as gods and using the secret gifts that God meant for mankind, illegally? Had these people welcomed a devil's presence?

We have "All" come short of the glory of God. The door (entry way or gate) to the realm (or dominion) of sin has been opened and made available to us, first by Adam. Sin had ENTERED our world, our realm of existence through him (Romans 5:12) and ended up affecting his son. Remember that just before Cain was thinking about killing his brother, God had said, "…if you do not do what is right, sin is crouching at the door; it desires to have you. You must rule over it" (Genesis 4:7). Many have been exposed to the wild beast crouching at the door, leaving them powerless to redeem or save themselves.

There is only one person throughout history who has ruled over the beast of sin. He never let it penetrate his personal thoughts, like Cain did. Remember, Cain was jealous and angry over the better sacrifice that Abel had offered to God. What character did Jesus portray, Cain or his innocent brother Abel? Jesus did not get angry with those who caused him to be cursed to die on the cross. He did not let anger in the door to rule him, when he became the one who was crucified.

The spirits can't bring you back to life when you pass away, and they certainly can't get you to heaven. The idol worshippers had attached themselves to the same judgement sentenced on those spirits who illegally used God's power (2 Peter 2:4-17).

God's Holy Spirit is the one we should give praise and worship to, because worshipping him provides cleansing for our spirits. He feeds us from his eternal life! His Spirit can release us from the grips of death, and he can get us to heaven.

God's power has been proven to be superior over and above the power of darkness. The power of God was proven in the story of the Pharaoh, Moses and Aaron (the high priest). God showed his miracle power, when he had Aaron cast his rod (staff) down before Pharaoh, and it became a serpent (Exodus 4:2-3 and 7:10-12). The Egyptian sorcerers also cast their rods to the ground, which also became serpents. But the rod that Aaron had cast down swallowed up their rods, proving the superior power of the real Spirit of God over their enchantments.

The Holy Spirit gives power over and above evil powers of the enemy. Jesus did good things after he was anointed of the Holy Spirit. He wants us to do good too! Why do you think he showed us all the works that the Holy Spirit could do?

Jesus had to die in order for the eternal Holy Spirit be released to the rest of us. When Jesus did die, he went into the realm of the dead just like anybody else. Did his companion who had kept him through the temptations, helped him do good for others, and to endure the cross, just leave him in the realm of the dead? Of course not! The bible tells us that the soul of Jesus was said to go there, but it was not left there (Acts 2:30-35). When Jesus rose from the dead, his body was quickened (or repaired and recreated) by the Spirit who had been his companion throughout his ministry (Romans 8:11, 1 Peter 3:18). Jesus rising from the dead proves that the Holy Spirit can do the same thing for the rest of us.

Jesus has now gone into heaven and is sitting on the right hand of God, which represents a special place of highest honor. He did the right thing with God's power legally. Angels and authorities and powers are made subject to him (1 Peter 3:22 and Ephesians 1:19-21). Jesus is the Lord over both the dead and the living (Romans 14:9, Ephesians 2:5 and Revelation 1:18).

So, we can see that the Holy Spirit is a good thing. He is a special companion that we can have ourselves. He is a Godsend! The Holy Spirit holds all secrets of God. All God asks of us is to be his body, his feet, his hands, his mouth, his heart, his mind to do good in this world. Thank goodness that all the angels did not know all secrets of God. But the Holy Spirit does, because he is the very essence of God.

We all can be born of his Spirit. And we all can become preachers or messengers of his words. The world cannot contain the whole and complete essence of the all-mighty God. There is more than enough of his Spirit available for us all.

John 1:12-13 (NKJV), "But as many as received him, to them he gave the right to become children of God, to those who believe in his name: who were born not of blood, nor of the will of the flesh, nor of the will of man, but of God."

Let's take two bible stories, the flood and the Red Sea, and see how they relate to us today regarding good and evil. They are believed to have really happened within our history. So, let's compare them physically and spiritually to understand how being born again and redemption works for us in the spiritual sense.

God can intervene and liberate us from an evil past and put it behind us to die out. He wishes all mankind to be saved. But neither those who were destroyed in the flood or those that drowned by the Red Sea were willing to turn from their wickedness.

God says in Ezekiel 33:11," As I live, I have no pleasure in the death of the wicked, but that the wicked turn from his ways and live..."

The drowning of the evildoers in the flood of Noah and the drowning of Egyptian slave owners in the Red Sea, both show us that God separates good from evil even though he loves every single person.

God saved the Israelites from bondage, just as he is the one who saves us from bondage now. It was a physical thing then, now it is a spiritual thing. Those who trust in God are freed and able to move forward from their undesirable past. The two stories use the physical realm that we live in to explain what happens to us each spiritually. So, you can think of or compare the evildoers that drowned, as your old self of sin crucified. God considers your past evildoing as dead or cutoff from your future. You can go forward with a new beginning and new adventures without your past overtaking you.

Romans chapter twelve tells us to abhor evil and cling to what is good. Judgement belongs to God, and God only. Leave past sins behind you and let him deal with them like he did in the two stories.

We are to overcome evil with good (Romans 12:9, 19 and 21), and if the bible says we can, then we can. Jesus did! Unlike Job, we have a redeemer who can fight back for us, because we have the Spirit of God living among us.

I believe God is fed up and is saying, "Enough, Satan! No more! I will put my Spirit in my people. And I will stand up against you through them. And, they will have my power to do what is right."

TAKE THE FULL ARMOR OF GOD

---◆---

LESSON 36

We read in an earlier lesson that just before David was going to fight with Goliath the giant, the king had offered him his own armor. It was way too big, and he had never used anything like it before (1 Samuel 17:1-50). In defeating the giant, David depended on the defense that God had already taught him. Let's just say that David went before Goliath equipped with the armor of God!

David had already defeated a bear and a lion while protecting his own father's sheep. He was confident that God would guide him in killing Goliath, who had been terrorizing the Israelite army for forty days. The giant had no fear of David and mocked and cursed him as he was approaching. But he had underestimated David and David's God. David knew that his God was bigger than the giant. The scripture tells us that he quickly <u>ran</u> towards the giant to kill him with just his sling and a stone. As he went, he said to the giant, **"...I come to you in the name of the Lord, for the battle is the Lord's, and he will give you into my hands." (1 Samuel 17: 47).** He had confidence in his God, just as he had in the past with the bear and lion.

Rather we realize it or not, we are in a battle against wicked spiritual giants. They are trying to overcome our souls. Like with David's predicament in the physical battle, he could not use the kings' armor because it did not fit him. He also had no past experience using that kind of battle gear. We can't fight a spiritual battle with regular military equipment. But we can fight with God's! God has been around since the beginning of time. He has all wisdom and understanding, and he is bigger than any giants that may come up against us.

Ephesians 6:13-17 (NIV), "Therefore, put on the full armor of God, so that when the day of evil comes, you may be able to stand your ground, and after you have done everything, to stand. Stand firm then, with the <u>belt of truth</u> buckled around your waist, with the <u>breastplate of righteousness</u> in place and with your <u>feet fitted with the readiness</u> that comes from the <u>gospel of peace</u>. In addition to all this, take up the <u>shield of faith</u>, with which you can extinguish all the flaming arrows of the evil one. Take the <u>helmet of salvation</u> and the <u>sword of the Spirit, which is the word of God</u>."

God's spiritual armor has been made to fit mankind. It is the same armor that fits King Jesus! It is something that you wear from the inside out.

Paul compared it to the armor of a soldier. It is made up of the **<u>belt of truth</u>** which is knowing the truth about Jesus and his authority. Knowing the truth helps to secures other pieces of the spiritual armor that we need. It secures all our protective gear, that represents authority and power given by Jesus.

Another piece is the **<u>breastplate of righteousness</u>**. It protects the most inner parts of the spirit man, especially the heart. We need to believe without any doubt that we have a right standing with God like David did. This knowledge shields the largest and most vulnerable parts of our being.

111

We are to guard our minds with the **helmet of salvation**. We are to remind ourselves of our redemption through Jesus and what he did for us. We are to think on the things of God.

As we walk forward in his **shoes** on the battlefield, we have assurance that his shoes will be more than sufficient in helping us to stand our ground firmly. We have confidence in the good news of peace that comes through walking the steps of Christ Jesus.

As we march forward to battle, we are to place the **shield of faith** in front of us. It protects us from the fiery darts of the enemy. There is another smaller companion shield referred to as a **buckler** that also helps deflect the blows of an opponent's weapon. Psalms 91:4 says that God's truth or faithfulness is our shield and buckler. The enemy's weapon can't penetrate the invisible shields of faith. Faith in the name and blood of Jesus as the anointed one, is our protection to block the enemy fire.

The last piece that is mentioned is the **sword of the Spirit**. It is the power source that we use to go forward in battle. It is much bigger than the enemy's darts.

Ephesians 6:17 says that the <u>sword of the Spirit</u> is the <u>Word of God</u>. It comes alive with power when we exercise our authority and use it. <u>The word of God IS the sword of God.</u>

Hebrews 4:12 (KJV), For the word of God is quick, and powerful, and sharper than any two-edged sword.

God gave us his word as a sword against our enemy. We can speak his word like Jesus did, when dealing with the devil. Jesus showed us how to deal with the devil by doing it himself. When he spoke, he was doing it as his defense (to defend) and his offense (to attack). The right words can be used as powerful weapons to protect us and help us fight back.

Proverbs 18:21 tells us that death and life are in the power of the tongue.

The bible is made up of stories and specific phrases that God wanted to be spoken into existence (or made law) throughout time. He was creating the needed verbal suggestions to accomplish his plan in the world.

Jesus used these inspired phrases as his defense against the mental and spiritual attacks of the enemy. He is our example! In the temptations of the wilderness, he spoke directly to Satan using words in the scriptures. He was not afraid, because he knew what to do and say to win the battle of wits. He overcame the temptations in the wilderness by the same Spirit that led him there in the first place. We have been given the wilderness story in the bible for a purpose. It was so that we could know how to defend ourselves.

There are two ends to the sword! The two-edged blade and the handle. For us, just holding on to the sword (or his word) gives us power.

Hebrews 4:12 (KJV), "For the word of God is quick, and powerful, and sharper than any two-edged sword, piercing even to the dividing asunder (between the two) of soul and spirit, and of the joints and marrow, and is a discerner of the <u>thoughts</u> and intents of the heart."

The word(s) of God that we see or hear electrifies and empowers us. As we listen to and/or read it, it infiltrates our thoughts. It affects the very core of our being. Hebrews 4:12 tells us that it penetrates into the marrow of the bones. And the marrow is what causes new cell production for the rest of the body. It has power to heal, invigorate and do whatever it is intended or targeted to do! Anyone that comes in contact with the sword of God is affected by it in some way.

As we take hold of the sword of the Spirit, it motivates us to go forward into battle. It is a type of spiritual surgery! Just knowing we have the ultimate weapon to defend ourselves gives us a higher level of confidence and strength. It is enough power to release God's courage within us.

Just like David trusted in God's armor and weaponry to stop Goliath, Jesus trusted in the same. It was fitted just for him. We need this same equipment in order to stop all the Goliaths that come up against us. God's power can be found in his written word, and when we speak it in faith, it is backed by God and all his angels.

A policeman has to first learn the laws and be trained how to use the authority given to him. He also has to learn how to use his weapons properly and be fitted in his uniform. Then he will be able to affectively use the authority given to him to act in the name of the law.

Jeremiah 31:33, God said, "I will put my law in their inward parts and write it in their hearts; and will be their God, and they shall be my people."

We are given authority in the name of "Jesus" by God himself. Spiritual law is his jurisdiction and it is far above all law. We are to uphold his laws and that is where the sword comes in. We have to learn, memorize and practice his word (his law) in order to properly use it. It is similar to the policeman, who has to learn what the laws are in order to uphold them and how to use his gun properly. Higher authority backs him or her when they act in the name of the law. God backs us, when we act and speak in the "name of Jesus".

Do you need to call on God for backup? Scripture tells us how to approach him.

Psalms 100:4, Enter into his gates with thanksgiving, and into his courts with praise: be thankful unto him, and bless his name.

When we do what Psalms 100:4 tells us to do, we get into his presence. If we do, he will get into ours because his word says so. There is power in praise. Psalms 22:3 tells us that God <u>inhabits</u> (dwells in or occupies) praise.

I had mentioned that when I first got saved, I still struggled with depression for a little while. Prayer and praise were both my biggest weapons in fighting back or blocking the enemy's thoughts. I didn't know the word very well, but I knew I could praise God when I needed him. Praise gets the attention of our heavenly Father, and as we call on him, he will hear us.

In Psalms 18:3 (NLT) it says, "I <u>called on</u> the Lord, who is worthy of <u>praise</u>, and he saved me from my enemies."

The one thing that the devil wants to do is to keep us from learning God's word that works against him. Satan wants us to reject the armor of God and stop using his shield and sword. It is our right and authority to enforce God's law against the influences that exalt themselves against the knowledge of God. 2 Corinthians 10:4-5 shows us in God's word a principle or law that works on our behalf.

2 Corinthians 10:4-5 tells us, For the weapons of our warfare are not carnal, but mighty through God to the pulling down of strong holds; casting down imaginations, and every high thing that exalts itself against the knowledge of God and <u>bringing into captivity every thought to the obedience of Christ</u> (2 Corinthians 10:4-5).

And, truthfully, good thoughts can replace destructive ones, if we speak the good ones to ourselves.

We can reject, disqualify or stop the lies of the enemy by just confronting him. We have that right! Speak out loud the word of God in order for the enemy to hear you. Even David spoke what he was about to do to the giant. As we fight with prayer and spiritual warfare, we can talk to God and run the enemy off.

There are many scriptures that refer to our mouths as the force behind the sword (Isaiah 49:2, Revelation 1:16, 2:16, 19:15 and 19:21).

Ephesian 6:18 is the last thing that is said regarding the armor. It says to <u>continually</u> pray in the Spirit, all kinds of prayers, and for each other. We can fight for each other with the armor of God.

Even though our enemy may still be at work causing havoc to destroy mankind, his destiny of doom has already been decided. If you want to find out what will happen to him and his defeated armies, read Matthew 25:41 and Revelation 20:10.

James 2:19 (NKJV), "You believe that there is one God. You do well. Even the demons believe – and tremble!"

Hebrews 4:16 tells us that we can approach the throne room of God to ask for help in time of need. In John 10:9, Jesus says that he is the door or way into God's presence. He connected the two realms by his obedience to the laws of God. Even though the Spirit of Jesus dwells in us, he also dwells in the throne room with his Father. Devils dare not enter, but we can through his Holy Spirit.

I want to say one last thing that God has brought to my memory from years ago. I think this message that God has brought to my attention is for someone in particular.

There was a young man who had been recently converted in a church that I was attending. He started playing an electric guitar in the worship part of the service. When he played, it was so easy for us all to sing and praise God. He put his heart into what he was doing, and you could just feel God's presence and peace. I believe he had a special gift. Before his conversion, he had used his talent to play in a heavy rock band under the influence of drugs. After his conversion, he struggled with thoughts that came against him in his mind. These thoughts told him that he should not be using his talent to play music for God because he wasn't worthy. The enemy had lied to him. This young man was so full of guilt that he wanted to quit even though he enjoyed playing the guitar for God. He had a battle going on in his mind. If you are in Christ, you are a new creature. This young man's talent did not come from the evil side. It was hijacked by the evil side. God gives us everything to use for the good of all. The young man really was on the right track and had to fight back against the lies. He didn't know in his heart yet that he had a right standing with God. He needed to keep going and doing for the Lord.

Use what you have for the Lord's sake and don't let the enemy tell you any different. This young man needed to look for the joy he was giving to others through his music. We were all blessed by him coming to the Lord and using his talents for the glory of God. Whatever talent you may have, use it for the glory of God and bring joy to the world.

Remember David spoke from his heart what he believed about his God. He had already known God all his life. Over time, he had built up a deep trust. He had been trained with the lion and the bear before he came up against the giant. He put his trust in the armor of God and won. So now when you think of "David and Goliath", think of this story and what he said. We can speak with the same authority that others like David did.

1 Samuel 17:47 David said, "I come to you in the name of the Lord, for the battle is the Lord's, and he will give you into my hands."

Submit to God and put on his Spiritual armor; resist the Devil and he will flee!

BAPTIZED, COME UP OUT OF THE WATER OR NOT

—◆—

LESSON 37

At one time or another, we have all been emotionally battered and scarred by disappointing life events, either of our own doing or through someone else. Picture your experiences as having a favorite shirt that you have had for years. It has been with you in the bad and in the good times. The bad times have left it in a sad condition. It has been stained and damaged by being torn, dragged through the dirt, or it could be just plain worn out. It would need some kind of tender loving care to bring it back to life again or it may need to be thrown out. We can be emotionally weighed down by all the hurt, guilt, shame, rejection and anger that can build up over time.

It is not healthy to be weighted down with too many misgivings. We all make intentional and unintentional mistakes. Some of these mistakes can damage us to the point of no return if we don't do something about them. Somewhere along the line, there needs to be a change.

There is a way to consciously free our own selves from these heavy weights, so that we can enjoy the rest of our lives in peace. The answer lies in giving the excess baggage to God. Psalms 55:22 tells us to cast our burdens upon the Lord and he will sustain us. Being baptized in water is one way of turning our burdens over to him. In most church baptisms, a person is totally immersed under water and then immediately brought back up. It is a symbolic gesture associated with good and evil, life and death. You are making a statement that you are going forward in your new life with him, leaving any old life of bondage behind. You are trusting God to purge it from your life, if need be.

Jesus himself was publicly baptized in water. He had made the decision to reject all (evil) works of the devil and to do the(good) works of his Father. He is a good example for us to follow.

We have a right to make our own decision rather we want to be baptized or not. When we get baptized and go under the water, it symbolizes cleansing and purification from the inside out. We are saying that it is our will to become emotionally, mindfully and spiritually separated from the influence of sin and dead works. Dead works are worthless, unprofitable or useless experiences that do nothing good for our lives. When we come up out of the water, we are purged consciously (Hebrews 9:14). We are claiming <u>freedom</u> from the unwanted feelings and mindset that has been formed by bad past life experiences. We can let it go, as we rise to our new life in Christ. We are resurrected to a new beginning and leave our past spiritual bondage of failure behind to die. And through our decision, God can now work to root out sin's power or stronghold over our lives.

Through the story of the flood and the story of the Red Sea, we can see the importance of what baptism means. The Red Sea parting of the waters and the flood of Noah both had a two-fold purpose. It was a good thing for some, but deadly for others. Evil was destroyed by the waters, while good was preserved by the waters. The defiance and rebellion of sin against God and his people got overtaken and destroyed by the waters. The waters were used for judgement and deliverance at the same time.

There is little difference between the process of being physically and spiritually baptized. Baptism covers all aspects of cleansing. When we physically wash ourselves with water, it can make our bodies clean on the outside from the things that are not supposed to be there. When we get baptized in water, we are making a confession of faith for the things that may not necessarily be seen on the outside of our bodies.

It is thought-provoking to me that those who had drowned in the waters had the waters overpower them from the outside in, but with the symbolic act of water baptism, living waters from God flow from the inside out.

At the Red Sea crossing, the enemy that pursued God's people was wiped out by the waters, while they themselves were set free or cleansed because of the waters (Exodus 14:21-30). The Israelites had to pass through by faith! They had to trust God that they could pass through safely without the wall of water collapsing down on them and it didn't! It only destroyed the sin and bondage that was pursuing them. Once God's people had passed through the Red Sea area, they entered a new beginning for their lives. Their old life of physical bondage was cut off. They could move forward free from their past. The Red Sea occurrence is one example of baptism.

In the story regarding the flood and Noah, evil of mankind had gotten so bad that God sent the flood to cleanse the land (Genesis 6:9-22). From what we understand in the bible, all living bodies were destroyed except Noah, his family and the pairs of animals that God told him to bring on board the Ark. The waters had a two-fold purpose which was to save and to destroy. God had the waters carry Noah and his family in safety, while he cleansed the land of the evil that was going on at that time, with those same waters.

Here is my take on the whole ordeal.

The only way that the race of people who were born from the daughters of men and sons of God could do anymore damage, was to do it without physical bodies. They lost their privileges of having one for themselves, when they drowned in the flood.

So, as mankind began to refurbish the world again, these beings resorted to stealing from the living. These evil spirits were jealous of and hated the living. They have been known to bind people with physical and emotional disorders, as well as cause sickness and pain through deception. They were robbing people of fully enjoying life that God had blessed them with.

So instead of people dealing with the real beings that lived in their own bodies before the flood, people dealt with spiritual bondage and disorders brought on by them as invisible spirits.

I am not saying that all sickness and disease come from evil spirits, but Jesus showed us that some of it does. Examples of dealing with evil or unclean spirits are found throughout the New Testament (Matthew 10:1, Mark 5:1-15, Luke 6:18, Luke 7:21, 8:2, 29, Acts 19:12-13 and many more). There were many times that Jesus had to stop them from harassing or hurting people that were living in his time.

Thank goodness, God has given his people authority and power over their influence. Jesus dealt with spirits a lot and so did some of his followers.

Paul had to deal with a woman having a familiar spirit (called a spirit of divination). She had claimed to predict the future (Acts 16:16-18). He cast the spirit out of her, and she could no longer be used for her employers' gain.

There are also spirits that can whisper information about another person, who has already passed on years and years ago. These spirits have been around for a very long time and could have had some kind of access to their personal life or be told the information through another spirit. Spirits can access and express themselves to or through other living human bodies.

As Christians, Jesus gave us jurisdiction over evil spirits that are operating illegally. Devils have to flee at the name of Jesus (Acts 16:18). They know who he is (Mark 3:11). Jesus said that he gives us power over all the power of the enemy, and nothing shall by any means hurt us (Luke 10:17-20).

We have to realize what Christ has given us. Baptized means to be immersed completely by his Holy Spirit, who cleanses us and gives us a new life connection with God. As Christians, we have been baptized into his death and raised to live with access to God's throne!

1 John 1:7 tells us the blood of Jesus Christ God's Son cleanses us from all sin. If we confess our sins, he is faithful and just to forgive us our sins, and to cleanse us from all unrighteousness (1 John 1:9).

Jesus was literally baptized by his own death and raised to new life three days later. Sin was never able to accomplish its mission against him. Jesus was not captured by it, or enslaved by it, like the rest of the evil doers, when they died and lost their bodies. Any influential evil that tried to put Jesus in eternal bondage was captured at his death, and sentenced, itself. Sin itself is what was sentenced to die. It had no right to Jesus or his body! And sin had no restraining order that could stop the Holy Spirit from raising Jesus from the dead either. Jesus no longer belonged under the law of sin and death. He is the first and only one who can now baptize (immerse, take us through and release us) by the baptism of his death into his resurrection. (Luke 3:16 and John 1:33).

We have to trust and accept the Spirit that raised Jesus Christ out from the dead for ourselves. We have to trust the Holy Spirit that Jesus baptizes and seals us with (Ephesians 1:13).

Jesus did not die on the cross and go into the realm of the dead for nothing! When Jesus was dying on the cross, one of the other men who was also being crucified asked Jesus to please remember him. **In Luke 23:43 Jesus told him, "Today <u>you shall be with me in paradise</u>."**

This same Spirit that raised Jesus from the dead can dwell in us and quicken our mortal bodies, if we accept this concept (Romans 8:11). We must be baptized or immersed in his Spirit to be born again, now, before we leave our bodies. **To be absent from the body is to be present with the Lord (2 Corinthians 5:8).**

If the story is true about what happened with the giants becoming evil spirits, then it just gives strength to the concept that Jesus as part human and part God can and is alive even now. I am not sure but have pondered the thought that when Jesus was dying on the cross, Satan was waiting for the moment that he could capture him and use him as a bargaining tool with God. He thought that Jesus would become a disembodied spirit like the children that came from the fallen angels. But he was mistaken! Jesus is alive and in his own perfected body!

We need a continual source of God's Spirit to live on forever. This is my take on the death and resurrection of Jesus. He was born to die here on earth and had to be forsaken <u>by God</u>, <u>as his God</u> (in Matthew 27:46), so that his soul could pass into the realm of the dead. According to Acts 2:27 and Ecclesiastes 12:7, the body, soul, and spirit that gives us life can be separated at death. This is a hard concept to understand, especially soul and spirit. Jesus never let go of the Spiritual hand of God <u>as his Father</u>. He said, "<u>Father into the hands I commit my spirit</u>" just before he passed away (Luke 23:46). He kept himself connected spiritually when he was baptized by death. God's power source is through the Holy Spirit. We connect with God's Spirit by our spirit. Staying connected with his life-giving power source is the key. God leaves the decision up to us.

The Holy Spirit (acting as the third party of God and companion of Jesus throughout his ministry) quickened or delivered his soul, (the very essence of Jesus) from the curse of death (1 Peter 3:18). Jesus was the first to be born again from the dead by and of the Holy Spirit, who gave him new life.

117

Being able to live in our bodies is a privilege. His body was now made invincible (unshakable and unconquerable)!

This new life or essence of the Holy Spirit of God is a permanent connection to God, as our Father, who resides in the highest spiritual realm there is. This gift couldn't be given to us until after Jesus passed from death to life to be rebirthed himself. The process of salvation has been created and established as law by God's Spirit. It can now be passed down to the rest of us through the name of Jesus.

At one point during his own death, resurrection and ascension, Jesus delivered those who had already passed on into the realm of the dead and had been waiting for their coming savior and Messiah. Jesus called their resting place "Abraham's bosom" (Luke 16:19-31). Some of these souls were souls that had been there since the beginning of time. Could Abel himself have been one of them? Were they the first to be born again of the Spirit, after Jesus? All those who accept Jesus are now with Jesus himself (Luke 23:39-43 and Ephesians 4:8-10).

The Holy Spirit has access to our realm and can live in each one of us as he did when he filled the body of Jesus to do good works. He is the living waters (John 7:37-39). He can be a part of us, as we become a part of him. Jesus said that we must be born again of his Spirit. It does not happen after we die. It has already been established at his death, resurrection, and ascension to his Father. It is a now thing for us all! The Holy Spirit is God working in our lives to help us, protect us and guide us as we yield to him.

In conclusion, the flood of Noah and the Red Sea were both used to bring death to the evil intent of others. These others had no desire or intent of changing their ways. They did evil while in their bodies and it meant death to their bodies.

In (Matthew 12:43) Jesus said that these unclean spirits roamed the earth. He also said that when an unclean spirit is gone out of a man, it walks through dry places, seeking rest and finding none.

What happened with the flood and at the Red Sea, saved people who had been tormented from the evil intent of others. Their past was wiped clean by the waters, so that they could start all over anew. They had gone through a form of baptism that literally saved and spared their lives (spirit, soul, and body).

The Holy Spirit is God in action. We can't see evil spirits in the world, but we can see their influence. We can't see the Holy Spirit, but we can see his influence in the world and in our own lives. The Holy Spirit controls the ultimate power that takes away or gives life, like in the flood and the Red Sea. The baptism is your declaration that you are going to trust God and yield to him. You are saying, "I am letting God deal with my physical bondage (like he did at the Red Sea crossing) and my spiritual bondage (like he did with the evil giants). I am going forward and leaving my sins behind for him to take care of, and with God I can do all things. He takes care of my past, my present and my future.

HE PAID THE PRICE

---❖---

LESSON 38

I would like to explore another very deep idea. Faith in Jesus is important not just to our spirits. It is important to our whole being which includes mind, body and soul, God promises to someday wipe out all evil and give everything that exist here on earth to those who has accept him and his cause. His plan is to save mankind from sin and extinction. Since the body of Jesus has been raised to an incorruptible state, and this same bodily state is promised to us, then the body must be important to God enough that he wants us still to have bodies forever.

I don't know if when Adam was first created from the ground, he had an actual body like we do today. He became a living soul only when God breathed into his nostrils. Adam started out as a healthy human being.

When he and Eve sinned, the bible says that their eyes were opened, and they knew that they were naked. Then the bible says that God made them coats of skin (Genesis 3:21). I don't know if the coats of skin came from sacrificed animals to make them clothes to cover their bodies, or if he did something supernatural to them, like alter their bodily state (or physical condition) to adapt to their new situation.

I want to delve deeper into the things of the bible that talk about the body. There are all kinds of elements that exist here on earth that can affect our health. Traumatic events can affect our health, as well as hereditary traits from our ancestors. Even our thoughts affect our health. There are so many things that our bodies are exposed to that can help or hurt us. We express ourselves through them. We obviously want to be comfortable, healthy and have the freedom to express who we are with our bodies.

Sometimes we let the wrong feelings be in charge of our thinking. We have all done some kind of stupid things that affect our lives in negative ways. Mankind has been that way from the beginning. Cain had lost control of his feelings and desired to end his brother's life.

Jesus taught life lessons about what could happen to people and their bodies when they do the wrong things. When he taught on this subject, he was trying to explain how sin causes corruption to the body.

There are some very harsh things that Jesus had said regarding offences or things that were considered wrong to do. In the next scripture, Jesus was talking to his own people, the Jews, that were under the old law or covenant. He was showing the impossibility of keeping the whole law. Adultery was one of the ten commandments and he used it as an example in his teaching.

In Matthew 5:28-29 (NIV) Jesus said, "You have heard it said, 'you shall not commit adultery.' But I tell you that anyone who <u>looks</u> at a woman <u>lustfully</u> has already committed adultery with her <u>in his heart.</u> If your right eye causes you to stumble, gouge it out and throw it away. <u>It is better for you to lose one part of your body than for your whole body to be thrown into hell.</u>"

Obviously, if we were to start getting rid of our body parts that we used to do something foolish or commit wrongful acts, we would eventually end up dying physically. You can't physically fix all the problems yourself by getting rid of your own body parts. In fact, that doesn't fix anything! It makes your life harder to live or kills you!

If we were to lose a hand because of committing sin, for example, then we wouldn't have use of that hand anymore to do good. It would be as if it was dead to you. Besides Jesus said in his example, that if you were to look at a woman lustfully, you have already done it in your heart. In other words, bodily desire can take over without considering any consequence for your actions. It is just a body and doesn't understand the problem. The sinful desire of the mind and heart is the problem that causes the body to get into trouble. Our body parts become captive to sin and sin is what destroy and decays it.

When we read about Jesus going to the cross, we can see that we have a choice to make regarding our own lives. Which would you rather do? Would you rather pay the price by losing a particular body part associated with your sin, or would you rather accept what Jesus had to go through when he paid the price for your sin already?

The crucifixion that he went through covered just about every area of the body. He was beaten, spit on, and had a crown of thorns place on his head. He had nails put through his feet and through his hands, and he was pierced in the side of his torso. He bled out and suffered all throughout his body. He was punished by man, and it was counted as recompence for our sins. Our consequence for our own sin can be transferred and accepted by him and his body. It is retroactive back to the time of Jesus on the cross.

Romans 6:11, 23, (KJV), ".... Reckon ye also yourselves to be dead indeed unto sin, but alive unto God through Jesus Christ our Lord. For the wages of sin is death; but the gift of God is eternal life through Jesus Christ our Lord."

As Christians, Paul said to consider ourselves dead (or disconnected, separated or divided) from the sin.

Through Jesus, the punishment for committing acts of sin, or violating principles that lead to corruption using our bodies, can be spiritually transferred back into his past, and to his body, that hung on the cross. There are no limitations with God through his Spirit in regard to the past, present and future. You can't physically go back into the past and lay it at the cross of Jesus. He is not there anymore anyway. He already paid the price for your sin.

God looks at the heart and sees what you mean when you ask him to help you. God who is invisible gave us a visible bodily image of himself suffering on the cross, so he could show us his mercy and forgiveness. He gave us a part of himself, so that he could express his great love to us all. He let mankind beat, bully, and kill him in his earthly body so that he could win our love. If he can win our love, he can save us from our own self-destruction.

In the Old Testament, the Israelites transferred their sin to the lamb that was to be sacrificed and offered on the altar of God. Its body was killed, and its parts were then purified by fire. It was innocent by itself until the sin was mentally, physically, and consciously transferred to the lamb by laying of hands on the head of the lamb. It was to be put to death for their sin. Sin was transferred by faith to the lamb.

The Israelites willingly and consciously performed rituals to appeal to God for forgiveness. The offender did not have to take the punishment for their sin on their own body when they followed this process for forgiveness. The Israelites actively used all their physical body parts (hands, feet, etc.) to bring the lamb, transfer their sin to the lamb, and then offer that lamb as atonement for their sin. They had to physically, consciously and mindfully carry out the steps that they knew would cover their sin. They used their bodily functions to clear their conscience before God.

They received forgiveness and healing instead of condemnation. This was the temporary fix until Jesus was pierced and punished like the lamb. We go forward with a clear conscience and learn to use our bodies and minds for good. If we can, we can make restitution to others that we hurt. But we make restitution with God through the lamb of God, who was Jesus.

Jesus used everything he had for good. We know that he kept the whole law. He is the only person who never used his body for evil. Colossians 1:22 tells us that God has reconciled us to himself by the physical death of the body of Jesus. I personally thank the Lord that we don't have to pay the price with our own body because he already did!

WHAT ABOUT MY BODY?

———— ✦ ————

LESSON 39

Our destinies are not set in stone. They are subject to change up until the end of our lives. What happens to us at the end of our lives depends on choices that we make now, while still in our original bodies.

God created different kinds of beings, including angels. They all have their own particular forms, functions, and personalities that identified them as individual entities.

We don't know a lot about other beings before our beginning, but we do know that the destiny of the fallen angels who had anything to do with us is final. Satan himself was an anointed angelic being, who was perfect in all his ways until iniquity was found in him (Ezekiel 28:13-19).

The first man of our species did not become a living soul until God breathed into his shell of a body the breath of life. This breath came directly from God, not the earth. Since our bodies are made from the dust of the earth, we are held here by earth's gravitational pull.

There is more activity going on around us than what we can actually see. We are somewhat protected from the chaos of seeing everything, because we have bodies.

There is a whole world of difference in an unseen realm of which we are a part of. For instance, can you see how your words travel through space almost instantly when you talk on your cell phone? What about using GPS? Can you see the signals that communicate back to your device? When the wind blows, can you see it? We can see the effect on the tree branches, hear the whistle of the wind or feel the gentle breeze, but can't see the actual wind. We have learned to react to things according to the feedback that we get through our bodily senses. With the natural body, we only experience the outcome from the invisible effects.

We have limits as to what we can see and do because of our earthly bodies. For example, if there was a solid wall between you and another person, it would block you from seeing them. And you would probably not be able to hear them very well either. On the other hand, a wall and a roof could keep you comfortable during a storm. The wall and roof could protect you from danger. It is good that we are made from the same elements as the earth and connect with the things around us.

Our bodies limit us to certain fields of vision, hearing etc. in our realm of existence for a reason. For example, we can only see a certain spectrum of light even though there may be additional waves of light around us. White light is visible and contains all the colors of the rainbow. One type of light that we can't normally see directly with our physical eyes is ultraviolet light. It has a shorter wavelength than the violet at the end of the visible spectrum that we can see. The lens in our eyes have a filtering effect that blocks most of the ultraviolet light. Some of this light is also blocked by the cornea. Ultraviolet light is invisible to humans. Some of these invisible waves of light can be dangerous to skin and eyes. Also, if we could actually see everything going on around us, it could be very chaotic.

It is good that we are made from the same substances that shape our world. It gives us boundaries. We all should know that everything that we are, and what we build or put together has its beginning with atoms. Atoms had their beginning when they were created by God.

Our bodies are made from some of the same earthly materials as other things, so that we can interact with them through our five senses such as touch, taste, smell, sight and hearing. We can also interact, feel and express love to each other because we are all made from the same substance. It is all meant to be a blessing. Our bodies are a gift from God to enjoy other tangible things.

We can build houses to live in and furnish them with beds and couches to make life comfortable. We cook delicious meals made with different ingredients, and we make roads to travel on. We can enjoy the environment around us because it is the same physical or tangible substance that our bodies are made of.

Matter is a substance that takes up space and can exist as a solid, liquid or gas. It is composed of atoms grouped together. Science is still finding new and fascinating information about this field of study. I am not an expert, but I know, and so do you, that things can either stay the same, decay, or change its form.

When we have to die and leave our bodies behind, we don't have access to the atoms that make up our eyes and ears. We don't relate to the things in this physical realm anymore even though we may have spiritual eyes and ears. All the things we will relate to will be in a different kind of realism.

As Christians, when we pass from this life, we leave our bodies and go to be with Jesus, if we have already accepted him by faith. When faith is first set into motion, it functions as an invisible presence or power. It starts changing things and circumstances throughout our lifetimes, even though we can't physically see what's happening. We evolve from the inside out. The words of life that come from God help us make any changes necessary to make it to heaven.

Paul tells us that God's words can have a profound impact on our lives. **He said that the word of God is quick and powerful, and sharper than any two-edged sword. It can penetrate to the dividing of soul and spirit, and of the joints and marrow. It is a discerner of the thoughts and intents of the heart (Hebrews 4:12).** Nothing can infiltrate a person any deeper than God's word. It affects the body, the human spirit, and the mind, will and emotions of the soul. It penetrates the very core of our being.

Our own DNA is some kind of chemical blueprint. It has to do with programming instructions that are needed to keep us alive and well. It is associated with historical characteristics from both our fathers and our mothers. We know this because people can see the similarity between our physical features and our parents. Genes are segments of DNA that link us to our ancestor's and their DNA.

The bible tells us that Jesus was born from both a human and the Spirit of God. He had human blood and human DNA just like us, but he also had something from his Father, who is Spirit.

Whatever it is that we receive when Jesus becomes a part of our lives, it is a perfected invisible element that relates us to him. I don't understand it all, but maybe we get some kind of spiritual or chemical (or both) alteration in our own bodies. Whatever we receive, it relates us to his life story. His life history is written in his DNA. Maybe there is some kind of change that happens to our own DNA when we decide to accept him.

For instance, and just maybe, we receive some kind of special Spiritual genetic material or processes that was completed in Jesus Christ after he ascended to the Father and present his blood of DNA. It had the experiences identified with him and his life story. In other words, his lifetime genetics was coded with his history. It had evidence of him being filled with the Spirit of God (while in his human form) to do great things for others. His DNA marker had the evidence of his body being raised to incorruptible life. This marker reveals his eternal inheritance of life after death. We may not understand the coding, but

God does! Maybe it is one of those things that we just can't see! Something from his own life is then made available to us.

1 Corinthians 15: 52-44, In a moment, in the twinkling of an eye, at the last trump: for the trump shall sound, and the dead shall be raised incorruptible, and we shall be changed. For this corruptible must put on incorruption, and this mortal shall put on immortality, then shall be brought to pass the saying that is written, death is swallowed up in victory.

Our bodies will be changed to be made like his, because it is all in the blueprint of his life. We can know that the Holy Spirit transforms lives and can make us immortal, because he did it for Jesus, who was the first new immortal man.

At the moment we receive Jesus, we received some kind of invisible element pertaining to Jesus and his eternal life. I looked up a few things that I thought were very interesting to share. I don't know what it is exactly that we receive physically because of Jesus, but whatever it is, it ties us to him and his Father.

There are three things that I discovered:

1) First of all, I found that scientists can alter DNA to add, remove or change something in a DNA segment or gene.

2) Secondly, did you know that it is possible to have two DNA models inside you, yours, and someone else's? It can happen through bone marrow transplants. The donor's DNA that is present in their donated bone marrow can stay in the patient for the rest of their lives.

3) Thirdly, there is also another interesting thing that I don't know much about either but found interesting. I read a little about "telomerase" which is a type of enzyme. Telomerase allow cells to keep multiplying and avoid aging because it elongates chromosomes. It is a good thing except for the fact that it can enhance cancer growth as well. The amount of telomerase in our bodies decline as we age. It has been called the "immortality" enzyme.

So, is it possible that we could live on forever? Did Jesus house two types of DNA, one coded from his own human spirit and the other from the Holy Spirit at his water baptism? In other words, did the infilling of the Spirit have some kind of direct effect on his DNA structure? I believe it did! What about when he rose from the dead? I believe it did! I do not know the exact answers, but it helps me to believe that the same Holy Spirit that effected his DNA can become a part of our DNA as well. The Spirit of God has all the secrets to eternity itself.

The devil lies to us! He is trying to disarm (deactivate or neutralize) the truth from our minds. He wants to have an effect on our DNA, as well. Sickness, disease, poverty and death are his devices! He tries to turn us from the truth about Jesus Christ that sets us free.

In general, words are invisible things with meaning. They are spiritual in nature. We make them more tangible or come alive to us, when we hear, see and write them. We use the physical senses to learn the spiritual.

Jesus is referred to as the "Word of God" that changes us from the inside out. When he walked this earth, he never got sick, he never sinned, he was able to ward off the devil, he raised the dead, and he lives with God. It is all in his DNA. If we are in Christ Jesus, there is no condemnation that says we should die for our own sin. He already did! The truth gives us strength and sets us free mentally, spiritually, emotionally, and physically.

God gave us bodies so that we can enjoy life. We hear the melody of chirping bird and the voice of our child or other loved one. We can feel and hug them. We see the beauty in God's landscape of the mountains, oceans, colorful flowers, and skies, and even in the darkest of the evening with the stars and the moon. We can taste a variety of flavors like sweet, spicy, garlicky, and so on. Life is meant to be enjoyed.

The future looks good! For now, we can still enjoy the things that God has placed in our midst because he gave us bodies! Use them wisely! Your DNA (one of the most important parts of your body) is capable of housing secrets to life itself.

KEEPING OUR FAITH FIT THROUGH COMMUNION

——◆——

LESSON 40

God wants us to talk to him as if he was one of our closest friends. We can tell him our deepest and darkest secrets since he knows about them anyway. And, we can ask him anything! He is well pleased with our efforts and will give us his undivided attention when we focus on him for guidance.

It takes faith to be able to reach out to a God that we can't see. Hebrews 11:6 says that he who comes to God must believe that he is coming to God. It also says that God is a rewarder of them that <u>diligently</u> seek him.

Scripture tells us how easy it is to reach out to him in faith. We don't have to go very far because he dwells within us (Ephesians 3:17, 2 Corinthians 13:5, Galatians 1:16 and Galatians 2:20.

Romans 8:9-11, But ye are not in the flesh, but in the Spirit, if so be that the <u>Spirit of God dwell in you</u>. Now if any man has not the <u>Spirit of Christ</u>, he is none of his. And if <u>Christ be in you</u>…But if the <u>Spirit of him that raised up Jesus from the dead dwell in you</u>, he that raised up Christ from the dead shall also quicken your mortal bodies by <u>his Spirit that dwells in you</u>.

1 Thessalonian 5:16-19 tells us to <u>rejoice</u> and <u>pray</u> continuously, and in everything <u>give thanks</u>. It is God's will and desire to hear from us. You may ask, why is he so interested in our thanksgiving and praise? It is because he takes delight in rewarding them who diligently seek him.

God is a real being and has real feelings, just like us. We normally reach out to those that we love, to let them know how much we love and appreciate them. We sometimes give them our undivided attention in order to express our good feelings toward them. And we also praise them for their accomplishments. So, why not do the same for the Spirit of God, especially when we need him? We should not ignore him, but to welcome his presence in our lives in the same way that we would do for anybody else that we love and care for. To pray, rejoice, praise and give him thanks is one of the best ways of communicating with him.

How does rejoicing, praying and giving thanks benefit us? Psalms 22:3 says that **God inhabits praise**. Inhabit means to live in or occupy. If you are nice to a guest staying in your home, they will probably want to visit with you more often. God wants to be with us as much as we will let him. Ephesians 5:18 tells us to be filled with his Spirit and Ephesians 5:19-20 tells us how to be filled with the Spirit.

Ephesians 5:19-20, Speaking to yourselves in psalms and hymns and spiritual songs, singing and making melody in your heart to the Lord; Giving thanks always for all things unto God and the Father in the name of our Lord Jesus Christ

If God inhabits praise, it makes sense to give him the praise that he deserves, because **he is drawn into our presence by our praises.**

We can praise him in song, meditation, prayer and discussing him with others. If God lives in us, by his Spirit, through his Son, then good things can happen. Jesus made a promise to be in our midst individually and collectively (John 14:23 and Matthew 18:20).

"Where two or three are gathered together in my name, there am I in the midst of them" (Matthew 18:20).

Even if you are alone and seeking him for any reason, you are not really alone because Jesus and you make two!

Jesus gave us instructions on how to align our whole being (mind, body, and spirit) into perfect harmony to bring him within our midst. You might say, "Why do I need to pursue his presence, isn't he already within me?" The simple reason is that **the joy of the Lord is our strength (Nehemiah 8:10).** We need a continuous flow of his presence to keep fit. Life events can wear us down, but Jesus can build us up again! He is fully capable of blessing us with health, wealth, long life, peace, and joy!

When we consciously and passionately attempt to get his attention, we do things like close our eyes in order to help us concentrate; reach our hands towards heaven to show our complete surrender and submission; and or get on our knees to show our respect and reverence for his majestic nature. We also involve other bodily functions to express our emotions. We use our lungs to breath out the air that causes our mouths to speak, when we sing to him or about him. We can get so emotional that sometimes we cry tears of either sorrow or joy. These are all faith steps that we can follow in order to get our focus on him, so that he can communicate with us.

The holy communion is another symbolic gesture that we can do to consciously bring into line our spirits with his. We can deepen our faith just by carrying out the instructions that he had recommended. At the last supper, he had taken the bread that represents his body, and the wine that represents his blood, and gave them to his disciples (Luke 22:19). He said to eat and drink it in remembrance of him! The communion is a special occasion where we celebrate Jesus.

In the process of acknowledging him through communion, we can receive something special from him. It is a serious ritual that should not be taken lightly. It is done in order to bring him to the forefront of our thinking! To treat it like an ordinary meal would be eating and drinking in an unworthy manner (1 Corinthians 11:24-30). Paul says in verse 29 that we must discern the importance, the power, and the influence of the meal. We can associate Jesus with our own lives through the bread (body) and wine (blood). The mind, body and spirit need to be focused on him in the whole experience.

We purposely use our bodily senses of sight, taste and touch as part of our focus during communion. For example, if you think about it, we first <u>see</u> the bread that he said represented his body. We then <u>feel</u> its material substance as we take it in our hands and put it into our mouths. As we <u>taste</u> it, we <u>feel</u> its texture again. We then feel its presence entering into our bodies as we swallow it. We do it because he said to do it. We sense the breads presence with our eyes, hands, mouth, throats, and bellies throughout the whole process. We are purposely and physically doing something with our bodies to acknowledge Jesus.

The communion is a conscious way of acknowledging his presence that is within us and it links us to all his benefits. I recently looked up a new phenomenon that I had never heard of before, called "synesthesia". It has to do with crossing of the senses. One of the senses response mechanisms can bleed over into another. Some people associate a number or sound with a color, hear sounds from images, see colors from music or even taste or smell certain foods when a particular word is spoken. The person being affected is really experiencing a reaction through their other senses. They see, hear, or taste and to them it is real. Even though synesthesia is thought to be rare, we all experience this phenomenon to some degree.

For example, I can just think of seeing a slice of my favorite chocolate cake and then experience the taste of chocolate in my mouth. It makes my mouth water, and in my mind, I crave it. I can even feel hunger for it in my tummy. All my senses work together to tell me that I want a piece of chocolate cake.

We can't physically see Jesus during communion, but we can connect with him through our imagination. We can get our minds on him by meditating and using our bodily senses. Using our bodily senses during communion helps to enhance our concentration and is a significant benefit in faith building. Faith is the substance of things hoped for and the evidence of things not seen. Jesus gave the command as a definite "to do" when he said, "do this in remembrance of me" (Luke 22:19, 1 Corinthians 11:24-25).

He knows that this event can consciously activate (trigger, initiate or cause) our subconscious mind to be focused on his realm of existence. In other words, we can think with our spirit. It is a powerful tool in reaching out by faith with our spirit to his Spirit because faith is spiritual in nature.

By faith we can receive new life. We can receive something from his healthy, sinless spiritual and bodily nature and presence. He is the perfect prototype (the perfect model citizen), who makes us fit for the kingdom of God. God wants us to focus on his Son's image and strive to become more like him. When we symbolically take in the bread and wine (body and blood of Christ), we are creating good thoughts that help our own minds, bodies, and spirits to heal and be more like his, through the Holy Spirit. It is impossible to please God without faith, "for he that comes to God must believe that he is coming to God, and that God is a rewarder of them that diligently seek him" (Hebrews 11:6). Faith is the doorway that we must go through to receive the rewards or inheritance that come through his own Son.

We can draw from his new and perfect life and image. I believe the word of God that was written in Genesis 1:26- 31 is not over. **God had said, "Let us make man in our image, after our likeness, and let them have dominion...." (Genesis 1:26). God created man in his image, in the image of God created he him, male and female (Genesis 1:27). And God blessed them and said, "Be fruitful, and multiply and replenish the earth, and subdue it: and have dominion...."** He went on to name everything that he blesses mankind with to meet his needs (Genesis 1:28-30). He saw everything that he had made and behold, it was very good (Genesis 1:31). God will have his word accomplished. His will is being done. He predestined mankind in the beginning, and he will see it through.

Isaiah 46:9-10 gives us a hint of how God thinks.

God had said, "Remember the former things of old: for I am God, and there is none else; I am God, and there is none like me declaring the end from the beginning, and from ancient times the things that are not yet done, saying, 'My counsel shall stand, and I will do all my pleasure'" (Isaiah 46:9-10).

In the book of Joel 2:28-29, God had said that he would "pour out his Spirit upon all flesh." The Spirit or life that came about because of Jesus is a never-ending fountain of pure and living water for mankind. It has been released into our atmosphere or realm, and has been made available to us all, if we want it. Why wouldn't we want any of the things that Jesus did for others, when he was here on earth. And, why wouldn't we want access to the throne of God in good and bad times. Why wouldn't we want good health, prosperity and eternal life.

Communion can be a therapeutic time of healing and restoration, if we have a real revelation of what takes place by faith. We can claim that as Jesus is, we are too. Paul had to tell some of the church people that they were not taking the communion in an appropriate manner, or understood the meaning behind the celebration. They treated it like a time to simply get together and eat. He also said that the reason some of the them were weak and sickly, was because they did not consciously acknowledge the influence or power that was behind the ceremonial act (1 Corinthians 11:27-30). It did some of them no good and they were missing out. Paul went on to explain that with the partaking of the body and blood symbolically, they could be made stronger in faith, and some were even healed from sickness.

The spirit, mind and body can have access to good things, when they are connected with the right source of information. God will not force himself on anyone. So, when we take communion, we are signaling to him that we give him are consent to touch our lives and improve it. We are asking him to empower us with healing.

Remember the lesson where I talked about the game show and hypnotist that I saw on TV? The contestants had given their consent to the hypnotist to hypnotize them. They consented to do whatever he told them to do. The hypnotist came up with a word, a sound or a particular type of touch that would trigger in their minds a thought to carry out his instructions. In other words, he gave his set of instructions a simple label, identifier, tag, or name. When they heard or felt the trigger with their senses, it activated the memory associated with his instructions. The contestants remembered his instructions and carried them out. They actually began to live out what he had implanted in their imaginations.

Just maybe, when we take communion, we are following the instructions of Jesus to cause our minds and bodies to fall in line with his word.

During the ministry of Jesus (before his death and resurrection), he had performed a miracle feeding thousands of people with five loaves of bread and two small fishes. The very next day, he taught a lesson about the bread, and his own blood to the people throughout the book of John chapter six. Communion using the bread and wine had not been established at this point in time. In John 6:32-35, 48, 50, 51 and 53-56, 58, Jesus had said that whosoever eats his flesh and drinks his blood, dwells in him, and he in them. They did not understand what he meant and took it literally, even his disciples (John 6:41-42,52 and 60-61). He was speaking of spiritual things, because in John 6:63 he said, "It is the spirit that quickens; the flesh profits nothing. The words that I speak, they are spirit, and they are life." So, in communion I believe we literally take from him spiritually. It's something invisible to us. Jesus is the blessing of God that comes down from heaven. Jesus is the trigger for the things of God!

Let's compare the consuming of the communion meal with consuming other nutritious and beneficial things that are good for us? What about healthy foods, prescription drugs and vitamins that we give ourselves in order to have better quality lives. Let's take the prescription drugs for an example. These medicines give us hope and affect our future. Let's refer to the bread and wine as taking faith enhancing capsules. **Faith is the substance of things hoped for and the evidence of things not seen (Hebrews 11:1).** This medicine is the only medicine that we can take whenever we want or need to. According to the written instructions on the bottle, there are no side effects, and it is always good for you. We could label the bottle Jesus!

The bread and wine are the generic or symbolic replica of the real favor and blessing (or medicine) that God made just for us. We may not be totally aware of what it does to fix our lives, but we are the ones that must make the decision to take it. Jesus said that it will work if we do it in remembrance of him. We don't have to know how it works. All we have to know is that it can drive or flush out the bad and give new life. This invisible Spiritual Substance has been made available to and for us all. It came at a great cost for the original Owner. It is now available to us for free!

Preparing ourselves physiologically for communion is the first step in the training exercise of faith. If we know ahead of time, when we are going to actually do it, we can prepare our minds and hearts to be ready to participate.

We can look forward to feeding our spirit man. If we want to make changes in our lives, the trigger word to inscribe within our minds and imaginations is Jesus. Everything about him is all good!

There are so many ways to train ourselves in the knowledge of our creator and the savior that he gave us. We can acknowledge them through music, reading, communion, listening and having conversations about him with others. The whole bible from the beginning to the end is centered around God giving us his Son, Jesus. Jesus is our trigger word. If we know his story, it can destress our minds, as well as calm our heart. We are not perfect yet and God knows this. He accepts us as we are. We are a work in progress, and we live and learn by faith in his Son.

THE SPIRIT PROMISE FOR ALL NATIONS

In the beginning of our time, God had blessed mankind. His purpose was for us to be fruitful, to multiply, and replenish the earth (Genesis 1:28). There may have been other types of beings here on earth before us that didn't work out, but God created man to exist in a life of peace and joy.

Any other false kingdoms, principalities and rulers of darkness will eventually come down because Jesus "made a show over them openly and triumphantly" (Romans 8:38, Ephesians 6:12 and Colossians 2:15). Since God had first blessed mankind, the sin nature has become fruitful and multiplied to replenish the earth along with mankind. There have been times when God had to clean up the blunders made by our civilization like he did in the flood story. After the flood, God had said a similar statement about replenishing the earth to Noah (Genesis 8:17). God's kingdom is the only empire that will stand forever.

Later, when Abraham came along, God made a similar statement again. This time he involved himself in the equation and vowed to see it through. Through the bloodline of Abraham, he (God himself) would bless all nations to become fruitful, and multiply to replenish the earth.

Whatever words that God had spoken back then, have become a part of our existence even today. If God decrees a thing, then he also supplies the needed resources to fulfill his plan. He always has! We can see that he still wants us to be happy and blessed and replenish his earth, even now. He took the time to give us his own Son (his redeeming Spirit) to save the world. Jesus was born to make us a part of his Father's kingdom of real peace and joy (Luke 12:29-32). His plan is for us to become the image of himself, just like Jesus is. His will is to express himself in his own creation.

There was something special that could be passed on to us by the redeeming Spirit that came through Jesus. It alters the final outcome of the sin nature that is trying to destroy our lives. Through Jesus, God gave us a holy pardon that supersedes the law of sin and death.

Luke 23:33-46 tells us that when Jesus was on the cross, he asked the Father to forgive or pardon his persecutors (who represented all of mankind). He even explained the reason why. In verse thirty-four, Jesus said, "Father, forgive them; for they know not what they do." He knew that his persecutors were oblivious to the truth behind what they were doing.

They did not know the two-sided significance of their actions. They did not know that they were putting God's own Son to death. There are people even today that don't believe Jesus was God's own Son, who was put on a cross to die. This unbelief is their greatest sin! God knew ahead of time what would happen to his Son. It was all meant to be! The other significance was that the people were playing a part in God's plan of salvation, rather they realized it or not.

Another thing that Jesus cried out while suffering on the cross was, "My God, my God, why have you forsaken me?" God as the holy or divine judge had to desert Jesus on the cross for a moment in time, just to give mankind forgiveness. He had to reject the old nature of man to give a new one.

There was a couple more things that Jesus had said before he breathed his last breath. In verse forty-six, Jesus had said, "Father, into thy hands I commend (or commit) my Spirit." Jesus was presenting himself as suitable for approval and acceptance. Jesus had done the work that he had come to do and the last thing that he said in John 19:30 was, "It is finished!".

Jesus had asked God to forgive us as he hung on the cross. He did not necessarily ask for God to forgive us for hanging him on the cross, for that had to happen to get forgiveness. It was much deeper! It had to do with unbelief, disobedience and rejection of his Father, our creator, and our God. Jesus was sent here on earth to abolish the death sentence, and to bring us life and immortality. He came with endless compassion for us all and gave his life to prove it.

God made a way that we could put our unbelieving and rebellious nature on the cross by the one man, Jesus. The opposite of the word forgive is to blame, condemn and punish. When Jesus said, "It is finished" I believe he was declaring our forgiveness. He was paying for it through his own God ordained desire of true love and sacrifice. We don't have to run from God or avoid him anymore. We can be fruitful, multiply, and replenish the earth because Jesus got us our pardon.

After Jesus had died, and before he ascended into heaven, there were different accounts from the disciple's and followers about seeing him. He visited with them for 40 days. The first account is in John 20:17-22. It was the morning Jesus had resurrected from the dead. The scriptures said that he appeared to Mary Magdalene (who was one of his devoted followers). He told her in John 20:17, "Touch me not; for I am not yet ascended to my Father." I believe that this meant he was transformed somehow, because he could not be touched. He had to stay pure in order to present himself as the living and pure sacrifice to his Father. Apparently, the process of whatever his body was going through was not yet completed.

After Mary had first seen Jesus, she went to his disciples and told them that he had risen from the dead and that she saw him for herself. Later that day, Jesus appeared to his disciples while they were assembled together behind closed doors. He showed them his hands and his side where he had been pierced.

In John 20:22, it states that <u>he breathed on them</u> and proclaimed with authority to them, "<u>Receive the Holy Spirit</u>!" He told them that he was giving them the authority to retain or forgive sins of others. They were sworn in to continue his mission. There was something powerful that happened at the moment he spoke the anointed and God ordained words with his own pure and immortal breath. He transferred something to his disciples, and John 20:22 says it was the Holy Spirit!

Thomas, one of his disciples was not there to witness seeing Jesus when the others first did. He did not believe them when they told him that he had risen from the dead. Eight days later, Jesus appeared again, and this time Thomas was there (John 20:26-28). Thomas immediately wanted proof that the man standing in front of him was Jesus, so Jesus told him to see his scars and touch them. When Thomas saw the scars and touched the body of Jesus, he was ecstatic! He knew without any doubt that it was Jesus and said, "My Lord and my God!" Something had changed from the first time Jesus was seen by Mary Magdalene when he could not be touched. He must have presented himself to the Father shortly after he talked with her (John 20:17), because now he could be touched. He even ate a meal with them all, including Thomas.

In Luke 24:45-49, it says that Jesus explained to them everything that was going on and that there was more to come. He told them that he had to suffer and die, and then rise again. He also told them that he was sending them to do the works that his Father had sent him to do. But first, they needed to stay put in the city of Jerusalem until they received the promise of the Father. This promised gift would provide them with power from on high to be a witness to the world. In Acts 1:4-5, Jesus explained that they would be baptized (or immersed) in the Holy Spirit to get it. He reminded them of the water baptism done through John the Baptist, but this was a new thing.

The Holy Spirit had a big part to play in the life of Jesus before and after his death. Just before Jesus had officially started his ministry, he was baptized by water. The bible says that he was immediately filled with the Spirit when he came up out of the water. He was then led by the Spirit into the wilderness to be tempted of the devil. After the temptations, he came out of the wilderness anointed with great power. He spoke and did works with such great authority and power that many were amazed (Luke 4:14, 18, 32, 36,37). It was the Holy Spirit of God who helped Jesus get ready for his ministry and stayed with him through it all.

We can be baptized in water as a statement of our faith that we are rising to new life in Jesus. In Mark 1:4-8, John baptized people in the water, as he preached repentance and the forgiveness of sin. This water baptism started before Jesus had died and rose again and is still going on today. It is an event where a person is literally dunked under the water and quickly brought back up again. The whole process is a faith step or symbolic gesture to say, "my sins are washed away". At the moment the water covers your whole body, it cleanses. At the moment you are raised out from the water, you are cleansed. It is one of those events (similar to the communion) where you use your bodily senses to make a statement symbolically. It is a faith step to spiritually purge the conscience.

When John had baptized people in the Jordan river, he said, "I indeed baptize with water: but he (Jesus) shall baptize you with the Holy Ghost (or Spirit). Matthew 3:11 and Luke 3:16 states the same thing as Mark 1:8, except they add that Jesus will baptize them with the Holy Ghost and with fire." So, there were two types of baptism's, one when we do something symbolically with water, and the other when Jesus does something spiritually.

When Jesus had risen from the dead, he rose on a yearly day of thanksgiving referred to as "First fruit". It was a time of celebration and feasting for the bountiful barley harvest that God had blessed his people with. After Jesus had risen from the dead, he was seen by many for forty days before his ascension into heaven.

The Holy Spirit baptism could not happen until after Jesus died, rose again and ascended into heaven to be with his own Father. The Spirit baptism took place 10 days after he ascended into heaven. It happened exactly 50 days from when he rose from the dead and seen by many. Fifty means Pentecost and the 50th day from First Fruit was referred to as the day of Pentecost. It was also a time of celebration like the First Fruit, where the people gave thanksgiving to God for the next harvest called the wheat harvest. So, in summary, Jesus died on Passover, rose on First Fruits (resurrection Sunday), and the promise of the Spirit was given seven Sundays later on the day the Pentecost.

On the day of Pentecost, 120 people were assembled together praying and worshiping God, when suddenly something out of the ordinary happened.

Acts 2:2-4 (KJV), And suddenly there came a sound from heaven as of a **rushing mighty wind, and it filled all the house where they were sitting. And there appeared unto them cloven tongues like as of fire, and it sat upon each of them. And they were all <u>filled with the Holy Ghost and began to speak with other tongues (or languages), as the Spirit gave them utterance.</u>**

This experience was the promised baptism that Jesus had told his disciples to wait for. The day had finally come! All 120 people that were in the upper room worshipping God were filled with the Holy Spirit.

They began to praise God in an unknown language that they did not know. They spoke in languages other than their own learned language (Acts 2:6-12). This was a miracle experience! The only way this miracle could have happened to them, is if the Spirit of God was involved. He is the only one who knows all things and all languages.

They were all baptized with the Holy Spirit and with fire. Jesus had said that they would be endued with power and be released out into the world. They could now lead others into the forgiveness of sin through the name of Jesus, just like he had said that they would in John 20:22. In that one day the church grew by 3,000 people. This baptism in his Spirit on the day of Pentecost was another very important event in history.

It was the actual account of the outpouring of God's Spirit. The man Jesus went to be with his Father, and his Holy Spirit was sent to us. There was an exchange, and it was now complete. His Spirit that he had committed into his Fathers hands had been accepted by the Father. And now, mankind can be made suitable for his Holy Presence because of what Jesus did. He was the first to be born of God with just the right fit and perfect in every way. This promised Holy Spirit has been given to us as a gift of new and eternal life.

This story of the Spirit baptism meant that they were filled so full of the Holy Spirit from the inside out, that the evidence overflowed through their mouths (Acts 2:4). There are scriptures that refer to this Holy Spirit baptism as drinking from living waters.

During the ministry of Jesus, he had said, **"If any man thirst, let him come to me and drink. He that believeth on me, as the scripture hath said, out of his belly (or from deep within him) shall flow rivers of living waters." But this spoke he of the Spirit, which they that believe on him should receive. For the Holy Ghost was not yet given because Jesus was not yet glorified (John 7:37-39).**

But now Jesus has risen from the dead and has been glorified. And, the Holy Spirit (or Holy Ghost) has been given.

The miracle of speaking in an unknown language began on the day of Pentecost or fifty days after the resurrection of Jesus. At the time of this actual baptism event, Peter stood up to explain what was happening. He said that this miracle was the fulfillment of prophecy written in the book of Joel.

In the book of Joel 2:27-28, which is in the Old Testament, the scriptures foretold of this occurrence long before Jesus was even born. **God had said, "I am the Lord your God, and I will <u>pour out my Spirit</u> upon all flesh." Jeremiah 2:13 and 17:13** (also of the Old Testament) says that **"the Lord is the <u>fountain of living waters</u>."** And then in John 4:10-14, Jesus explains that **the <u>water that he gives is a well of water springing up into everlasting life</u>**. These scriptures are all referring to his Holy Spirit!

So, you may ask, what is there in this Spirit baptism for me? Why do I need it? Isn't it enough to mentally and verbally accept Christ as my savior? There is a good reason why we need this special gift or power (Acts 1:8). It gives us some more of the same ability, strength, and power that Jesus had in order to help ourselves and others. We need to access everything he offers. If he is for us, who can be against us?

I believe there are some ministers that have access to this ability in them already, but don't realize it. They could do more in their own ministry to edify the church, if they chose to search the newest part of this spiritual gift from God (1 Corinthians 12:27-31 and 14:12).

There were two new supernatural gifts made available to the followers of Jesus through the Holy Spirit baptism. His disciples had already been doing some of the same things that Jesus had done, like heal the sick and cast out devils. This new function of the Holy Spirit was language gifts referred to as the gifts of tongues and interpretations. Tongues means to speak an unlearned language and the interpretation is the actual message spoken in a learned language.

If you think about Jesus and all the adversity he had to go through in his own ministry, you may wonder how did he keep up his strength and not give up? There were so many people who were against his teaching and tried to stop him. Nonetheless he never let the mocking of others get to him. He somehow still went about doing his best and he had the power and endurance to do it!

As Christians, we need times of refreshing like Jesus did when he lived here on earth. Does it sometimes seem hard to go forward and live your life with peace on the inside, or know what to do when you are facing a difficult situation? Jesus did! He went off by himself frequently in order to pray. He drew his strength by talking to his heavenly Father.

The character of Jesus was one of perfect control over his feelings and desires, and he loved people. He shows us that we can accomplish a lot more with others if our personal feelings and desires are in check. It can be a very hard thing to do on our own. believe me, I know!

When Jesus would get alone with his Father, I wonder what dialog or language they had between them? Could it have been the same universal language (called tongues) that was given to the 120 on the day of Pentecost? Was his prayer language with his Father now made available to others?

Jesus had the Holy Spirit to help him throughout his ministry and now it is available to us. The Spirit baptism is a special gift to help ME and YOU rather than the other guy. And in turn, can do something good for the other guy. You need his power, endurance and attitude for yourself first, in order to help someone else.

The baptism of the Holy Spirit gave the 120 an enhanced power source on the inside like Jesus said it would. You could think of this special gift as a comparable to a dimmer light switch. You can turn the power of the light up or down yourself when needed. The choice is yours as to when you want to turn it on or off. Jesus had told his disciples in advance that they would be baptized with the Holy Spirit and receive power, and they did (Acts 1:5,8).

The evidence of their baptism was the speaking in an unknown tongue. Maybe the language they were speaking was the real and complete language of God. Paul himself said in 1 Corinthians 4:9 (KJV), "... I speak with the tongues of men and of angels..." After all, God is working towards all of us being united as one in Christ.

Maybe, this language is a small revelation to what is to come in the new heaven and new earth under his rule. We will all be able to communicate with God and to each other, and we will live in peace, health and harmony. I believe we won't need healing, prophecy, miracles, or even the need to speak in different languages. We will all be made perfect as he is perfect.

Jesus had fulfilled his destiny as one of us, and now we are to fulfill our destiny as one of his. God released his Spirit into humanity itself, in order to change the world and bless all nations. We are being suited properly from the inside out with his Holy Spirit, and it all started on the day of Pentecost. I believe all sin and temptation that has hurt mankind will be dealt with and gone for good. Without a tempter, we will have the perfect mind (or thinking) that Jesus Christ already has. I don't know how it is all going to happen, but I believe we are a work in progress.

Let's look into what happened while the people praised and worshipped God on that special day of the Holy Spirit baptism. The people had all began to worship and praise God in their own language that had been taught to them in their early childhood. Their praises were voluntary praises to God. In other words, they did not have to yield their mouths, lungs, and vocal cords to give God praise, but they did. They had made a decision to speak what they wanted to say. And the thoughts of course had to come from their minds. The whole process of praise had to involve the language part of their brains, their lungs, vocal cords, and mouths. In other words, they used their bodily functions and learned language to express what was on their minds. They were all in one accord praising God.

During or while they were praising God and thanking him for his Son, a miracle happened to their speech. In an instant, things shifted. While they were giving God their undivided attention and consciously yielding to him, he filled them with his Holy Spirit. The result was that their words of praise were transformed into different languages, and it was not coming from their learned language portion of the brain anymore. They had entered into the realm of faith by yielding body, mind and spirit with their praise. God literally inhabited their praise.

The expression of their worship began to shift from coming out from their own minds, to coming out from deep within each one of them. It was likened to a flowing river of water, spiritually speaking. They did not have to consciously think about what they were saying. But they were aware of their feelings associated with their praising God. Their praise was flowing out from their inner belly area just like Jesus had said it would. He had said, "out of the belly shall flow rivers of living waters (John 7:38)." It flowed out from the center of their being, where the Holy Spirit came in and made his dwelling.

Jesus had said "if any thirst, let him come unto me and drink (John 7:37)." A river is a flowing stream that can connect with other waters like itself. We are spirit beings, and so is he.

The water baptism was an outward bodily thing that we do. This was an inward thing that God does if we let him. They are both important activities that God definitely takes part in. And they both have to do with the living waters.

When God activated his promise in them, the effects filled them so full that it overflowed from their inner being outward through their mouths. They had become so focused on praising him, that he now had their undivided attention. The unlimited love and power of God began to overflow from deep within their spirit into their minds and bodies like a flowing river. They were now connecting with him and his presence with great joy. They felt so much joy coming from God on the inside that it could not be contained. Psalms 16:11 says that in his presence is fullness of joy. The more joy they felt, the more joy they wanted. This was the presence and promise of God through the living, breathing, and flowing spiritual waters.

The multi-languages of praise that they spoke from their lips was a sign that the promise was given for ALL NATIONS, just as God said to Abraham. These people tapped into the realm of God's Spirit (far above all chaos, evil, pain and sorrow) when they focused on worshipping and thanking him for his Son Jesus. They became intertwined with the Holy Spirit as they yielded to his presence. They were speaking from a universal language that they had not learned and the evidence was witnessed by bystanders. Only God knows all languages from man and from angels. It was proof that the Holy Spirit came to dwell in and with them. The Holy Spirit helps all nations of people in their connection with the Father.

Have you ever felt so much excitement or joy that you could not contain yourself? Would your excitement explode into expressing itself through your body and speech? What if you won millions of dollars? What would come out of your mouth? Would you shout for joy or jump up and down in your excitement?

Whatever we focus on and allow ourselves to feel can spill over into our interactions with those around us. In this case, their countenance had changed, and through them, the Holy Spirit was able to draw many others.

In Acts 1:8, Jesus had said that they would receive power from the Holy Spirit and go out to the "uttermost parts of the earth." From this experience, the ministry of his Spirit exploded. The church began to be fruitful, multiply and replenish the earth, as they went forward in the power of his Spirit. This experience of the baptism has been a continual thing. It didn't just happen that one day, on the day of Pentecost. That was just the first time. There were people baptized in Acts 8:12-13, Acts 19:2-6 and Paul himself according to Acts 9:17. It apparently was a necessary addition to the church and its growth.

There were some people who received the Spirit baptism before they were ever baptized in water. According to Acts chapter ten, there was a time, place and day that a man named Cornelius and others who were gathered together in his home received this same baptism. When Peter preached to them the story of Jesus, the bible says that the "gift of the Holy Ghost" fell on them all, and they were heard speaking in tongues while magnifying God. This time it happened to the non-Jews (or gentiles). Peter said that they should also be baptized in water, and so they were. That means these two baptisms are two separate things, and that they can be done in either order or together. You can read about it in Acts 10:43-48.

It is a good thing to have limitless access from the Holy Spirit of God when needed. That is why Jesus associates the Spirit with flowing and living waters. We can drink from it at any time and for any reason as we pray and seek his face. We need times of refreshing. Just as our bodies need refueling and rest, so does our spirit man. We don't have to get baptized more than once. But we do need to keep filled with his Spirit. The gates of Heaven have been opened and God's Spirit and blessing are being poured out on all flesh.

God could have just written us off as a lost cause because of so much evil in the world. Maybe, he could have made a different man from the ground and breathed into him the breath of life similar to what he did to the first Adam. He could have just started all over.

He could have made the new man more robotic and unfeeling, so that this new man would not be tempted by desire. But then, what would be the purpose? There would be no true love between man and God. We would just be like puppets.

God wanted mankind to have his own choice to desire him in their lives. We inherited the desire of Adam and Eve to be our own gods. This desire (or temptation) was transmitted to us all. If it hadn't been presented to mankind in the first place, it would have never been a problem. We wouldn't be making all kinds of wrong decisions. This sinful desire can keep us hiding from our creator and we would eventually die without him. Sin is a huge problem for the whole world. God could have just wiped out everyone in the world, but he didn't. He gave us a helper instead! He gave us a part of himself!

THE GIFTS OF THE HOLY SPIRIT

LESSON 42

Paul found that there was a big benefit to the powerful baptism of the Spirit and related gifts. To him, these gifts became an ongoing blessing in his ministry. In 1 Corinthians chapter fourteen, he gave a lot of details about them. He explained that they worked to edify the whole church, as well as being a communication line with God. They were gifts that could be used to reach the world to spread God's blessings.

Everything about all the gifts is good. They give life-altering resources for our whole mind, body and spirit. And someday, our mortal bodies will be quickened to exist forever like Jesus and his immortal body, when it is time. It is the gift of eternal life promised to every believer.

It is a good thing that all of mankind does not live forever in their present state. I want you to think about a "what if" moment that could have been for all of mankind. What if we were all able to live forever in our present state, body and all? It may seem like a good idea, but if you think about it, this idea would include all the criminal minded people that will not repent and change their ways. They would also live forever terrorizing the rest forever. God has dealt with this kind of tragedy before with other beings that were pure evil. He is putting a stop to this problem by giving us his Spirit and power directly, as well as the help of his angels. The "what if" of evil has been taken out of the equation because he made a way to cut it out and save the good.

When God had said that Eve's seed would crush the head of the serpent, he meant it (Genesis 3:15). The serpent was Satan in disguise, and the one who was really behind the attack on humanity in the garden (Ezekiel 28:12-19, Revelation 12:7-9, 11 and Revelation 20: 1-3). When we are spiritually born again of God's seed that was first planted through Jesus, then in us, we become the seed of God who crushes the head of Satan to stop his works.

Thank goodness God will not allow the bad to overlord the good and destroy it. This is why he wants us to get born again of his Spirit who is all about good. The old nature that has the capability of ruining the lives of many will be wiped out totally when Jesus comes back. We must be born again of the HOLY Spirit in order to live forever in peace. As for now, even though we have evil and good still among us, we have access to the benefits and gifts of the Holy Spirit. His gifts can change things from bad to good!

In 1 Corinthians 12:4-13 Paul named nine different gifts that can operate through God's people. I believe that these gifts had operated within Jesus without measure, when he was physically here on earth ministering. They have been made available to us. These gifts overcome evil with good.

NINE GIFTS OF THE HOLY SPIRIT

- **Three revelation gifts**
- **Three Power gifts**
- **Three utterance or inspirational gifts**

The first three are the **"revelation gifts"**. They reveal or make something known that is not already known to the natural mind. They are referred to as the <u>word of knowledge</u>, the <u>word of wisdom</u> and <u>discernment of spirits</u>.

The first gift is the word of knowledge, and it is a message of truth from God.

It is a fact or principle that is revealed to a person, so that they can use it for good. It is usually given as a thought or feeling. For example, God may reveal or show someone a sickness or disease that another person may have. God never intends it to be used to expose or belittle anyone. It is gifted for that moment in time to minister properly. It is Jesus (his Holy Spirit) working through the one who is ministering. This knowledge can be about anything that God needs his ministry workers to know. Sometimes it can lead to a miracle, healing or other answers to prayer.

There are many examples in the bible of the knowledge gift given to men for particular situations. Jesus himself was given knowledge about people so he could heal them all throughout his ministry. One example is the story about the woman at the well (John 4:5-19). Jesus knew about all her husbands, even though he did not know her personally. Another example is when Jesus was about to be taken away to stand trial. He foreknew that Peter would deny even knowing him, in fear of persecution (Luke 22:31-34, 54-61). But knowing this, Jesus reassured Peter that he prayed for him already, so that his faith would not fail. If you ever think God has given you a word of knowledge, pray about it, in order to know what to do with it.

Later on, after Jesus had gone to heaven, the word of knowledge was given through a prophet named Agabus. It was a warning for Paul. Agabus was given vital information regarding Paul's future (Acts 21:10-14). Paul was told through the prophetic message that he would be a prisoner of the Gentiles. Paul could have made the decision to not go forward, but he said he was willing to be imprisoned and even die, if necessary for Jesus. The gift of knowledge is vital information given from God, and it could be of the past, present or future. It can be a crossover of other gifts like the gift of prophecy.

The second gift is the <u>word of wisdom</u>. It is a supernatural revelation or answer for a particular situation, and it can affect the future.

Acts 7:10 reminds us of the story in the Old Testament regarding Joseph, who was sold by his brothers to be a slave in Egypt. He ended up going to prison by no fault of his own. While there, he had interpreted a dream that troubled the Pharaoh. And, because of God giving him the interpretation of the dream, he was promoted to one of the highest positions in Egypt. God had given him the meaning of the dream and the wisdom to deal with it. God supernaturally gave him a plan! Through the wisdom that God gave him, Joseph was able to save the people from the famine and have his relationship with his family restored.

1 Kings 3:5-15 has another great story regarding God's wisdom. It was the story about King Solomon, who was King David's young son. Solomon had become successor of his father's kingdom, and God was so pleased with him that he wanted to grant him his heart's desire. God asked him what he wanted. Solomon asked God for a wise and understanding heart to rule the people. God was so pleased that he gave it to him, as well as great riches.

King Solomon used the wisdom given to him from God to handle a desperate situation between two women (1 Kings 3:16-28). The two women lived together, and both had given birth to a son. One of the woman's babies had died in the middle of the night, so she switched babies with the other woman. When the other woman woke up, she knew that the dead baby that was in her arms was not hers. They took their dispute before King Solomon, and he ordered the baby to be cut in half and given to each of them. The real mother of the living child begged him not to kill the baby. She said she was willing to let the other woman take her son, if it meant her son would not die. The king realized from her quick response that she was the real mother of the child, and he gave it to her unharmed.

Jesus verbally gave his disciples wisdom to minister properly. He had already showed them what to do to heal people and cast out devils, when he was here physically on earth. Then he said that when the Holy Spirit comes, he would guide them on what to say and do in a pressing situation of any kind, if needed (Luke 12:12). That would be the gift of wisdom in operation. If we have accepted Jesus Christ, we have the mind of Christ (his Holy Spirit) in us (1Corinthians 2:16). The Holy Spirit is Jesus being with us and we are given access to the power and wisdom of God (1Corinthians 1:24).

Wisdom is the power of discernment and to know and judge properly. Wisdom knows what to do. We can ask God for wisdom according to James 1:5. Supernatural wisdom can be gifted at a particular moment in time for a certain situation. It can be used to correct or make things right for the future.

The third gift is the <u>discernment of spirits</u>. It is the supernatural detection of a presence from the spirit realm of something good and/or bad.

There were (and still are) people who could see in the spirit realm when God showed them. Jesus did! He had to deal with the devil himself in the temptations, as well as other evil spirits that were tormenting people.

2 Kings 6:8-23 is the story of Elisha the prophet and his servant. God had revealed to Elisha (through the knowledge gift) where the camp of the Syrian enemy was hiding out. So, Elisha took the information to the king of Israel to warn him. When the king of Syria found out that Elisha was the one who told the king of Israel where his camp was, he set out to pursue him with an army. Early one morning, the servant of Elisha woke up to see the great Syrian army surrounding the city and became afraid for their lives. At the request of Elisha, **God opened the eyes** of his servant, and he was allowed to **see a mountain full of "horses and chariots of fire"**. He was allowed to see in the spirit realm around them.

These first three gifts, the word of knowledge, the word of wisdom and discernment of spirits can reveal information supernaturally that would not necessarily be known already or it could give confirmation of something already speculated.

These gifts and all the other gifts are thru the Holy Spirit. They can be expressed in different ways. They can manifest to us by a vision, a dream, an audio voice, an inward revelation, seeing into the spirit realm, or just by reading God's word. These gifts reveal things that we would not normally know or see. They are messages that God wants to reveal to his people, and they operate as the Holy Spirit of God wills.

The next three gifts are the **"power gifts"** and they do something out of the ordinary. They are the <u>gift of faith</u>, the <u>gift of healings</u> and the <u>working of miracles</u>. They can be activated and work along with any of the other gifts.

The fourth gift of the nine gifts is the <u>gift of faith</u>. It is a supernatural ability to believe God for something to come to pass without having any doubt.

You just know that you know! Hebrews 11:1 says, "faith is the substance of things hoped for, the evidence of things not see." God gives supernatural power in one's heart and mind to believe for a particular miracle, healing or for any other desired outcome to come to pass.

Matthew 9:20-21 is the story of a woman who was healed of a rare blood disease that she had for over twelve years, just by touching the garment of Jesus. She had heard of his healing power and believed in him. God honored her belief in his Son, and I believe God gave her supernatural <u>knowledge</u>, <u>wisdom</u> and <u>faith</u>. She just knew that she knew that Jesus was her healer.

I also believe that God gave her the wisdom to know what to do in order to get her healing. Faith was the substance of the healing that she hoped for, and the evidence of the thing she did not consciously see yet. She imagined the whole scene of being healed before it actually happened in the natural. She visualized in her mind that as she touched the garment of Jesus, she would be healed. She set up her own trigger point of contact (his garment) in her thoughts.

God is well pleased in those who believe in his Son and honors them with supernatural faith to receive. I believe she pleased God, and he gave her the thought (or divine insight) that would activate the power to heal her. Faith to me is power! Faith connects us! As she touched his garment, the power of God shot through her.

The gift of healing is the fifth gift. Jesus was the Christ meaning he was the anointed one. Healing was and still is associated with Jesus.

Jesus was on his way to heal someone else, when the woman reached out and actually touched his garment. The bible says that when she did, he felt the healing virtue flow out from himself to her (Mark 5:30). This miraculous event involved many of the gifts in operation. They were all rolled up into one. This story also tells me that when the healing virtue is flowing, anyone with faith can receive. Jesus was on his way to heal someone else and had no idea that she was about to touch his garment.

After Jesus had ascended into the heavens, the gifts exploded, and the church started growing into the multitudes. People were being healed by the ministry of his followers.

Peter played an important part in one of the stories and gifts regarding healing. People were bringing the very sick and vexed with unclean spirits into the streets and placing them on beds and couches. Faith was flowing strong among the crowd of people. They actually believed that when Peter was to pass by their sick loved ones, his shadow would overshadow them, and they would be healed (Acts 5:14-16).

Multitudes became followers just by seeing the gifts in operation. They were moved by what they witnessed for themselves and believed. Healing can be for any kind of sickness or ailment (mentally, spiritually, bodily or emotionally). It can happen instantly or over time as your faith progresses. It is found throughout the bible even in the Old Testament. This power gift was and is still active in the church. Even today, there are many stories of people who were instantly healed by the gift in operation.

Jesus had demonstrated all the gifts himself. He commissioned his followers to heal and deliver others from the bondage of Satan. There was a woman with a spirit of infirmity for eighteen years (Luke 13:11-16). According to Jesus, Satan was the one who had bound and crippled her up to where she could not lift herself (verse 16). How did he know this? Remember that the gift of discernment reveals that there is a spirit behind the sickness, disease or torment. Jesus laid his hands on her, and she was healed and delivered from Satan's grip. He has access to all gifts.

The gift of healings can operate through people as they yield to God's Spirit. We can pray for ourselves or another to receive healing. I have received healing without even asking for it, myself. I was just sitting quietly soaking in the reality of how good God was, and it just happened, instantly. We have got to realize the awesome goodness of God in order to receive something good from his Spirit.

The sixth gift is the working of miracles. It is divine intervention to miraculously change the outcome of a current situation of any kind.

There are lots of miracles that happened in the bible. Some of them I have already written about in this book. God did miracles when the Israelites were captive in Egypt. He sent plagues, parted the Red Sea, gave manna from heaven, and turned bitter water into drinking water. What about Abraham, David, and Solomon? God made them all very rich men because of their connected with him. Jesus himself turned water into wine, fed thousands of people and was financially set in his ministry. Healing itself is a miracle! The Holy Spirit that is given to man is a miracle! Jesus was the greatest miracle that ever happened!

The last three vocal gifts are the "**utterance or inspirational gifts**". These gifts are spoken words or statements from the Spirit of God through a spokesperson. They can operate in conjunction with any of the other gifts. For example, the information that comes from the first three gifts (word of knowledge, word of wisdom and discerning of spirits) can be made known through these vocal gifts. These three gifts are the gift of prophecy, the gift of tongues (or unknown language) and the interpretation of tongues.

The seventh gift of the nine gifts is the gift of prophecy. It is a supernatural and divine message spoken in a known language by a spokesperson on behalf of God himself.

There were prophets all throughout the old and New Testament. Jesus was considered a prophet and spoke the things from God to mankind all the time (John 12:49-50). He told his disciple that when they were to go forth and minister, the Spirit of his Father would speak from within them (Matthew 10:20).

Earlier, I mentioned that a word of knowledge was given through a prophet named Agabus and that it was a message to Paul about his future (Acts 21:10-14). The prophetic message was that he would be a prisoner of the Gentiles as he went forward to preach. If you think about how Paul was able to travel all over the place to preach God's message, he did it while being a prisoner. He was able to get God's message out to thousands as he traveled far and near.

There are times when God has a special message for someone, or a group of people gathered in his name. It can be a message that he directly speaks through someone. It may be for a special mission, situation or to give encouragement.

There are false prophets in the world who may think they hear and speak from almighty God. The only sure way to know that the message of prophecy is from God is to get to know God and have a relationship with him. And, if the message does not line up with his will and word, and it doesn't feel right, then pray about it and seek the truth. It may be true, and your feelings need to catch up with what his word says, or it may be false or wishful thinking from a human perspective.

The last two gifts are the newest of the "**utterance or inspirational gifts**" from God.

The eighth gift is called the gift of tongues. It is speaking in a language not known to the speaker.

It is speaking directly from a person's spirit by his Spirit. The mind is not necessarily active and understanding what the mouth is saying, even though the mouth helps in the coordination of expressing the message.

Isaiah 28:11, For with stammering lips and another tongue will he speak to this people.

Romans 8:26-27 (NLT), And the Holy Spirit helps us in our weakness. For example, we don't know what God wants us to pray for. But the Holy Spirit prays for us with groanings that cannot be expressed in words. And the Father who knows all hearts knows what the Spirit is saying, for the Spirit pleads for us believers in harmony with God's own will.

When we decide to accept Jesus as our Lord, mentor, advocate and protector, we have access to the Holy Spirit gifts and promises. Romans 8:26 tells us that the Spirit helps us with our weaknesses. We do not always know what to pray, or how, especially when we are desperate. The Spirit itself makes "intercession for us with groanings which cannot be uttered" or expressed. He knows what we are trying to say because he knows what's in our hearts.

Since God knows all languages, he also knows the language of all other creatures and things. Birds make different sounds to express themselves to each other and God knows what they are saying. So do dogs and cats and other animals. Does language expression always have to be in words that we understand?

Jesus himself made a comment that tells us that rocks (or stones) can cry out or speak in their own language that God understands (Luke 19:40). Jesus talked to a fig tree and cursed it to die and it did. We can talk to plants and science says it affects their growth.

Let <u>everything that has breath</u> (or breathes), praise the Lord (Psalms 150:6).

We can't see the invisible that breathes to express itself. It may not necessarily have complete words that we understand like with a bird or dog. But we can learn what they are trying to tell us, as we become familiar with their language. God recognizes or hears the vibrations and frequency created by the breath and body of the person or thing speaking out.

The ninth gift is called the <u>interpretation of tongues</u>. Some messages spoken out in an unknown language can be interpreted into a known language.

This gift translates the message either in one's own mind or through another spokesperson. The spokesperson does not need to know the unknown language. The benefit of this gift is so that the hearer(s) can understand it in their natural minds. That is why it is called the interpretation of tongues.

The interpretation (or meaning and translation) of the message can be given by God to the original spokesperson, who spoke in the unknown language, or, God may choose to give the understanding of the message to a different person that is nearby.

If there is no one who has an understanding of the message, it is probably the Holy Spirit interceding and communicating to the Father in secret for the speaker or on behalf of another. When God reveals the translation of a message in the mind of an interpreter, it is up to the interpreter to speak out what the message is.

Talking with God either by saying what is on our minds in our native tongue, or by praying through the prayer language, we can keep his presence active in our lives. They are both important in staying in tune with his Spirit and hearing from him.

God interacts with us through Jesus, his spokesperson. When Jesus was physically alive here on earth ministering to people, he ministered to and through their spirit. His words pierced deep between soul and spirit to create change in that person's life. He still ministers to us and through us, spirit to Spirit.

Most of these nine gifts have been active throughout time except for the gift of tongues and interpretation. Maybe Jesus used this language already to communicate with his Father when he lived here with us as a natural human. I don't know for sure! But it was a new thing he gave to the church. He might have already had it for himself.

All these gifts can manifest together or alone as the Spirit wills, and as his people yield to him. The Holy Spirit brings power to the church to overcome evil with good. We may be many members of his church, but we all drink and receive from the same Spirit (1 Corinthians 12:13).

1 Corinthians 12: 7 says that the manifestation of the Spirit is given to every man to profit all.

Regarding the tongues of fire

In Exodus 3:1-6 of the Old Testament, Moses heard God speak to him from a bush that appeared to be on fire. The bush was not being consumed by the fire. This shows us that God can reveal himself through anything. Was there a similarity between this event and the baptism of the Spirit on the day of Pentecost? Was it similar to the tongues of fire that sat on each of them and did not consume them in the book of Acts? Like with the burning bush, could the tongues of fire be carriers for the language associated with the Spirit of God?

There was a time when the whole earth was of one language and one speech (Genesis 11:1-9). It is a story where all people decided to build a city and a tower whose top would reach into heaven. The Lord came down to see what they were building and said, "The people is with one language...now nothing will be restrained from them, which they have imagined to do."

Their imaginations were becoming united as one, and they were capable of doing anything their hearts desired to do. They could not be fully trusted! It would have been a disastrous outcome because their hearts were not without sinful tendencies. God knew this and confounded their language, so that they could not understand one another's speech. He then scattered them abroad all over the earth.

He had to separate them for the sake of saving them all from becoming as one with sinful intentions. We should all be united together under God, but we are not! We see even today that people can be influenced by a majority. Herd or mob mentality is the likelihood of adapting to beliefs and behaviors of others, either good or bad.

The baptism and evidence of speaking in an unknown language united God's people as one. Paul had said that he himself spoke with the tongues of men and angels (1 Corinthians 3:1). God's presence, his Spirit unites us as one under one language, his! We speak his language to accomplish his will for our lives as a whole people.

So, the flip side of what God said regarding the tower of babel is good. His people are with one language, and now nothing will be restrained from them, which they can imagine to do till Jesus comes again.

Genesis 11:1-9 "The people is with one language...now nothing will be restrained from them, which they have imagined to do."

A lot of good things developed from the baptism of the Holy Spirit. God is continuing his work that he started in his Son, Jesus. His Son is revealed in us, as we exercise his power by the Holy Spirit here on earth. We should be sensitive to his Spirit and his gifts. God wants to express himself and his love to and through us to save his world.

HIS POWER LIVES ON

---◆---

LESSON 43

Jesus had said that the gifts of his Spirit would operate through those who believe in his name. He wants to work through us to continue his mission. While he was physically here on earth in our realm, he gave healing and deliverance to all who believed in him. The ministry of Jesus exploded and began to spread throughout the world.

In the previous story of the woman who was diseased with a blood issue for twelve years, she had already made up her mind that she would be healed if she could get to him (Matthew 9:20-21). He was on his way to heal someone else when she found him. When she got close enough, she took her step of faith and reached out to touch his garment. She was activating faith.

Matthew 9:21 (KJV) tells us that she said within herself, "If I may but touch his garment, I shall be whole."

Jesus felt his healing power flow out from himself. He turned around to see who it was who touched him and told her that her faith in him has made her whole. She was healed that very hour.

At first, he didn't know who it was who had touched him. She got her healing without him even acknowledging her presence until after she touched his garment. She had her attention focused or fixated on an action of faith and believed in him for her healing. I know this may sound controversial, but it was like if she hypnotized herself. Nothing else would be acceptable to her, except for her healing when she touched his garment. Touching his garment was her trigger for healing and she acted on it, and then she got it.

Then later on in Matthew 14:35-36, the bible says that many more were brought to Jesus for healing. It says that <u>all</u> those who <u>touched the hem of his garment were made perfectly whole</u>.

Jesus was appointed and anointed to redeem us from all evil. **In Luke 4:18 he said, "The Spirit of the Lord is upon me, because he hath anointed me to preach the gospel to the poor, he hath sent me to heal the brokenhearted, to preach deliverance to the captives, and recovering of sight to the blind, to set at liberty them that are bruised."**

Acts 19:11-12 says that after Jesus had ascended into heaven, God wrought special miracles by the hands of Paul. After Paul would get done ministering at his meetings, his handkerchiefs and aprons would be taken to others that were not able to be there. The freshly anointed items were meant for others in need of healing and deliverance. They could be used as a point of contact to activate or spark the power for healing. It was just like what happened with Jesus and his garment. Paul did not have to personally be there to lay hands on the sick and tormented.

They believed they would be healed when they touched Paul's clothing, just as the women with the issue of blood was healed when she touched the hem of Jesus garment. They believed and had a point of contact for their faith, and they were healed.

Jesus had said in **John 14:12 (KJV), "He that believeth on me, greater works than these shall he do; because I go unto my Father."**

Mark 16:17-18 gives details of some of the things that Jesus commissioned his followers to do.

Mark 16:17 (KJV), "And these signs shall follow them that believe; <u>In my name,</u> shall they <u>cast out devils</u>; they shall <u>speak with new tongues</u>; they shall take up serpents; and if they drink any deadly thing, it shall not hurt them; they shall lay <u>hands on the sick</u>, and they shall recover."

Then in **Luke 10:19** Jesus had said**, "I give you <u>power</u> to <u>tread</u> on serpents and scorpions, and <u>over all the power of the enemy: and nothing shall by any means hurt you."</u>**

Jesus said, "I give you power." He gives us power to run the devil out of our lives and the lives of others.

Genesis 3:15 is where God had told Satan what would happen in the future because of what he had done. God said that the seed that would come out of Eve (which was Jesus) would bruise his head. Now Jesus tells us to do the same and crush the works of Satan.

God works through us, by his Spirit, who is alive and active in our realm. There are so many things that show his power working in the world even today. People still get healed and delivered and have miracles happen in their lives. It is all due to the Father, the Son and the Holy Spirit. God is now with us! He DWELLS with and in us, not just in a general term, but can be deep within our being. He is with us in Spirit, and is our connection to the realm of heaven. God wants us to be his representative to the world!

DOWNLOADING HIS SOFTWARE

— ❖ —

LESSON 44

We struggle to believe the things regarding a God that we can't see. It has not been part of our nature. But through him we can have healing and miracles because they have already been provided for. We can study his word about healing and pray until we get to a point that we just know that we know. We can know that we are healed or free from some kind of spiritual bondage, even though we don't physically feel better yet or see that we are.

We can just have an intuition (or revelation) about it without trying to consciously reason it out. We believe because his word says so. This is faith in action! It may not seem logical to us. Things just don't normally or instantly heal by themselves in this physical world that we see, hear, touch, and feel. But we do know that our bodies can heal on their own by experience. We can get to the point that we believe in our hearts that we are healed, and the rest can follow, even if we don't understand how. Our conscience will accept the things from God as good for us, even if we don't understand spiritual concepts. The thought or image of healing becomes alive and real, because he is alive and real within us.

Unbelief, uncertainty, and doubt are ugly words that can discredit and dishonor God's words for healing. The battle comes in play, when the enemy of unbelief tries to sway our thinking into not believing for the good things that God wants to do. That is when we have to fight back even harder with the words of God to get our miracle or breakthrough.

The subconscious mind is in between the conscious and unconscious area of the mind. The unconscious part of the mind is inaccessible to the conscious part of the mind, but still affects our thoughts, feelings and actions. Thoughts do exist without us consciously realizing it, so we have got to put the right information in our heads. If we give our heart to Jesus, we will read and see in his word that he healed everyone who asked him. Knowing this information helps our faith to grow.

If you ask Jesus to come into your heart and save you, does that mean you have to first feel that he saved you before he actually does? It took me a while before I actually felt that I was saved. I just had to trust him in the beginning. The feeling came later. Your own confession to accept him is enough if you mean it.

Jesus said when we turn our lives over to him, we become born again. When we are born again, we are entering a whole new reality of existence. In techy terms, he has updated and finished his new spiritual software that will not fail us. He wants us to download it into our spirits. We become part of his kingdom realm and can learn about all the new things associated with it. God gives us purpose and our final destination is already determined. It is a good one! There is no evil, poverty, sickness, sadness, or loneliness where he is. We can access his benefits from where we are right now, because the power of his Spirit is connected through his Word with a different kind of WIFI (Wireless Internal Faith Included).

147

JESUS, ARE YOU MY LORD AND MY GOD?

———— ❧ ————

LESSON 45

There are numerous scriptures that refer to Jesus as God. There is the Father, the Son and the Holy Ghost. Luke 11:13 refers to the Holy Ghost as the Holy Spirit. The three, Father, Son and Holy Spirit are one as God. They make up the whole presence called God.

The original King James version implies that Jesus is God. **John 1:1-18 explains their existence. John 1:1-3 (KJV) tells us that "In the beginning was the Word, and the Word was with God, and the Word was God. The same was in the beginning with God. All things were made by him; and without him was not anything made that was made."**

John 1:14 (KJV), "And the Word was made flesh, and dwelt among us." (God made himself known through the body of Jesus.)

John 1:18 (NIV), "No man has ever seen God, but the one and only Son, who is himself God, is in the closest relationship with the Father."

1 Peter 1:18-19 tells us that we were not redeemed with perishable things like silver and gold. God himself stepped down to redeem us by creating his own life-giving bloodline. Thomas recognized Jesus as his God in **John 20:27-28 when he said, "My Lord and my God!"**

These scriptures tell us that Jesus was foreordained before the foundation of the world (1 Peter 1:18-20). He was revealed for our sake and for our benefit. He was born into our realm to save us. We are redeemed by the precious blood of Jesus Christ, who is the incorruptible seed of man and God that lives forever.

Before God created us to be like him, he had already dealt with a fallen nature through other eternal beings that existed before our time. There have sadly been those who have rejected him. He has secured our destiny from the beginning. He gives us free will to choose him and live or choose to be without him if we want.

We have opportunity to choose life or death now before our eternal destination. We are already envisioned as eternal beings when we are conceived. He has great plans for us. We are in temporary housing conditions (through our bodies) that are not eternal yet. Eternal means to last or exist forever. Most things on this earth will change, our bodies will age, certain things will rust or decay. Most things do not last forever.

God reveals himself to us through the historical stories and by helping us when we need it. He gives us opportunities throughout life to make the all-important decision from our own free will, to accept him or reject him. Now is the time to learn of him. He wants us to choose him on our own free will. Sin destroys lives! He wants us to realize it before we get to a permanent eternal state of being and residency.

I have read a few stories of people who have temporarily left their bodies through the dying process and then were revived back to life. Some of the testimonies of people who had died and visited the spirit world can be seen on "You tube". The stories were somewhat different from each other depending on the circumstance.

Some of the stories where inspiring stories of people who had left their bodies and had a chance to see heaven, loved ones and Jesus himself. There are also stories of people who did not believe in God until they had a near death experience. They had a bad experience that ended in a good one. The experience always made a believer out of the person who almost left our realm of existence but was given another chance.

There was one particular story of a man who while in his childhood heard about Jesus, but did not believe or accept him when he became an adult. He got very sick and at death's door. When he left his body, he says he was being led into another realm by others. He then says that they started harassing him and trying to force him to go with them somewhere else. All of a sudden, there arose something on the inside of himself, giving him hope. In his desperation, he tried to access any memories that he had that could help. He remembered learning about Jesus as a child. Long story short, He called out to Jesus and Jesus saved him. He was restored back into his body and now witnesses to others about his experience. According to a lot of the stories, there are apparently different levels and stages of the afterworld experience. This man was able to reach out to Jesus, just in the nick of time, while entering the spirit realm and in his dying stage. He was given another chance at life because he had heard about Jesus as a child.

A person may go on into eternity and make residency with Jesus if they choose before it is too late. I believe some have chosen Christ as they were leaving their bodies. In the back of their minds, they knew that he was a savior, and they stopped rejecting him. Joel 2:32 and **Acts 2:21 tells us that "whosoever calls on the name of the Lord shall be saved".** Always remember to tell others about Jesus so they can choose before they cross the line of no return.

Some have been given another chance in life. But isn't it better to be safe than sorry? We don't know when our own time will come for us to meet our maker. This man made it because he reached out to Jesus. It didn't matter what he had done in his life. What mattered was that he reached out to Jesus and Jesus became his savior.

ENTERING HIS COURTS

———◆———

LESSON 46

The word of God takes precedence over everything no matter what it is. Nothing ever existed until he spoke things into existence. His word is the final authority that is documented by the highest court in the heavens. God has established his name here on earth through his Son and his authority supersedes all others that govern our lives.

Man does not live by bread alone, but by every word that proceeds out of the mouth of God (Deuteronomy 8:3 and Matthew 4:4).

We live or die by his own words, and all of heaven stands behind his authority. God sent his own Son to let us know who he is. Jesus is the spokesperson and mediator between us and God. He is our advocate of faith to plead our case if we sin according to 1 John 2:1. His blood that was shed on the cross paid the price for our sin, so we could come boldly before the throne room and highest court without judgement. We have to stand in complete innocence! And the only way is to come through Jesus Christ who is sitting on the right hand of God (Psalms 111:1).

I want to explore more about the story of God, the faithfulness of Job and Satan the accuser. There was a time when Satan had presented himself before God among some of the other "sons of God" (Job 1:6-12 in KJV). When God asked him where he had been, he said that he had been roaming back and forth on the earth. Then God asked him what he thought about the man Job.

(Keep in mind that Satan is a very judgmental and angry being, who is set on persecuting and prosecuting us. He hates us and he attacks us to hurt God.)

When God asked Satan what he thought, Satan gave God a piece of his mind about the whole situation. In my own words to paraphrase what was said, Satan told God "Well, of course he is faithful! It is only because you put a hedge around him and blessed all he has. That is the only reason he is faithful to you! If you take it all away, he will turn on you! He will curse you to your face! Take away his blessing and see if he rejects you! He will stop serving you!" Satan was on a mission to take Job down.

Satan was basically putting Job on trial before God for something he hadn't even done. Job never committed a crime, and he never turned his back on God. God lifted the hedge of blessing and protection from Job's life at Satan's request, maybe to prove Job would stay faithful, or maybe to invalidate Satan's accusation, or both. Without God's protection, Satan was able to do horrific things to Job. He lost his wealth, his children and then his health. Job had no one to plead his case before God. He was now on trial by himself. He had to prove his faithfulness to God, all because of the accusations of an enemy that he himself couldn't even see. He had no idea that he was being put on trial. Satan's plan was to get God to impose judgement and curse Job for no reason.

God is a righteous judge. He watched Job carefully and I believe he knew his heart. In this case, the story ends where Job proved himself faithful. If anything, this made Satan look ridiculous before God.

His own thoughts were exposed. He revealed his own feelings and broken relationship with God. He didn't want to serve God, and he was trying to prove that humans won't either. Who was really on trial here, and who won their case?

As we can see through the story of Job, mankind needed a protector, defender, and redeemer. This story of Job happened a very long time before the event of where God made a promise to Abraham. God promised a savior through Abraham's bloodline. We basically needed a lawyer to plead our case because of the accuser.

Sometimes, I wonder if Satan says to God, "You bless mankind, and he doesn't have to do anything in return to get his blessing. These people do bad things all the time and you still love and bless them. That is not fair! Why am I doomed, but they still get to live out their own lives?" So, was Satan so jealous that he was calling mankind God's spoiled brats?

If there is anything that the devil can use against us, he will. He has never changed for the good! He pays attention to our weaknesses. In order to stand against him before God, we need to be pardoned and have a cleared conscience.

Satan is not allowed to bring accusations for those of us that are in Christ anymore. Jesus our advocate pleaded our case a long time ago and won! We are free of any fault that says we are guilty. We can honestly confess all we know in our hearts that could be wrong and still win our case.

What is the evidence that the enemy would have to use against you? He is not your righteous judge. Even though he points his finger of accusation, your own repentance covers you. If you confess your faults before God, the bible tells us that God is faithful and just to forgive and cleanse you from all unrighteousness (1John 1:9). Forgiveness and **pardon** come by repentance. God promises to forgive if you ask. God gives you pardon based on the blood covenant between you and him.

According to Romans 2:16, God will judge the secrets of men by Jesus Christ. In John 5:22-23, Jesus had said that the Father judges no man, but commits all judgement to the Son, and that all men should honor the Son, even as they honor the Father. Isaiah 3:13 and 33:22 says that the Lord is our judge.

Hebrews 4:14 says he (Jesus) is still our great high priest, and for us to hold on to our profession of faith in him. He finished his 1st assignment here on earth and has been promoted into the highest court. He is literally in a position to help us stand before the Father. He tells us that he will acknowledge our name before his Father and before his angels. John 5:24, 26-27 says he that believes, has everlasting life, and shall not come under condemnation. Jesus said himself that he came to give us life abundantly (John 10:10).

Does God have a place in the chapters of your life? Romans 8:31 says "**If God be for us, who can be against us.**" Revelation 3:5 says that whoever overcomes shall be clothed in white raiment and their name will not be blotted out of the book of life. Is your name written in the lamb's book of life?

In a court of law, there is a defendant and a plaintiff. The defendant is the one on trial being accused of committing a crime, and they are being sued. The plaintiff is the one who brings a case against the defendant. They go to war using the written laws against each other. You could be on either side of this argument in a court of law.

How do you stop yourself from being a victim in God's court? Tell God the truth. The enemy could be tempting you, harassing you, or tormenting you, and you want freedom from it. Put the enemy on trial for making you a victim.

2 Corinthians 10:4-6 (KJV), "For though we walk in the flesh, we do not war after the flesh. For the <u>weapons of our warfare</u> are not carnal, but mighty through God to the <u>pulling down of strong holds; Casting down imaginations and every high thing that exalts itself against the knowledge of God and bringing into captivity every thought to the obedience of Christ</u>."

How does this happen, and how can we legally fight an enemy we can't see? How do we protect our thoughts and imaginations? First of all, we renew our minds by learning God's written word of love, mercy and grace. It is the founding principles acknowledged in God's Supreme Court. Then we plead our case in the name of Jesus. This is our legal weapon of defense. The word of God comes in to play to enforce and release the powers of heaven. It is the law of love, mercy and grace that will defend our case to set us free and stop the enemy in his tracks. We can say, "I am in right standing with God, the Father, the Son and the Holy Spirit! The price is paid in full! I have been redeemed by the blood of the lamb, Jesus Christ!"

The law of Moses was written to expose sin caused under the rule of the first Adam. But the law also reveals what the blessing is. It shows what life could be for each individual depending on what they do with thoughts of good and evil.

Do you act from an evil conscience as Satan did with Job? Do you love or hate? When you are wronged by another, do you choose to retaliate with hate or turn the other cheek? We all have faced these situations and have failed at some time or another.

Just because someone or something tells you what to do, it doesn't make it the right thing to do. We have to learn to discern good from evil. We need to learn how to pull down strong holds, cast down evil imaginations and any thoughts that exalts themselves against the knowledge of God according to 2 Corinthians 10:4-6. We can take foreign and evil thoughts as prisoners of war and force them to give up their mission against us. They must surrender under the rule of Christ. We **must come to realize are rights** and to implement them in the name of Jesus. We can go to battle and change our mindset to choose life, even after we have made a wrong decision and messed up. We have the option to change things.

In Luke 4:6 and in the wilderness temptation, Satan had showed Jesus all the kingdoms of the world and offered him kingship. He then said that it all belonged to himself, and that he had the right to give it to whomever he wanted. Was Satan lying to Jesus to get Jesus to accept and obey him, as if he was ultimately in charge?

Satan also tempted Jesus to defy the law of gravity to prove himself. Later, throughout all the gospel stories, we see that Jesus walked on water, turned water into wine, and did other miracles. I believe he could have defied the law of gravity at the time Satan had been tempting him, but he would not do it at the devil's request. Jesus stayed within the directions of his own Father.

Satan would have deceptively gained power over Jesus if Jesus would have listened to him. But Jesus knew Satan was a liar, and told him who he believed was in charge, God. Satan only gains his power over someone if he can deceive them into believing his lies. He already tried it with God himself, when he came against Job.

When Adam and Eve had submitted to the words of the serpent, they had let Satan have an open door to work on trying to take over their domain. Satan deceptively took a position of authority over the things that God had given to Adam. Adam didn't know any better. I was wondering, when was the authority given to Satan by God? It wasn't! It is only given as man gives it to him. Satan gets it by deception, and he could not deceive Jesus.

So, why hasn't God already rid us of Satan? If God would have taken him down already, he would have had to take us down with him too, because of sin. There will be a day when the wheat will be separated from the tares. The bad from the good. It is the day when God's harvest of people will be ready to reap and the tares will be destroyed (Matthew 13:24-30, 37-43).

In Matthew 28:18, after the earthly man Jesus died and rose from the dead, he was seen by his disciples. He said to them, "All power is given unto me in heaven and in earth". He has been promoted into a higher position and gives his available and obtainable position of power to us here on earth (Matthew 18:18-20).

Jesus wants us to know that Satan is a liar and has no authority over us as long as we don't give him power. Satan tries to get people to be in agreement with him, and to disregard what Jesus did on the cross for us. Jesus represented the law under mercy and grace for he paid the price himself, and that puts Satan in contempt of court (or in violation of court order). The court is made up of God the Father, Jesus his Son, and high-ranking angels. They are all ruling in our favor. Satan can't deceive the courts because they already know all the evil that he has done. He really has no case for those who know their position in Christ. If you realize you can't break free from the enemy, then take him to the highest court and tell the Judge about it. Tell God that this is not of your free will and that you don't want to want it.

We ourselves should always approach the throne in prayer with boldness, but also with respect of his court, even if we are in desperate need. All those in the courtroom are pulling for us and we are loved from above.

Psalms 100:4-5 (KJV), "Enter into his gates with thanksgiving, and into his courts with praise: be thankful unto him and bless his name. <u>For the Lord is good; his mercy is everlasting</u>; and his truth endures to all generations."

LIVING BY GOD'S NEW LAW, THE COVENANT OF FAITH

❖

LESSON 47

Genesis 3:15 (NIV) God said, And I will put enmity between you (Satan) and the woman, and between your offspring and hers; he will crush your head, and you will strike his heel.

I have come to realize that everything God said to Adam and Eve, when they took of the forbidden tree, was to help all of mankind. I used to thing that he was so angry with them that he was condemning them to die. As I questioned all the things that he said to them, I realized that he was telling them what their action caused for themselves and what he was going to do to fix it. He set in motion a prophecy that would create the faith substance to save humanity over time.

Adam and Eve were both banned from the garden of Eden for their own sake. God banned them for the time being, so that they could not be tempted to eat also of the tree of life and live forever in their current fallen condition. It is interesting that the tree of life is mentioned in the first book of the bible and in the last book of the bible. **Revelation 2:7 says that whoever overcomes will be able to eat from the tree of life which is in the midst of the paradise of God.** Revelation 22:2 and 22:14 also confirms the same thing. There is a final stage to God's plan regarding the tree of life. According to what God said in Genesis about the tree, it can give life to live forever.

God set into motion a plan that would redeem his creation from extinction. He does not will for us to die. His plans are to make his creation indestructible. When God said he would put enmity between Satan's seed and Eve's, he was talking about her future seed Jesus. Jesus would be the redeemer, who would lead a revolutionary revival of restoration called the church to come against Satan. It will eventually affect the whole world in one way or another. Jesus would bruise (crush) Satan's head, meaning Jesus would stop Satan's plans of dictatorship over the whole world. Jesus, who was made from the God seed and human seed will not only restore the broken relationship between the Father and his people, but make it permanent.

God purposely put division or a spiritual partition of enmity between us (his church body) and Satan. Romans 16:20 says "The God of peace shall bruise Satan under your feet shortly." In fact, metaphorically speaking, we are to put pressure on Satan as we come against him, and this is what pushes him under our feet. We are to crush his leadership of principalities and powers of the darkness, through the leadership of Jesus Christ.

Satan and his band of evil beings have been trying to raise up human followers through deception. He thinks he can convince people to disrupt Gods' plan by making it unappealing. He thinks he can get his own empire and eventually rule the world his way. He wants to play God!

We can defend ourselves against evil and get restitution because we can claim that we have been redeemed through Jesus. There are more benefits in learning about the divine laws, then just having to go before the courts of Heaven to plead our case.

The commandments in the Old Testament books give detailed information about each of its laws regarding good and bad. The bible tells what the law pertains to, the punishment for breaking it, and what restitution there is if any, that can be made to make things right again. The laws of Moses are referred to as the laws of sin and death (Romans 8:2).

These laws also show a positive side of doing good things. It shows the rewards for being obedient (Deuteronomy 7:14, 12:7, 28:3-6). If it had not been for Jesus coming along and paying with his life for our sin, we would be doomed. We don't have to live by the law of sin and death, even though it shows us what sin is. Just like with our own children, we have to be taught what is right and what is wrong for our own good.

We have all heard about some of the laws that govern our universe. The law of gravity, the law of relativity, the law of attraction, and the cause-and-effect rule. There are so many variables to the laws that govern our world to cause things to happen in a particular way. Some things happen because of an action that we take. Jesus taught lessons using parables and real-life experiences to explain laws that govern everything. He used stories to help explain the positive side of the laws of God and how to use them for our benefit.

Jesus taught us to do unto others as we would have them to do unto us. Every action does cause a reaction of some kind. The law of attraction for example, shows that positive or negative thoughts bring more positive or negative thoughts. Even words that we speak cause responses. Like attracts like! We can attract what we believe and speak. We can cause a situation to become worse if we respond in a negative way. I know because I have been there and done that.

Jesus showed us how to get the principles of the new covenant law to work in our favor. He gave so many examples through telling stories. Just read his stories and see how they relate to a principle that can work for you in your own life. The bible is the book of instructions and Jesus shows us that good overcomes evil, as it did in his own life.

Our words and actions affect our own brain waves, so don't focus your attention on a thought of trying not to do the wrong thing. Focus on the right thing! Over stimulation of the wrong thought in certain brain activity can lead to depression, agitation, insomnia, anxiety, and metabolic and impulse disorders. An unproductive thought can bleed over to the rest of our thinking.

Overstimulation of the body and brain regarding hurtful addictions, worry, and burn out can also cause everything to be out of balance. It can even be expressed in pain. It affects the mind, body and spirit, and it can make it harder for our whole being to function all together properly.

To purposely think happy thoughts is a real thing. In stressful situations, it helps to focus on things to be thankful for, and on thoughts of the things in life that make us happy. I understand that it produces or releases a hormone chemical that can impact emotional, cognitive, and social behaviors in a good way. It can create a feeling of relaxation and stability in highly emotional situations. Philippians 4:8 tells us to think on things that are: honest, just, pure, lovely, and of good report. If there be any virtue (advantage or benefit) and any praise (approval) in the thought, think on these things.

Everything can have a good side to its existence. Jesus said give and it shall be given to you. If you concentrate on what you can give or do for others and for the cause of God, you are in a positive energy stream of God's laws. God sees what is done in secret, bad and good and rewards openly for the good (Matthew 6:4). Everything belongs to God. Jesus tells us to be good stewards with what we already have, and to be good to others, and most of all, to God himself. Make it a lifestyle choice. Jesus said it will bring you into a more positive, fulfilling, and joyful life.

The Word of God reveals life changing secrets. Jesus taught universal laws of physics by illustrations and by giving his advice. And, obeying them will cause good things to come back to you.

Jesus had said, "Father forgive them for they know not what they do," as he hung on the cross to die. He activated a law in his own life and ours. He forgave us, so we should do the same to others. Forgiveness is the secret to defeating the devil from coming against you through others.

It all works together. So, take what is wrong and make it right. Jesus said to forgive others their trespasses, as you ask God for forgiveness for yourself, so that your prayers would not be hindered according to the Lord's prayer (Matthew 6:9-15). You don't have to feel like you want to forgive others, you just do it by faith. Offenses block God's laws of blessing. Get rid of offenses by talking to God about it.

We should be mindful of what we say. The hardest thing I have tried to control is things that come out of my mouth. Satan wants us to use our mouths to activate negative forces into our lives and the lives of others. Proverbs 18:21 tells us that death and life are in the power of the tongue.

In the book of James, chapter three, it says that the tongue may be a little member of our body, but it is one of the hardest to tame. James says that if a man can control his words, he is able to bridle the whole body (James 3:2-4). He used an example of a horse's bit that is placed in its mouth to help control its direction. He also gave an example of using a large ship. He said the helmsman can control the course of the very large ship with a very small piece of equipment called a helm. What we speak does affect our future, as well as the future of others. It sets things into motion, keeps a good or bad situation going, or it can set free.

In the beginning, God did not curse Adam and Eve. He did level with them about the truth. The spiritual law was already in place regarding the tree. They put the wrong thing in their mouths and now we have to work on the things that come out of our mouths. Satan figured out a way to flip the law and use it against them. He tricked them by telling them a lie and they believed his lie. They put themselves on the opposite side of the law.

Every word God spoke to Adam and Eve after their fall was creating faith substance for the future.

Hebrews 11:1 says that faith is the substance of things hoped for and the evidence of things not seen.

This faith substance (or seed) was God's Son Jesus. He was spoken of or prophesied into our existence.

Every word that Jesus spoke to his followers was God's faith substance being released. They let us see who the real enemy is and how to STOP listening to him. God wants humanity to believe in him, not a lie. He made a way of escaping the wrong side of the law by activating his new covenant of faith. We can step out of the line of fire and into the peace of God. All it takes is faith in God's Son.

TRUE KNOWLEDGE

---◆---

LESSON 48

In the beginning, Adam and Eve was part of God's extended family and had it all with little effort. There was safety, peace and provision until Satan took the truth and twisted it into a lie.

God wants us to all grasp his truth. We can become perfected or infected by what we allow into our minds. We would choose good if we knew the real truth about the bad and the good.

Hosea 4:6 The Lord God said, "My people are destroyed for the lack of Knowledge."

God's desire is to redeem us from the clutches of the originator of deception. It is our right to make our own decisions regarding our own lives because God has given us a free will! If we could look into the future of our decisions and see the two different outcomes for ourselves, we would know what to do about it. God's book of knowledge regarding our lives has a beginning and an end, and it is a happily ever after ending for some, but not for others. God's word gives us warning about the ultimate outcome of consciously or willfully exercising and/or accepting bad behavior as a good thing. We can look into our future by what we read in his word. It has two opposing outcomes. The end of the book tells us that God restores mankind's rightful place and rids them of all evil influence.

In Genesis 1:28 the bible says that God pronounced blessing on mankind. He told them to multiply, replenish and subdue the earth, and to have dominion over every living thing. He expects us to take care of his creation, so we can live in it.

The laws of the universe are taking part in God's finished works. He works within his own principles. If not, he would be a liar, and everything would fall apart. The law of attraction says that positive or negative thoughts bring positive or negative experiences. This is so important! Jesus taught laws through his stories and by giving his advice. He taught how to make God's laws work for us. If we read from some of the scientific research that has been done on how everything works, we could see that Jesus taught some of these same principles himself. Science has given them labels to identify each one and how they work in our universe. We attract God's divine favor to release his kingdom benefits in this world when we take action, because action causes reaction.

Jesus said, "Seek first the kingdom of God, and his righteousness; and all these things shall be added unto you," in Matthew 6:33.

God owns it all and all good things come from him! Adam was not placed in the garden of Eden until after he was formed from the dust of the ground. Then God placed him in the garden to dress and keep it according to Genesis 2:15.

Any authority had to be established and given to Adam by a higher power, since Adam did not own the garden. Thank God he didn't! He would have lost it to Satan too! God gave Adam some of his authority, but he had to place some boundaries so that Adam and Eve could not overstep his own authority.

The tree of good and evil was a connection to the powers outside the realm that Adam and Eve knew anything about. True knowledge belongs to God, and only he (the creator and owner) could decide what happens with its balance of good and evil, so that life itself does not collapse.

Adam and Eve were given rule and authority over some things on earth except the one tree. They could enjoy their life and have fun with all the things that God gave them to enjoy. But the rights that God gave them charge over was limited. They did not have all authority or all ownership as God did. The tree was the indication of God's ultimate ownership and high-ranking authority in and of the garden.

When they took from the tree, God had now been illegally violated of his own free will and authority, by their free will. When they went too far by taking from the tree of good and evil, Satan had gained legal ground to use against them. They had rejected God's own will regarding the tree.

In a brief moment Adam and Eve had given authority over to Satan by following his instructions and will. It wasn't the serpent's right to say what was to happen to the tree. The authority had never been given to him either. He just took it through tempting Adam and Eve.

As Adam and Eve took from the tree, their thoughts were focused on the words that the serpent (or the devil) had fed them. This was just like with the hypnotizer on the game show that I mentioned earlier. They consciously accepted and allowed him to take control. Adam and Eve consciously accepted and allowed the devil to take control.

Adam and Eve trusted Satan over what God had said and acted upon his suggestion. At the moment that they ate from the tree, the devil became in charge of their thoughts. He had led them to believe it was okay and would make them to be like gods, knowing good and evil. Satan had an evil agenda in mind, and he led Adam and Eve astray to cause trouble between them and God himself.

Isaiah 14:12-15 tells us what Satan's own endgame is and what God's endgame is for him. He had said in his own heart that he would ascend into heaven and exalt his throne above the stars of God. He also said, "I will ascend above the heights of the clouds; I will be like the most-high", but verse fifteen says that he will be brought down to hell, to the sides of the pit.

God had created Adam and Eve with a free will regarding most things. Adam and Eve encountered and perceived thoughts that could give them negative reactions, feelings and outcomes. There full joy had turned into feelings of fear, insecurity and uncertainty of what was to happen next. Things had changed! They chose to be their own god!

They were banned from the garden to make sure they would not make the mistake of eating from the tree of life and be stuck with their decision forever. Now they had to learn how to make life comfortable for themselves.

It is all too dangerous to put the knowledge of whatever the tree has, into the hands of those who know nothing about it, Or, to put it in the hands of those with an evil purpose. I would rather the decision stay in the hands of God. He knows his own laws and how they work for the good of all his creation. God gives boundaries for our own protection. He had given things to Adam and Eve in the beginning because he wanted them to be happy. He takes pleasure in blessing his people! God wants us to realize we are better off letting him be in charge.

Psalms 35:27 (NKJ), "Let them shout for joy, and be glad, that favor my righteous cause: yea, let them say continually, let the Lord be magnified, which hath pleasure in the prosperity of his servants."

THE REAL WORLD IS THE SPIRIT WORLD! It is a good thing that our state of being right now is temporary and subject to change until our final destination, when we will fully get God's full blessings for our lives, forever.

LIVING SACRIFICE

————◆————

LESSON 49

Since our bodies are made from some of the same substances as the earth, we can use the resources of the earth to improve our lives. Over time, we have learned how to mix elements together from the earth's substances to make things that enrich us for the better. I am thankful for comfortable things to sleep and sit on, technology to keep in touch with my family, heat, air and electricity. I am thankful to God that he has blessed others with inventive minds to create new things. God gives things of the earth to his children to bless them, but he also expects them to use some of these things for his purpose as well.

There are some things made out of this earth that are used for evil or greedy intent that can hurt us. It all depends on its purpose. What about illegal drugs or weapons? Is drugs a good or bad thing? Can they help us or hurt us? Do you see guns as a means of protection or to steal, kill and destroy a life? What do you want from their power? There is so much division over these issues because good and evil intents are both present with us. There are people who unjustly take from others to make themselves rich.

The earth and everything on it, is meant to give us tangible things to feed and heal our bodies, make life comfortable, and if used wisely can make one rich. **Deuteronomy 8:18 tells us to remember the Lord God, for he gives us power to get wealth, so that he can establish his covenant.** This is another good reason why God wants to bless us in abundance.

God had made the man Abraham a wealthy man. He was generous as well as thrifty with what he had. Everything that he had was because God blessed his life abundantly. Abraham did not technically own everything he had. He knew his wealth came from God. He obeyed God with all the substance that he was entrusted with.

Let's look at the bond between God and Abraham more closely even though we have the details about their relationship in a previous lesson. Genesis 12:1-3 and 17:1-20 give us details regarding their covenant. Abraham was known as the friend of God. He was very thankful and made sure that God knew his presence would always be greatly welcomed in his life no matter what. Whenever Abraham had stopped to rest in his travels, he would take the time to set up altars of worship and pray. He had a wonderful relationship with God and trusted God with everything including his own son, Isaac.

I had said in the earlier lesson that when Isaac had grown into a young boy, God asked Abraham to go up to a mountain in the land of Moriah and offer his son as a burnt offering (or sacrifice on an altar). It took Abraham three days just to get to a place where he could see the place in the far-off distance. He'd had lots of time to think about what he was going there to do. Before he traveled any farther on to his destination, he told the others that had been traveling with him to wait behind, while he and his son continued on to the place that God had told them to go. Abraham said to them, "I and the lad will go

159

yonder and worship and come again to you" (Genesis 22:7). It sounds like Abraham was telling them that he <u>and his son</u> would be back to join them later.

When Abraham and his son got to where God had told them, he prepared everything including his own son for the sacrifice. He was going to follow through at God's command, if he had too. It took the greatest faith he ever had to have, in order to trust God with his son's life! Hebrews 11:19 says that Abraham believed that God was able to raise his son up from the dead. I believe he was planning on going through with the sacrifice of his own son if he had to, because he trusted God to bring his son back to life.

He knew the importance of God's plan and that he had to be faithful in order for it to come to pass. He knew God had given him his son, Isaac and that this must be part of the reason why. Abraham agreed to obey God even though he did not fully understand what God was going to do to bless the nations (Genesis 22:1-18).

Through Abraham offering his own son at God's request, God saw Abraham's willingness to trust him with the very best thing that he had ever given him, Isacc. Abraham proved he was prepared to let God be in control. When God and Abraham first made the covenant with each other, Abraham may have agreed in word, but this was the physical proof of his loyalty and acceptance of the agreement.

Through this event, **God had Abraham's permission and cooperation to accept a sacrificial offering of a future son of one of Isaac's descendants, instead of Isaac.** What if God could not have raised Abraham's son up from the dead, after Abraham put him to death? Did this thought ever go through Abraham's mind? I doubt it! He had such a close relationship with God that he just knew that he knew that God would not let him down! Abraham believed God and it was counted to him as righteousness (Genesis 15:6 and Romans 4:3). This is what God wants from us. He wants us to believe and trust in him. God proved himself faithful when he raised Abraham's future son Jesus, a descendant of Isaac from the dead!

Abraham did not have to actually give his son; God supplied an animal substitute instead. Eventually it would be God's own Son who would become the substitute sacrifice for all. The plan was a joint effort. Jesus came from both the lineage of Abraham and from God himself. Jesus is the fulfillment of their covenant through both sides!

There are some similarities and differences between the events of Abraham and the events of Job. Abraham had made the decision to give up his son in that moment of testing, but he did not have to. The fate of his son was in his own hands. But in the story of Job, Job had no choice about his own children and lost them all. Satan had caused Job to lose his children rather he was willing to give them up or not. The good news is that Job is with all his children now in the afterlife because of what a future descendant of Abraham did. Both Abraham and Job are with Jesus who saved them and their family.

In the story of Job, the devil wanted God to take away the hedge of protection, so that he could get to Job and destroy his life. He put Job on trial before God, and Job couldn't even be present to defend himself. He didn't even know that he was on trial. Satan told God that Job was only serving him because he had been given a blessed life. Satan wanted to prove to God that if all the blessings were taken away, Job would curse him to his face. Of course, Satan was proved wrong. Job stayed faithful to God even in all his misery of losing everything.

The two stories about Abraham and Job are similar in the fact that both men stayed faithful and trusted God with their life situation. The stories are different in the fact that the devil was behind the accusations about Job, and Job never had a choice regarding his own family members, while God was the one behind what happened with Abraham. Abraham had a choice regarding his family. Satan would have loved it, if Abraham would have said "no way" to God, when God told him to offer up his son. Maybe with the story of Abraham, God had actual evidence to prove Abraham's faithfulness, just in case Satan were to object like he did with Job. Either way both men stayed faithful in their circumstances.

I believe that God was revealing his future plan to Abraham through an illustration. God wanted Abraham to know what it felt like to willingly give up one's son to die. Isaac was Abraham's closest son! God was expressing or relating to Abraham his own feelings of giving his own son to die in the future. Of course, I am sure that neither one of them wanted to make the sacrifice to carry the plan out, even though it was necessary. Through this experience, Abraham was able to feel the pain, sorrow and agony that would come from the death of his own son, (without actually losing his son). He was relating to the Father!

God (the Father) was showing Abraham what he himself was willing to go through. Abraham was able to feel God's heartbreak himself. Not only was Abraham able to experience the grief through a fathers' broken heart, but to experience the agony that his own son would have also had to endure. The Father and his Son both had to suffer for the rest of the world. God sometimes reveals his feelings to us by using illustrations.

Isaiah 53:4 (KJV) reads "Surely, he hath borne our griefs, and carried our sorrows, yet we did esteem him stricken, smitten of God, and afflicted."

Our acceptance of the sacrifice that God and his Son endured gives God permission to complete his promise in us. The Father appointed his Son to be the one to crossover death's door into the spirit world, so that his Son could be the man who would lead us to himself.

In Matthew 16:25, Jesus had said, "…whoever shall lose his life for my sake shall preserve it." Why and how do we lose our lives for him? Romans 5:8-10 says that Jesus is the only way to preserve our lives. Romans 12:1 tells us to "present our bodies as a LIVING SACRIFICE, holy and acceptable unto God."

Satan has no right to trespass on our hedge of protection that gives us love, health and wealth. The accusations have already been dealt with by someone who had no choice in the matter, Job. He ended up with twice as much of everything that he had lost. And the test has already been passed by Abraham who had a choice in the matter.

Jesus was faithful even to the point of his death. He is the true living sacrifice that was raised from the dead! God wants us to be a living sacrifice like Jesus is now and live for him. Jesus already paid the price for Satan's accusations. God had stepped down from heaven through his Son and proved his unconditional love for us by the sacrifice on the cross. Everything is covered by the protection plan of God.

GIVE AND IT SHALL BE GIVEN

◆

LESSON 50

God was the first giver of love, and he wants us to pay it forward. When Jesus started his ministry, he taught some of the principles regarding the kingdom of God. One of the principles that Jesus taught was about giving. There really is something powerful to learn about this particular principle. Jesus had said that when we feed the hungry, clothe the naked, visit the sick and those in prison, we are doing it to him. We are multiplying his goodness. He also said that for those who pay it forward, they shall inherit from his kingdom (Matthew 25:31-40).

There are lots of stories that teach on the concept of "giving and taking" verse "giving and receiving". It is possible to take something without permission but receiving is getting something that is offered or given to you.

There are two stories that give us some knowledge regarding the subject of giving, taking, and receiving that affect our lives rather we realize it or not. These stories were written long before Jesus came and died on the cross. Both stories give an example of "what happens next" from either doing the right thing or doing the wrong thing. The result ends in either gaining reward or reaping the consequences.

One of the two stories is in regards to the tree of knowledge that pertains to good and evil (Genesis 3:1-19), and the other is in regards to the knowledge that God gave his people pertaining to blessing and cursing (Malachi 3:8-11).

Both of these stories refer to taking something that belonged to God. In the first story, Adam and Eve could not give back the fruit that they had taken, since they had already ingested it. It caused a curse (Genesis 3:17-19). And in Malachi, God's people were not giving him the tithes and offering that they were supposed to. In this latter story, God rightfully accused them of robbing him and told them that they were cursed with a cursed because of it (Malachi 3:8-9). In both stories they all had actually caused hardship for themselves with a curse.

They had robbed themselves of God's blessings, when they took from what he claims as his own. The one difference between the two stories is that Adam and Eve could not fix the problem, but the people in the book of Malachi could.

In Malachi, God tried to explain the importance of giving, and how it would affect their lives in a very big way. There were different types of giving that God expected from his people. He had a system that worked for the good of all and he expected them to follow his instructions.

Malachi 3:10-11 (KJV), "Bring all the tithes into the storehouse, that there may be meat in mine house, and prove me now herewith" saith the Lord of hosts, "if I will not open you the windows of heaven, and pour you out a <u>blessing</u>, that there shall not be room enough to receive it.

And I will rebuke the devourer for your sakes, and he shall not destroy the fruits of your ground; neither shall your vine cast her fruit before the time in the field", saith the Lord of hosts.

162

God wanted them to give (or pay forward) a minimum of 10% as a small sacrifice, and he would multiply it, bless it and pay it forward, as well as back to them with increase. He had multiplied their possessions like their animals, grain, corn, wine, oil, spices etc., and he expected them to pay a little forward. Some of the resources that they were to give was to take care of the priests and those who were in need. God told his people that if they gave back to him like they were supposed to, he would bless all of them abundantly, as well as protect the other 90% of their resources.

If we connect God's concept for giving, taking, and receiving to today's world, he would be referring to our incoming resources of any kind. These stories may have happened in the Old Testament times, but it shows how God feels and reacts to giving, even now.

Let's look at current ways that we have protection or security regarding our possessions and our health. We buy insurance policies to cover us in case we have some kind of future catastrophe. It can give us protection over our homes, our cars and even the cost of our health. Another way we can secure our future is by making investments. We can become a partner in a business venture in hopes of securing more income, peace of mind, or even to be involved in an elaborate mission. We invest a little to hopefully secure something even better.

God is the business owner of the largest insurance company in this world. He said in Malachi that when we sow or give into his hands, he gives back with benefits. He tried to explain to his people that if they wanted to be covered for disasters, they needed to invest into his system. It is important for God to be included in our affairs because he takes care of his own. When we give to God, we are coming into agreement with him. We are giving him something to work with. God shows us that a little sacrifice covers us from losing it all.

The tithes and offerings received in Malachi were used for God's overall purpose in his business. His business is his people. The rest (90%) of the product that God had blessed his people with was for them to keep and enjoy. That tenth made a big difference in someone's life, especially when multiple people had given a tenth. Ten people can make a big difference in just one person's life. If his people had given him back at least a tenth of whatever they had gotten from him, he promised them that he would open the windows of heaven and pour out such a blessing that there would not be enough room to receive it all. This means that there would be more than enough to share with others who need it.

So, how does this lesson in Malachi relate to the story of Adam and Eve in Genesis chapter three? Adam and Eve had access to the whole garden of God except for one tree. It was just a small part of the whole garden. The rest of the garden had all kinds of vegetation for them to choose from. It was all there for them to enjoy. God's multiplication principles worked to make sure they had food in abundance as long as they did not touch the one tree. It belonged to him! Maybe the tree and its fruit were like the 10% belonging to God in Malachi. Maybe he had his own good purpose for its use. Maybe he used the fruit on the tree to bless the garden for them. I don't really know! But once they stole from the tree, it caused a curse regarding reaping and sowing for the rest of their lives (Genesis 3:17). So, the situation in the garden and the situation in Malachi both somehow affected God's principle of multiplication. In both cases, if God was robbed, the principle of blessing stopped working the way that it was supposed to!

These lessons also teach us that if we don't give God something that he can work with, his principle of multiplication may not work on our behalf. Whatever is given to God, he treats it as seed that can multiplied. A seed can be anything.

God was and is the first giver of seed. In the story found in Malachi, God multiplied their crops with a bountiful harvest, which produced even more seed. They would then give 10% back to God's cause before they took hold of the 90%. This cycle worked to multiply more the next time.

In the beginning when God was robbed, Adam and Eve did not have anything that they could give back to him to make things right again, so God gave them a way to pay him back. His word is faith substance and he spoke it into existence by a word of prophecy that very day! He basically said that it would be by their own future seed, Jesus (Genesis 3:15). God was going to give them a way to make restitution and put an end to the curse.

God's word was planted in the womb of a woman as his own seed. This seed had come from God himself and was given to the world through the birthing process. It was a new thing created by God. Jesus belonged to God first before God gave him into this world.

While Jesus was with us, God gave and multiplied all kinds of blessings through him. He was the blesser of life itself! God gave him to us as a gift, so that we could have life more abundantly. All good things came by Jesus Christ. Jesus belonged to God. He became the sacrificed offering that nullified the curse over are lives, when he gave up his whole life (not just 10%) but 100%. He gave up to God the powerful seeds of blessing that was given to him first, just so that God could multiply and rebirth them into our lives.

We have to make up our minds to trust him in everything. We have to give our lives to him. We have to believe what he said in his word, and then give him the opportunity of making it good through his own principles. Money and resources are not the only things that God accepts from us. Jesus gave his whole life back to God already and look where he is.

Give God 10% of your time, effort and anything else that you think he could use for his own purpose, like with the tithes and offerings. As he uses it to bring about the blessing, it will include you.

Jesus was born for the sole purpose of stopping Satan from operating in God's rightful position of influence and power. He came to take back what Satan had stolen from God through Adam and Eve, and to restore all things to their rightful place of authority.

If Jesus would have been in the garden during his ministry, he would have never touched the tree without God's permission. He made sure that his Father was the final authority over whatever he did with his own life as a human being. All the actions that Jesus, the Son of God had done throughout his life was to willingly restore the authority back to his Father. He was the future seed that was spoken of in the garden.

Jesus was deeply dedicated and loyal to his Father's service. When he died, he gave his Spirit into his Father's hands. He gave his holy life as a gift to the Father. He was his own perfect offering. He was the best offering ever, morally and spiritually!

God took him and gave him back his life with increase. What does that mean? Jesus now has no need for anything and owns everything. Not only that, God his Father also officially gave him the highest position of authority, directly under himself (as the first immortalized man). **Jesus said, "All power is given unto me in heaven and in earth" (Matthew 28:18).** He is the one human who has been given all power over good and evil!

Jesus proved himself faithful to his Father. He proved that he would never devour (demolish or destroy) his Fathers belongings. His Father knows he can trust him to do the right thing for all of his creation. He can trust him with our lives.

To sum up what it all means, Jesus had said to give, and it shall be given back to you in good measure, pressed down, shaken together, and running over (Luke 6:38). It is the same principle as in Malachi. The good that we give of anything unto God and to others, blesses more than just were we give it. It is part of the multiplying process. When we give, we start or activate the process of paying it forward from ourselves. We are activating a law of blessing that affects all involved including ourselves.

In Matthew 25:14-30, Jesus told a story about the importance of giving and receiving. He starts out talking about talents. A talent was a measure of silver or gold comparable to how we define the worth of money and wealth today.

In the story, a wealthy man goes on a journey and leaves charge of his finances to three of his employees. He gives the first employee five talents, to the second employee two talents, and to the third employee one. He distributed the talents according to what he felt their ability was in handling his own wealth.

When the man returned home, he asked what each employee did with what was given to them. The first and the second employee had doubled the owner's talents. The owner was well pleased and praised them because of their faithfulness in multiplying the talents. He promoted them both into a higher position over his empire. The third employee had done nothing with what he was given accept bury the original talent in the ground. He presented the original talent back to the owner and said what he believed about the owner (Matthew 25:24). His attitude toward the owner was not right. He considered the owner as a hard man who reaped for himself what others had sown. The employee saw no value in helping the owner who he worked for.

He did not realize that the owner was giving him a chance to be blessed and promoted like the first two employees with a higher position of authority and use of his kingdom.

First of all, the owner was the one who gave them the talents to multiply for his purpose. It was all his, and as we would read later in the same chapter, the owner was a very goodhearted and generous businessman, and his business was thriving. Secondly, he was promoting them on their merits. He even told the first two employees to enjoy their promotion. Any owner needs his business to flourish and be successful or it will crumble.

The employee who did nothing for the good of the whole company was considered useless. He should have traded or paid for a commodity more useful to the owner's business. In Matthew 25:27, the owner told the employee he should have at least put his talents (money) to the exchangers, so that when he came back, he would have his money and any interest that it made. Since the slothful employee did nothing good with the one talent given for him to multiply, he was cast out of the owner's empire.

The Father in heaven considers his empire here on earth as his pride and joy. He put his son, Jesus in charge of it all. You could say it is his own family business. He is dedicated in taking care of those who want to be a part of it. I look at this temporary life as a trial period for the eternal life. If you read the rest of the chapter in Matthew, you will read that Jesus is like the man in the story of the talents. He has left on a journey and will come back to collect or gather from his harvest of people when the time is right (Revelation 14:14-15). The Father's business is all about people and he loves and cares for his own.

We are to treat others as we would want them to treat us (Matthew 7:12). If we all followed this principle, the world would be a better place. The only problem is that there is still an evil presence trying to keep us from being united in Christ.

Jesus had said that when we take care of others by feeding, clothing, and giving them shelter, we are doing it to him (Matthew 25:34-40). People are his assets, and he does not want to lose any of them. They are his investments. He wants his kingdom to grow and be blessed in the whole world. This means in wealth, resources, and people.

The principle of sowing and reaping is important to God. To the person who did nothing in the talent story, he reaped what he had sown which was nothing. God gets things done through us and he does give reward through the sowing and reaping principle. His principles work.

Tithing may have been in the Old Testament, but it is still practiced today. It is essential in the reaping and sowing principle. God loves a cheerful giver (1 Corinthians 9:7). We have to remember that everything really belongs to God and is entrusted to us. When we give into his cause through organizations that serve a purpose for us all, or to those in immediate need, he sees it as a willingness to accept him in our own finances. We are giving him permission to carry-out his promises in that area of our lives. He sees the giving and blesses the giver (Malachi 3:10-11).

When we give him permission to use some of our finances, we tie it to his corporation. We are in essence helping God multiply and prosper the whole business, which also includes all our own finances. We take part in his, and he takes part in ours. The principle in Luke 6:38 about giving can come into play. Give and it shall be given back to you in good measure, pressed down, shaken together, and running over. As we saw in the story of the talents, God was well pleased with what the two good stewards did for his corporation, so he rewarded them!

The assets and the time that we give to God's cause is given to advance his own business, his own kingdom. It is sharing God's blessing to others throughout the world to bringing them to Christ.

It takes giving, to reach and change the world. It is an action of promoting God's love. We have to spread his love, for it is a multitude of good seed. Good will not be overcome by evil, if we all do our part! We are the ones to plant his love in the world and his word says his love never fails (1 Corinthians 13:8).

God taught us about covenant through his Son Jesus. Did you know that when you give to God, you are **entering into the agreement** that Jesus taught in Luke 6:38? "Give and it shall be **given back to you** in good measure, pressed down, shaken together, and running over." Do you know why he could boldly teach this principle? It was because he was doing it himself. His efforts did not go unrewarded. He has thousands and thousands of followers and businesses, especially today.

Jesus taught the multiplying principle using five loaves of barley and two small fishes (John 6:1-13). There was a great multitude of people that followed Jesus up into a mountain. He showed them a miracle by taking a young lad's basket of food (five loaves and two small fishes) and multiplied it to feed 5,000 men and their families. When everyone had eaten and was full, there were twelve full baskets left over. He showed that he can take what you give him to work with and then multiply it abundantly so that it can meet the need at hand.

There was a strong similarity between the tree and the tenth both belonging to God. There is a part of God's assets or resources that he keeps for himself. He is the only one who knows what to do with it appropriately.

We need to become the image of God's Son by accepting his Spirit. We give our lives to him and he gives to us from his. The Holy Spirit is a spirit of guidance, deliverance, protection and love. We don't become him, but he does come and live and dwell in us.

Jesus has power over all the power of the devil. We can run him off in the name of Jesus because Jesus lives within us by his Spirit. We have to know this truth for ourselves, so that the enemy cannot deceive us. When the enemy sees the evidence of Jesus involved in our affairs, he can't take over or destroy what has been entrusted in the care of our savior. We are bonded with our savior through the Holy Spirit. We have been given the authority of Jesus over the enemy. We can put the enemy under our feet! Instead of giving in to him, we can take our rightful place of authority through Jesus Christ, and he will have to flee. The word of God says so!

James 4:7 (KJV), <u>Submit</u> yourselves <u>to God</u>. <u>Resist the devil</u> and <u>he will flee from you.</u>

God wants us to do the best that we can with everything he gives us. When we give him anything like prayers for our families, money, time, energy, efforts, or other resources for his cause, we are doing it for and to Jesus. When we give back anything to God, we are saying that we want him to be in our lives and we want him to protect what we have. Jesus proved himself as the God of giving.

Our own children are a blessing that came from the Father. He wants us to enjoy them, protect them, have a deep love for them and raise them for him. When we dedicate our children and make a commitment to raise them for him, we are lovingly giving them into his hands. They are on loan like the talents. God blesses us with them to love. He wants us to know and feel some of the same deep holy love that he feels for us as his children.

Everything we do in his name makes us a part of his business. We can put everything that we have, household, children, parents, friends, finances, ourselves and even our sin into the hands of God through prayer and giving. If we give our lives to Christ, it will be preserved! That is why he said give and it shall be given.

One last thought about giving. In John 15:4-5, Jesus had said that no branch can bear fruit unless it stays attached to the vine. He said he was the vine, and we are the branches. We can't produce his good fruit without him.

Galatians 5:22-23 (KJV) says, "But the <u>fruit of the Spirit</u> is love, joy, peace, longsuffering, gentleness, goodness, faith, meekness, temperance: against such there is no law."

SONS AND DAUGHTERS

—◆—

LESSON 51

There is some evidence that other life forms were here on our planet before people like us existed. From what we read in the first couple of chapters of the book of Genesis, Adam was the first like us. He was a man created with a body that was formed from the elements of the ground. And, then God breathed into his nostrils to give his body life. In the New Testament book of Luke 3:38, Adam was referred to as a "son of God" because he was the first human being that God created of our kind.

As I study to learn more details about the story of our beginning, I have more questions. There are other ancient scrolls that have been found which were not included in the bible that we have today. They contain information that may or may not be totally true. There was a legend about a female who was created from the ground just like Adam, when he was created. She rebelled completely and somehow became very evil. There was also ancient text that tells some things about the life of Jesus as he was growing up. And, still another that tells the life of his mother and her family before Jesus was born. I don't know if any of these stories are true, but my focus is on things that affect us from our first father and mother, Adam and Eve.

The first few chapters in the book of Genesis talk about the one male and the one female, and how they both came to be. Genesis 3:20 says that Adam called his wife's name Eve, because she was the mother of all living. This tells me that if she was the mother of all living, then Adam was the father of all living. He was the original man over those of his kind, us. Sometime after Eve was created from his rib, they both fell from the graces of God.

Then in Genesis chapter four, we read the story of their two sons Cain and Abel. We already covered the details of the story where Cain killed his own brother and was sent away by God.

After Cain killed his brother and was sent away, he went to live in a place called the land of Nod, where he started a family of his own. Genesis 4:17 tells us that he conceived a son from his wife. Where did his wife come from? Was she a daughter from Adam and Eve, and just not mentioned as a child born from them? I assume that the bible story focused only on Cain and Abel because they were their first two children and the first recorded murder. If Adam and Eve were the first people to have children, then Cain probably took one of his own sisters as a wife or took a niece that may have been born before Abel was killed.

People lived a lot longer back then. Adam himself lived 930 years. There were probably many generations of children that were born from Adam and Eve, and a lot of them could have been living at the same time. Genesis 5:4 tells us that there were numerous sons and daughters who also had sons and daughters as the human race multiplied.

Genesis chapter five is a short summary of creation from Adam to the sons of Noah. It starts out talking about God creating male and female, blessing them, and calling their name Adam. I could be wrong, but I do believe this was in reference to these first two people, Adam and Eve. Eve had been created from Adam's rib, so maybe she was also called Adam. She was not born from another. She was the first created woman made from the substance of Adam. Sometime after the death of Abel, Adam and Eve had another son and named him Seth. The rest of the chapter gives a list of the descendants from Adam to the three sons of Noah through the line of Seth.

The summary only lists the males that were born. This could be the reason why we don't know who Cain's wife was in Genesis chapter four. The daughters were not recognized or named in the beginning of history.

All the children that were born through the womb of Eve were not directly created or born by God, so they were not sons and daughters of God. They were sons and daughters of Adam and Eve. Their sinful tendencies came from their parents. The bible tells us so many stories that prove sinful tendencies have trickled down throughout time. But it also tells us that God has never given up on our species, since the time that Adam and Eve fell. There was to come a time, when there would be a seed born from both God and mankind through Eve and called the "Son of God".

When God was addressing the situation in the garden about the tree, he spoke to the serpent regarding his future plan to redeem mankind. He told him exactly what was going to happen. In Genesis 3:15, he told the serpent (referred to as the great dragon, the old serpent, the devil, and Satan in Revelation 12:9 and 20:2) that he would put enmity between him and the woman, and between his seed and her seed. God was referring to Jesus as her seed of the future. Her seed would come up against Satan to amend the damage that he caused Adam and Eve to do.

In Genesis 3:15 (KJV) God said to the devil, **"And I will put enmity between thee and the woman, and between thy seed and her seed: it shall bruise thy head, and thou shalt bruise his heel."**

Whatever God speaks into existence becomes law. God was actually making a declaration of love, compassion and mercy for Adam and Eve and their descendants, through a hidden message. He spoke a prophetic word. The prophetic meaning of what God had said, had not been revealed in Adam and Eve's lifetime. It was a plan that was unfolded over time. We can understand what God meant now about her seed, because of all the stories in the bible that led up to the birth, death and resurrection of God's Son. God's spoken word does come to pass.

When Jesus was born, he was called the Son of God and the son of man. He was the first of his kind from both God and mankind. He was the seed to come from the woman that was spoken about in the prophecy. The seed had to be given from a higher power or authority than mortal man and Satan himself. Satan was an angelic being. He was not equal to God. The seed that was to take down the devil's stronghold over the human race had to come from God himself. Even though Jesus was born through the womb of a woman, he was the seed that came directly from God. He was born both God and man in one.

Jesus did say that all power had been given to him. Adam may have lost our right standing with our maker, but Jesus gets it back with legal and binding force. He defied and rejected the power of Satan. Defy means that he challenged, confronted, rebelled, disobeyed, and resisted everything that the devil threw at him. He is the earthly man to bruise the head or dictatorship of the serpent. I doubt if Adam and Eve understood what God meant by his prophecy to restore mankind to himself, I know the devil didn't!

In the New Testament, there are many scriptures that refer to us as the sons and daughters of God. We are born of God when we accept Jesus Christ into our lives. It is a real thing! It is not in the way that a man and woman conceive. God actually plants his own risen Son's Spirit of Sonship into us, and God becomes our Father, when we allow him to do it.

Sonship could not be given to us until after Jesus was immortalized. We had to wait for his transition from death back to life, and for him to present himself (his Sonship) to the Father for approval. Jesus was the first to be transformed into an <u>incorruptible</u> being as the Son of God (Spirit) and the son of man (spirit) combined. A son of man can now also be a son of God. Children of mankind can now also be children of God. Sonship is now possible!

In the next several paragraphs, I hope that I can effectively explain how I think God used his principle of giving that is explained in Malachi chapter three to fix our relationship with him. I want to show the connection between the giving in tithes, offerings and crops talked about in Malachi, to what God did to give us legal status as his offspring. The comparison can help in understanding the big picture regarding why Jesus died, and how we became sons and daughters through his death.

In John 12:24 Jesus said, **"Except a corn of wheat fall into the ground and die, it abides alone, but if it dies, it brings forth much fruit."**

Jesus was the seed of Eve (similar to the example of a corn of wheat) that produces more like himself. He was the first to literally be forced (or planted) deep within the ground, and then be raised up in newness of life. Like the corn of wheat, he brings forth much fruit after his kind.

God accepted the spirit of Jesus that Jesus had offered to him, not just as a human spirit, but <u>as his own Son</u>, when he was put on the tree to die. Jesus had said, **"<u>Father</u> into your hands, I commend (commit) <u>my spirit</u>" (Luke 23:46).** Jesus entrusted and offered the Spiritual Relationship with his Father back to him, so he could give it to us.

God has his own soul (mind, will and emotions). His nature is to express his love through blessing his creation. We know this because of his ever-expanding universe. He gives (multiplies and supplies) the resources needed for our survival, and for us to enjoy. Since he has feelings, he wants to be loved back.

In Isaiah 42:1 of the Old Testament, God had said, **"Behold my servant, whom <u>I uphold</u>; mine elect in whom <u>my soul delights</u>. I have put my Spirit upon him."** God was referring to Jesus, his Son to born in the future. He confirmed his own feelings about his Son, two different times in the New Testament, when he actually said, **"This is my beloved Son, in whom <u>I am well pleased</u>" (Matthew 3:17 and 17:5).**

So, how is principle or law mentioned in Malachi chapter three regarding tithes and offering related to God giving us legal status as his offspring?

The whole process of giving had its beginning with God blessing and multiplying their crops and other resources for their own benefit. Then, they were to give back 10% of their increase. This was a continuous cycle that supplied them with more than enough. As everybody gave their small amount of just 10%, that small amount added up to an abundant supply to meet the needs as a whole community. It met the need to keep the priestly activities of God's temple, and to feed those less fortunate. As God's people gave their tithes and offerings, God continued to work his principle of giving for the next cycle of sowing and reaping. If they did not sow or give God the tenth, then the cycle of reaping would be broken.

If you look at the scriptures in Malachi about giving, the people were supposed to give back to God the portion that belonged to him in tithes and offerings. They couldn't directly give it to God because he was Spirit. They gave it to the priests who were the representatives for him, so that the priests could distribute it where God saw fit.

So, what basically started or activated the cycle was that God gave them increase in their crops, as well as other necessary commodities. We already know that seeds grow into plants that give food to eat and produce more seeds. Even a handful of seeds can produce an abundant harvest of food. God gave, so that they could be blessed abundantly and have enough to give back. He believes in overflow, so that all his own people would never go without. He gave and blessed them with more than enough, so they could give to bless others. And, when we give to others, we are doing it, or giving it to him (Matthew 25:35-40). It all pertains to the cycle of life.

For the most part, we see in Malachi that God worked his blessing for his people through a small portion of what he had given them, and it all ties back to what happened in the garden. God made the garden and moved Adam into it. He kept a small percentage of the space within the garden for himself.

It is like giving him a room of his own in your own home, that he created and gave to you in the first place. The stuff in his own room is his and he blesses you in return for the space.

Before the fall of Adam and Eve, God had supplied for them abundantly. But then Adam and Eve went into his space and took from his things without his permission. They made it theirs, not his. God was robbed! Maybe, when they actually stole some of God's fruit that contained seeds and ate it, they stole seeds that he used in the blessing and multiplying process.

The purpose of the fruit itself is to protect the seed that is within it. It is kind of like our bodies that provide protection for the real you and me inside. Maybe that one tree, a small portion of the garden, had a purpose in **blessing and cursing**. We do know that it had to do with **good and evil**. When Adam and Eve ate the fruit, they devoured a small portion of God's seeds as well.

Let's switch gears for a moment and look at a different kind of seed than an actual corn of wheat that is planted in a field. God was the first giver in a cycle of giving, when he gave us his own Seed, which was his own Son. God planted him among us for the sole purpose of distributing Sonship seeds all over the world. Jesus was the very first to be born as God's seed, as well as Eve's seed.

While Jesus was here on earth, he planted and distributed the good things from his Father. He came to give people an increase. He healed, he delivered, he multiplied food, he raised the dead and he gave this same power to some of his followers. He spoke to people through parables and prophecies as he gave sound advice to those who would listen. He was cultivating a harvest of people to give to his Father's kingdom. He was distributing God's blessings. He was sowing God's seeds into the lives of others.

He was sentenced to die while distributing his Fathers seeds of blessing into the lives of others. Satan knew who Jesus was and influenced others to rob God of his own Son's life, God's own Seed! Was Satan up to his old tricks to rob again, first with the tree in the garden and now with God's own Son? He had already caused people to doubt God in the beginning and now to doubt his Son.

While he was here physically, he never mistreated the relationship between his Father and himself. He protected it with his life. In fact, he was cursed and put to death because he said he was God's Son. Think about it, what if out of fear of them killing him, he denied being the Son of God? What if he thought it would save him from dying a torturous death? He knew he was God's Son and would not deny his relationship to the world. He would have lied if he said otherwise. He claimed his Sonship and paid a great price for it! He thought his Sonship to be a high honor and was proud to be God's Son.

Jesus was sentenced to hang on a tree by the actual religious leaders who represented God's law to defend it. They were jealous of the attention that he was getting. People were following him as their leader. They wanted to keep their position of control and authority over the people, so they wrongfully put Jesus under the curse.

Jesus as a man was judged under the law of his own people, so that his soul would descend into the spiritual realm of the dead. Satan may have wanted this to happen, but little did he know, the Father and his Son let it happen on purpose. It was so that Jesus could legally (as a human) enter the realm of the dead to take over before ascending into the highest heaven.

There are numerous scriptures that tell what happened to Jesus when he died, and after he was resurrected to go to be with his Father in heaven (Ephesians 4:8-10, Psalms 16:9-11 and Acts 2:22-36).

One reason why Jesus went into the lower parts of the earth is in 1 Peter. It reads, **"For Christ also hath once suffered for sins, the just for the unjust, that he might bring us to God, being put to**

death in the flesh, but quickened by the Spirit: By which also <u>he went and preached unto the spirits in prison</u>" (1 Peter 3:18-19).

Not all of God's plan of salvation was accomplished on the earth's surface. I believe it continued into the heart of the earth for he had to make an appearance their too!

Now, if we are in Christ Jesus and he in us, when we die, we go to be with him. In one of Paul's letters Paul said, "For me to live is Christ, and to die is gain." He had no fear of dying! He had the desire to be in heaven with Christ, but he also said it was more needful for him to be here on earth until his mission was complete (Philippians 1:20-24). We are all here for a reason. As for now, we can live out God's vision that has been given to us through his Word, his Son.

Jesus willingly gave the most magnificent offering of any man. He gave up his blessed life here on earth 100%. He offered himself as a perfect unblemished sacrifice, so that we would not experience the curse of death for ourselves.

The law that was used to punish him, **owed him his life back**. He should not have legally been punished for sin. The old law could have someone killed, but it couldn't bring one back from the dead. The new law of Christ can! If we accept Christ (God's seed), the curse (like in the cycle of giving in Malachi) has been taken out of the equation, and what is left is the blessing 100% through Christ.

<u>What is the difference of the blessing and the curse?</u>

Deuteronomy 28:4 (KJV), "<u>Blessed</u> shall be <u>the fruit</u> of <u>thy body</u>, and <u>the fruit</u> of <u>thy ground</u> and the fruit of <u>thy cattle</u>, the <u>increase</u> of thy cows (kine), and the flocks of thy sheep."

Deuteronomy 28:18 (KJV), "<u>Cursed</u> shall be the fruit of <u>thy body</u>, and the fruit of <u>thy land</u>, the increase of thy cows (kine), and the flocks of thy sheep."

The blessing and the curse have to do with things associated with our own wealth, health, bodies and offspring. It includes our accomplishments, as well as everything else in our lives.

What Jesus did for us all, meant more to God than any other offering, ever! He broke through the stronghold of the curse! God saw that he was the picture-perfect man and was very proud of him. Can you imagine their joy of reunion? God was so pleased with him for completing his complicated mission and to finally receive him home.

There is great joy in heaven because of the new covenant that was established between the Father and his Son. Jesus cleared the way for human reunification to his Father and the curse is not even an option. I believe Jesus first descended into the spirit realm of the dead to confront the real thief and to redeem mankind to himself. He has taken control back, but leaves the choice up to us to accept him. **There is great joy in the presence of the angels when any one person gives their life to Jesus (Luke 15:10).** Even when we die, we will get our full life back too, just like Jesus did. And it will be a glorified life forever. All of heaven celebrates our victory, when we accept Spiritual Sonship from Jesus to become joint heirs.

I believe that the curse was not meant for mankind in the beginning. For all we know, the law was already in force because of Satan and his efforts to overthrow God. He is still influencing people today to rob God of his rightful position of authority. According to the bible, hell was originally meant for the devil and his angels (Matthew 25:41). Mankind had been tricked into becoming an accomplice and accountable to the same fate.

Jesus knew that he came to die for us all. He did not have to let them put him to death, but this was the only way to stop the curse. It could only happen through his death. When Jesus was put to death, he and all the religious leader who sentenced him to death, were following God's plan to break the curse, even though the religious leaders did not know it. It was meant to be!

172

What they did only ushered in the rest of God's plan. The religious leaders meant evil against Jesus, but God meant it for good. This was similar to the story of Joseph (Genesis chapter 37 through 50). Joseph's brothers meant evil against him, but God meant it for good. God turned both situations around by putting Joseph and Jesus in high positions in order to save the lives of others. And Jesus, like Joseph forgave those who meant it for evil. It was all a part of God's plan.

We have all been in some kind of slavery like the Israelites or even Joseph himself. Joseph showed us to come out of the slavery mentality and do great things like he did. He left it behind in the past and made something good from it. He went forward and even forgave those (his brother's) who put him in bondage in the first place. If his brothers would not have done what they did, Joseph may have never made it to Egypt to be promoted to a high position. Whatever slavery you have come out of, forgive and move forward to do great things for the good of all.

Satan is the real culprit behind all bondage and slavery. So, does it mean that God used Satan's own weapon of jealousy to carry out his good plan? God knew how Joseph's brothers felt towards Joseph, just like he knew how the religious leaders felt about Jesus. I believe that this is also the way that Satan felt about the first man Adam. I believe this is also similar to the story of Job, when Satan caused a curse in his life. Jealousy was the weapon that was used to hurt Adam, Job, Joseph and then Jesus. Satan tried to curse them all.

In the bible, we see that every time Satan messed with the people of God and their affairs to hurt them, God turned it around for something even better. God knows how the mind of Satan works and his motive to destroy us, even when he tries to do it by using others. God can use and turn any situation around for the good.

Even though Jesus was human, he was born with something more than what we were born with. He came directly from the Sonship position of God. He could offer or give more than 100% of what any human being could possibly give to God. This position was immeasurably higher than that of the first Adam! He was born from the essence and life force of God's pure and Holy Spirit as well as human spirit. He was the perfect hybrid!

Jesus had to die without committing any sin in order to give his Father back the best seed ever from mankind. No one else could do it. Jesus was the perfect mold, model or prototype from mankind itself that could be generated, multiplied and given to others.

If we accept that Jesus is the Son of God, we are no longer affected by the curse of Genesis 3:17-19 and Malachi 3:8-9. Knowing this truth is the pathway to freedom. Jesus has already given back to God exactly what he needed to fix the problem that caused the curse in the first place. Jesus justified the law of sin and death. He willingly paid the price with everything he was made of for what was wrongfully done in the garden. It only took one man to cause a curse, and one man to stop the curse.

God needed someone willing to justify the law of the curse by satisfying its terms. (Justify means to prove that the law of the curse is right or reasonable for the crime.) Satan wanted to prove that the law of the curse wasn't justifiable, because it will affect his life in the future, when he will be permanently dealt with for his horrific crime(s). He figured that if he was going to be punished, so should we. And, he has set out to prove it. Jesus never set out to prove or say that the law was unjust, but he did pay the price of death written in the justifiable law for mankind's crime.

In Isaiah 45:7 God had said, "I form the light, and create darkness: I make peace, and create evil." In Isaiah 54:16 he said, "I have created the waster to destroy." When I first read this, I was surprised at the thought that God creates evil. But he showed me that the purpose was to destroy what comes against his own law that keeps life going. It was to keep his balance of life in force.

Jesus used seed, ground, and harvest time to explain the development of his kingdom. In Matthew chapter thirteen, Jesus had told three parables regarding the sowing of seed. One of the parables was about a man sowing good seed in his own field, in order to reap a bountiful harvest. In the story, he said that the man had an unseen enemy that was sowing bad seed among his good seed while he slept at night (Matthew 13:24-30). He would not weed out the tares that were growing until his wheat was ready to harvest, because he didn't want any part of his wheat to be destroyed in the process of destroying the tares. He had to wait till harvest time before separating the wheat from the tares! Jesus likened himself to the one sowing good seed and the devil sowing the bad seed, the field was the world, and the wheat and tares the people of the world (Matthew 13:37-38).

Faith is a spiritual idea or substance that can cause or produce good or evil fruit. It can go either way. It has been misused to activate evil in the world. It goes back to the garden where Satan planted the selfish desire for power. He has caused division, dividing us with our differences of color, culture, or any other factor. There are tares among the wheat! But there is a final race of people cropping up everywhere that will stand forever, the brothers and sisters in Christ.

The tree in the garden, the tenth and the Son of God all belonged to God, and they have been supernaturally restored to their rightful owner. We have to accept his concept. It is how the principle of giving works. God gave his Sonship first! And if we give ourselves to him, then there is no curse over our lives because Sonship is no longer cursed.

Sonship for us refers to a relationship with God as our Father. It has been created from the life of Jesus that was planted in the dust of the earth through death and then raised to new life. Jesus was the first hybrid of the spirit man and the Spirit of God. He was the "first fruit" that had risen out from the ground and accepted by God as a sweet offering. Sonship could be duplicated and multiplied as seed to the rest of the world. Sonship makes us sons and daughters of almighty God.

1 Corinthians 15:20-24 says, "But now is Christ risen from the dead, and become the firstfruits of them that slept. For since by man came death, by man came also the resurrection of the dead. <u>For as in Adam all die, even so in Christ shall all be made alive.</u> But every man in his own order: Christ the firstfruits; afterwards they that are Christ's at his coming.

I know this has been a long lesson, but it shows processes and principles of sowing and reaping, seed time and harvest time, good and evil, blessing and cursing. It shows how they have made a difference to shape our future.

God, as the Father is well pleased with his Son. God listens and sees us through a Father's eyes and ears, when he sees his Son Jesus accepted in us.

The concept of Sonship is very important! It may be hard to understand that we must be born again of the Holy Spirit. Regardless of whatever you believe, it is more of a real thing than being born through an earthly father and mother. This may be hard to hear, but at death, permanent separation is possible, unless you are born again of the Spirit. Sonship through Christ doesn't end at our death. Sonship is a permanent blessing given to us by our Father and his Son Jesus Christ.

1ST HISTORY OF THE FIRSTBORN RIGHT

Part I

LESSON 52

Firstborn rights of Jesus (as God's firstborn Son) are an important key to understanding our rights. I think that if we study the subject regarding "firstborn" in more detail, it will help us to understand who we are, and why we can trust in God's way of doing things. I have already written some things about Adam's sons, Abraham's sons, Isaac's sons, Jacobs's sons and God's Son, Jesus. God used a firstborn traditional law of the Old Testament to bring about his own Son, who would inherit everything that belonged to him, including us.

The world was designed to be a very blessed place. We are meant to have divine favor and protection, and to be fruitful (productive and successful) in our health, family and in our finances. But there are people all over the world that are living under the effects of the curse, only because it is not a perfect world system, as of yet.

<u>History of Firstborn Rights</u>

We can see that so far, what one man did or did not do, made a difference between a blessing and a curse for us all. Adam put us all under the curse by the one thing that God told him not to do, while Jesus did everything he was told to do.

There is a lot of material in the bible regarding a firstborn son's right in the family line that Jesus was born from. Jesus was a firstborn son under the old covenant and a firstborn Son of the new. He was the first born again from the dead, when he rose to his new and eternal life. His FIRSTBORN RIGHT connects us through the eternal Spirit to the promises and blessings of God.

When Jesus was here in the flesh, he had to follow all the laws of the Old Testament without breaking any one of them. The laws of blessings and curses that were written in Deuteronomy for God's people had very strict guidelines.

In Deuteronomy 28:1-14, there is a list of all the blessings, and then in the rest of the chapter there is a list of all the curses. It is a pretty intense chapter. We see the effects of both sides all over the world. The chapter in Deuteronomy is very long, so I would like to mention the verses that sum up everything that is affected by a blessing or a curse.

Deuteronomy 28:4 (KJV), "<u>Blessed</u> shall be <u>the fruit</u> of <u>thy body</u>, and <u>the fruit</u> of <u>thy ground</u> and <u>the fruit</u> of <u>thy cattle</u>, the <u>increase</u> of thy cows, and the flocks of thy sheep."

Deuteronomy 28:18 (KJV), "<u>Cursed</u> shall be the fruit of <u>thy body</u>, and the fruit of <u>thy land,</u> the <u>increase</u> of thy cows, and the flocks of thy sheep."

God's will for us is to be blessed! To be blessed is to be fruitful, multiply, and replenish the earth even in abundant of substance. The whole chapter of Deuteronomy gives details of what one could expect in reward or punishment by their actions. The result would be either to be blessed or cursed in one's body and health, as well as, with their earthly resources for survival and prosperity.

The first two sons born from Eve were both greatly affected by a curse. When they grew up, Cain had killed his brother and then lied about it to God. From his action, he caused a direct curse upon his own life, and for his brother.

The ground had already been cursed because of their father's sin, but now there was another serious problem. Cain caused the lifeforce from the blood of his own brother to bleed out into the ground. We know this for a fact, because God told Cain that he had heard his brother's blood cry out to him from the ground (Genesis 4:10). God also told Cain that the ground would not "yield its strength" for him anymore, because he caused a curse for himself. He would be a "fugitive and a vagabond" (Genesis 4:9-11). Abel became cursed when he was put to death at no fault of his own, while his brother Cain was cursed for causing it.

Before Cain had actually killed his brother Abel, they had both presented an offering or gift to God. God was pleased more with Abel's gift than with Cain's gift. In fact, this is what caused Cain to get upset and kill his brother. Abel's particular offering would be the last offering that God would receive from him before his death.

Abel had given God his best, when he gave a first year, first-born, perfect animal from the flock of sheep that he managed. As far as we know, the death of Abel was the first time that God had felt the pain and hurt brought on by death of someone he loved so much. God's last good memory of Abel was the pleasant offering of the lamb as a gift. I was wondering if this particular offering had a part to play in the purpose for the sacrificial offerings of the lamb mentioned all throughout the Old Testament.

Abel's lamb offering was a pleasant memory of Abel to God, instead of remembering his death. When someone passes away, we try to remember the good times by repeating their favorite songs or reenacting and recreating the good parts of their lives. The sacrificial offerings of the lamb throughout the Old Testament may have been partly related to what happened with Cain and Abel.

Maybe the lamb sacrifices are partly symbolic of Cain, who represents the cursed of mankind for his sin. Maybe the sacrifices are a way of making amends to say "I am sorry! Please forgive me!" The sacrifices are a way of giving something back to restore or undo the curse. Are the sacrifices symbolic of Cain's sin being put to death, instead of Cain himself for his sin?

The sacrifice and offering rituals were temporary solutions. Jesus was given as a permanent and perfect offering that could not be destroyed. Maybe symbolic gestures spark good memories, reminders and feelings for God. Maybe not only his feelings for Abel, but the good feeling of his own Son who was born, died and then returned back to him.

Most people are excited when they first hear that they are going to have a baby in the near future. Every thought up until the birth are filled with excitement and anticipation.

In the Old Testament, God had already known that he was going to have an earthly Son. Maybe the temporary sacrifices throughout the Old Testament reminded him of his Son to come. He knew that Jesus would become the sacrifice and be rebirthed to live forever. No one can ever take God's Son or one of his own children from him ever again, like what happened to Abel! Spiritually speaking, God is excited with every single person who becomes born again as his own children.

God now has more good memories, and he has the life of his Son with him. Believe it or not, God was well pleased with mankind's offering of his own Son. God is satisfied with Jesus offering himself as all the "Cains" of the world, because he got his Son back, including the lives of millions.

Remember the last thing that God heard from Abel was his crying out from the ground after his death. God hears and knows our voice by the blood, because the life of the flesh is in the blood (Leviticus 17:11). The blood has a voice that God understands!

The sacrifice of the lamb in the Old Testament was definitely a placeholder that covered sins up until God's Son went to the cross. God heard Jesus asking him to forgive us, as he bled to death on the cross. One sinless man interceded and made a difference for the rest of us. After Jesus had died, God heard the voice of Jesus from deep within the ground (like he did with Abel), but this time he was able to do something about it. The innocent blood of Jesus that was shed on the cross spoke of better things than that of Abel (Hebrews 12:24).

Cain and Jesus were both first's that opened the womb of their mothers. But Jesus was born through the womb of a virgin, while Cain was not. No man touched Mary until after Jesus was born. I may be mistaken, but I believe there was a part of Jesus that could not be permanently cursed because it involved God himself. God's word, his prophetic spoken word, his plan was alive in his Son, Jesus. Cain and Abel had ties to the ground through their mother and father. Jesus had ties to the ground through his mother, but he also had ties to God in heaven.

Cain and Abel both needed help! Cain brought the curse of death on his brother prematurely. Abel should not have been cursed to die at the hands of another. Cain became cursed because he played God when he took his brother's life. It wasn't his place or right to do it! I don't think God was happy with how things turned out for either one of them. Here are two good questions to think about. Was Jesus the final substitute that took care of the curse for both types of circumstances like with Cain and Abel? Could they both be saved through the sacrifice of Jesus Christ and living with him even now?

In the story of Abraham and his two sons, Isaac and Jacob, some interesting things happened regarding firstborn sons and firstborn rights. On the next page, I have listed their wives and their children that pertain to the family line of the 12 tribes of Israel, which led to the birth of Jesus.

Abraham

<u>Hagar</u>	<u>Sarah</u>	<u>Keturah</u>
Ishmael	Isaac	Zimran
		Jokshan
		Medan
		Midian
		Ishbak
	↓	Shuah

Isaac

<u>Rebekah</u>
Esau
Jacob

↓

Jacob

<u>Bilhah</u>	<u>Leah</u>	<u>Zilpah</u>	<u>Rachel</u>	
Dan	Reuben	Gad	Joseph ——→	Joseph
Naphtali	Simeon	Asher	Benjamin	<u>Asenath</u>
	Levi			Manasseh
	Judah			Ephraim
	Issachar			
	Zebulun			
	Dinah			

In the story of Abraham, God had told him that he would have a son even though he and his wife Sarah were already past the age of childbearing (Genesis 15:2-5, Genesis 16:1-2 and Genesis 18:10-14). We have already explored this story before, but I want to explore it again through another angle. When God told Abraham that he would have a son, it didn't come to pass right away. Sarah wanted a child so bad, that she tried to make it come to pass in another way. She gave Hagar her concubine to Abraham to conceive a son through her. Hagar gave birth to her first child and named him Ishmael. Ishmael was the son of Abraham, but not the son of Sarah.

God kept his promise to Abraham and Sarah, and she had her firstborn son and named him Isaac. Isaac was born about fourteen years after Ishmael. So actually, Ishmael and Isaac both were the first to open the womb of their own mothers. But what mattered the most in the promise from God was the seed who came out from the womb of Sarah. She was the one that God had chosen.

When Isaac grew into a young boy, God told Abraham to take him to a certain mountain region and to "sacrifice him there as a burnt offering" (Genesis 22:1-18). When Abraham took his son and laid him upon the altar, the angel of the Lord stopped him immediately and told him not to harm his son (Genesis 22:12). Abraham then looked up and turned around to find a ram tangled up by the horns in a cluster of bushes. He offered the ram as a substitute burnt offering instead. In this moment, God was revealing something about the sacrifice. It meant that Abraham could offer his son for God's purpose, just by offering a token. In this case, the token represented the offering of his son for God's own purpose.

God needed Isaac alive as a living sacrifice in order to bring about a descendant who would save all nations. Abraham proved to God that he was not withholding his son in their agreement. From that moment, God considered the deal a blood covenant and officially adopted Isaac as his own.

God wanted Abraham's approval to use his son, so that he could begin the process leading up to the birth of Jesus. Through his bloodline in the distant future, Jesus would be born as Abraham's son, as well as God's Son.

Going forward in time, Isaac had twin sons. Isaac's first son that was born of twins was Esau and the second was Jacob. Jacob became a father of what is known as the twelve tribes of Israel.

By tradition, Esau as the firstborn son had a birthright to be blessed with a double portion of the inheritance of their father, when their father was to pass away. When the two boys grew up, the birthright was switch from Esau to Jacob, even though Esau was born first.

What happened in the story, was that Esau traded his birthright to his brother for a hot meal when he was very hungry. The story tells us that there was a day when Esau returned from an exhausting trip. He approached his brother Jacob who had just made a pot of stew and asked if he could have some. Jacob took advantage of the opportunity to get Esau to give him his birthright inheritance. Jacob knew it was the best position of inheritance, and he really wanted it. It meant that he would become the overseer for all the others in the family after their father dies, as well as the double portion of paternal inheritance (Deuteronomy 21:15-17). He told Esau that he would make a trade by giving him some of his food for the birthright position (Genesis 25:24-34). So, Esau sold his birthright for a meal consisting of bread and lentil stew.

This agreement between the two brothers was binding in the sight of God. Even though Jacob was born as the second twin, he became the owner and heir of the birthright as the firstborn son of their father, Isaac.

The right of the firstborn was not set in stone, and it could be passed on to another as it was with the two brothers. Even though Jacob received the birthright promise from Esau, the transfer did not actually happen until their father Isaac had passed on (Genesis 27:1-41). Jacob's descendances were called the Israelites and Jesus came through them.

When Isaac was mostly blind from age and his time to die was drawing near, he decided to tell Esau what his inheritance was as the firstborn. Isaac must not have known about the switch between his sons because he called for Esau first. He asked him to go out and kill a deer, make it into a stew, and then bring it to him to eat. He also told Esau that when he got back with the meal, he would tell him what his blessing would be.

Rebekah, the mother of both men, heard the conversation between Esau and his father. She knew about the deal that both brothers had made with each other about the birthright. She knew that Esau had already given it to his brother Jacob. While Esau had been standing in front of his father, he failed to tell him that the birthright was no longer his.

So, after Esau left his father to go hunting, Rebekah set Jacob up to claim the birthright before Esau could get back. She sent Jacob in to see his father and to pretend to be his older brother. Isaac who could not see clearly had a feeling that something wasn't quite right. But Jacob convinced his father that he was Esau, and that he had returned early. Isaac went ahead and blessed Jacob with the right and inheritance of the firstborn. When Esau came in later to receive from his father, he had to take the rights as the second born, because it had already been given to Jacob.

So, from this story, the right of the firstborn can be given to another, which leads to a second reason Jacob received the birthright. God has his own purpose for any child that is still in the womb, even before they are born. He even had a purpose for Jesus long before he was created in the womb of Mary. Before Esau and Jacob were born, God had said that it would happen. He, himself had told Rebekah earlier (while she was still pregnant with them as twins) that "the elder would end up serving the younger" (Genesis 25:22-23).

Jacob who owned the birthright was renamed "Israel" by God. He became the father of twelve sons known as the twelve tribes of Israel. He and his family became well-known as the Israelites. So far, Jacob now known as Israel had received the birthright of the firstborn even though he was not the actual first born. He and his family became the leading figures in the bible and are talked about all over the world even today.

Israel (Jacob) had his children through his two wives, Leah and Rachel, as well as their two maidservants (Genesis 35:23-26). Israel's actual firstborn son was named Reuben, who was born through Leah, his first wife. She had four sons before Rachel had her first son, Joseph.

When Israel was old, it was time for him to talk to all his sons regarding their inheritance. The birthright position became complicated. Some of his sons had gotten into deep trouble with him, so he shifted the firstborn right to the brother's that he felt deserved it. Reuben as the firstborn son should have received the birthright, but he committed adultery with his own father's concubine (Genesis 35:22). The next two sons of Leah were Simeon and Levi. They had taken revenge on a whole city after the prince of that city had defiled their sister, Dinah. They killed all the men and took their possessions. Neither one of them, deserved the right either, for what they had done. (But years later, the tribe of Levi proved to be very important to God in the office of the priesthood because of something that they did in God's honor.) The next in line of Leah's four sons was Judah.

Judah received a good blessing. From what I understand, Israel knew by a revelation from God that there was something special about him. I don't totally understand the blessing pronounced over him, when his father had said "the scepter will not depart from Judah until Shiloh comes." A scepter has to do with royalty and rule. And I believe Shiloh was referring to Jesus Christ. I do know that King David and Jesus both came out of the tribe of Judah, the fourth son of Leah.

As Israel prophesied to each of his sons, he declared the best blessing over Joseph, Rachael's son (Genesis 49:22-26). He said the blessings of God shall "rest on the head of Joseph, on the brow of the prince among his brothers."

If you remember, Joseph was the one who ended up being sold into slavery by his elder brothers, when he was about seventeen years old. He became second in command in Egypt and saved the people from starvation.

Before Israel had actually spoken to all the brothers together regarding their inheritance, he had first requested to talk to Joseph without the others present (Genesis 48:2-5, 8-16, 17-20, 21-22). At the time, Joseph was still living in Egypt and had his own family. When he went to see his father, he brought his own two sons with him. It was the first time that Israel had got to meet his two little grandsons. He told Joseph that he was going to give him one portion above all the other brothers and this double portion included these two little grandsons, Manasseh and Ephraim. None of the other brother's children were given this privilege of the inheritance like Joseph's two sons. Manasseh and Ephraim were to take part in the division of the inheritance between all the sons of Israel.

Here is a quick interesting fact about Joseph's two sons that he conceived while he lived in Egypt. They were born from his Egyptian wife named Asenath, who had been given to him as a gift from the Pharaoh. So first of all, his sons were half Egyptian. Second of all, his wife was the daughter of Potiphera, who happened to be a priest for the gods of Egypt (Genesis 41:44-45). But because the two sons belonged to Joseph, they were accepted by God and Israel himself, even though they were part Egyptian. They became known as the half-tribes of Israel.

1 Chronicles 5:1-2 gives a quick explanation of what transpired between Reuben, Joseph and Judah regarding the birthright of the firstborn. 1 Chronicles 5:1-2 says that the birthright of Israel's very first son Reuben (born from Leah) was given unto the sons of Joseph (Racheal's first born). Verse 2 says Judah (Leah's 4th son) prevailed above his brethren, and of him came the chief rulers; but the birthright of Reuben was Joseph's.

God's Firstborn

After Israel and his sons had all passed away, the next generation of Israelites were still living in Egyptian territory (Exodus 1:6-22). The story about them becoming slaves under the rule of a new Pharaoh has already been explored in a previous lesson.

The new Pharaoh was a tyrant to the Israelites. At one point, he even ordered their newborn sons to be cast into the river to drown, all because of his fear of being overtaken by so many of them, when they were to grow up. The Israelites were kept in bondage for 430 years.

Things got so bad for them that they cried out to God for deliverance. God heard their prayers and ended up having to put ten plagues on the Egyptians before the Pharoah finally let them leave Egypt.

If you can remember the last plague, God had sent a death angel to take the life of all the Egyptian's firstborn sons and firstborn male animals, when the Pharaoh would not let the people go. I believe that the murder of all the Israelite's own newborn sons angered God deeply, and his anger was expressed in his message to the Pharaoh.

God identified all the Israelites as "his firstborn son." He said, **"Israel is my son, even my firstborn......Let my son go" (Exodus 4:22-23).**

God was referring to all of Israel's (Jacob's) descendants. They were the evidence and existence of Israel himself. At this point in time, when God had given Moses this message to tell the Pharaoh, Israel himself had already passed on. Remember that Israel had been given the right as the firstborn son instead of his older brother Isaac, over a pot of stew. And, according to the covenant that God had made with Abraham (Israel's grandfather), his own Firstborn Son Jesus was to come from these descendants.

In the rest of Exodus 4:22-23 when God had said, "Israel is MY son, even MY firstborn ...", he gave the Pharoah an ultimatum. He said, "LET MY SON GO that he (his family) may serve me: and if thou refuse to let him go, I will slay your son, even your firstborn."

When the Pharaoh would not let them go, even after God sent multiple plagues, God began to execute his plan regarding all the firstborn males of both man and animal. But before he could, there had to be a distinction between the two groups. God had to set apart the firstborn of the Israelites from those of the Egyptians, so that the plague of death would not touch them.

It wasn't the Egyptian son's fault that they had to die, they paid the price for the Pharaoh's sin. It wasn't God's own Son's fault that he had to die, but he paid the price for our sin.

Just before God's death angel (or it could have been God himself) was to pass through Egypt, each household of the Israelites were to kill an unblemished, firstborn, first year male lamb. It was then made ready through the sacrifice, and its blood applied on the doorpost of their homes. The blood acted as a shield of protection that the death angel could see. He knew not to touch those redeemed by the blood of the lamb.

Besides applying the blood on the doorpost, the Israelites were also told to roast the sacrifice itself by fire, and then eat it along with unleavened bread. They had to eat the lamb and be prepared to hightail it out of there in a hurry when they were told to (Exodus 12:3-13, 27,39). A whole household or two could share in eating one sacrificed lamb to cover them all.

This event would become known as the Passover celebration that was and still is carried out all throughout the years. It commemorates the death angel passing over them without killing their own sons.

I believe that there were others that lived among the Israelites that took part in the Passover meal and were also saved from the curse. Some of the Israelites had intermingles with Egyptians by marriage. Remember that Joseph's two sons were half Egyptian. God accepted others outside of the original Israelites. The one big thing that the males had to do in order to be part of the Israelites, was to accept their Abrahamic covenant and be circumcised (Genesis 17:10-11). God had said that all these others should be loved and treated as if they were born an Israelite (Leviticus 19:34).

After the Israelites were allowed to leave Egypt, God told them to sanctify and set apart all their firstborn males. This meant all males that opened the womb of both the Israelites and their animals. God had kept them safe during the last plague that killed the firstborn sons of the Egyptians. and claimed them as his own, for he said, "they are mine" (Exodus 2:13). He had a purpose for them in the starting up of the wilderness church and serving his people.

There is a whole list of animals that God accepted as clean and unclean in Deuteronomy 14:3-21 and Leviticus 11. The Israelites were told not to eat some of these animals or even touch them after they had died. To God, they were considered impure or unclean. These two chapters also list the animals that God considered as already clean and could be eaten. Some of these clean animals were also acceptable and presented as sacrificial offerings before God. For example, the people were told to redeem every firstborn donkey with the sacrifice of a lamb, if they wanted to keep it (Exodus 13:13). The donkey was considered unclean while a lamb was considered clean. They had to sacrifice the life of a lamb as payment for the life of the donkey. God said that if they did not redeem the unclean animal by offering a clean animal as a sacrifice (or substitute), then it was to be put to death itself. I don't totally understand how this law worked back then, but it makes me think that we are all considered unclean before God without the sacrifice, where Christ died in our stead. Only the clean can redeem the unclean.

Once the people had been delivered from Egypt and was traveling through the wilderness, Aaron the eldest brother of Moses (who had been the spokesperson during the negotiations with their enemy the Pharaoh) became the high priest. Moses and his brother were part of the Levi tribe. God assigned Aaron the highest duties between himself and the people. He was the chief religious official, and the only one who could go into the holiest part of the sanctuary on the day of atonement to offer a sacrifice. This day was once a year, and it was to atone for the sins of all the people. The firstborn sons of the Israelites were given a special assignment as helpers for Aaron and his sons who were also priests.

The firstborn sons became the liaison between the priests and the people, and the keeping of the temple, as their part in God's service. There were laws given to maintain a healthy and well-structured body of people under God's protection. There were special rules regarding the firstborns who were spared on the night of their deliverance from Egypt. It was their responsibility to do a variety of services for the wilderness church and for the priests. Later on, the duties of all Israelite firstborn's changed to the tribe of the Levites themselves.

2ND HISTORY OF THE FIRSTBORN RIGHT

Part 2

LESSON 52

All the Israelites had been physically redeemed from slavery and from the curse of the plague. Their bodies are what was protected and set free. Their thoughts regarding their bondage became the only thing that haunted them after their escape. It stopped them from accomplishing God's dream for them. Most of these adults did not continue to go forward into the promised land because of their mental and emotional bondage, but their children did.

The Jewish holiday that is called the Passover was born out of the story of their deliverance from the Egyptian bondage (Exodus 13:1-16). It has been celebrated every year. It is remarkable to note that the Firstborn Son of God gave his life for the good of all, during one of these Passover seasons of celebration.

There were lots of activities that happened around the death and resurrection of Jesus. According to different verses, he hung on the cross to die on a day of preparation for the Passover meal. The Passover animal was to be put to death as the people began their holiday festivities. And, on this day they were to also put out all leavened bread from among them. Luke referred to this day as the day of "unleavened bread", as well as "Passover" (Luke 22:7-8).

The whole celebration was to start on their 14th day of their 1st month according to sources in the Old Testament (Exodus 12:1-20). When I tried to figure out the timing of all the different requirements for the killing of the lamb; Passover meal(s); week-long feast which included eating unleavened bread; the two high sabbath days called "holy convocation" at the beginning and the end of the week-long feast; as well as the day of the "firstfruits", things got a little complicated (Exodus 12, Leviticus 23:3-8, Deuteronomy 16:3, Numbers 9:4-5, 28:16-14).

So, I made a chart that could be very helpful in looking at what happened and the timeline. I also go into more detail about the whole event that started in the Old Testament. There is a lot to absorb, in regards to understanding how it all plays out.

CHART

The first few rows of the calendar chart show the relationship of our days to their days.

Yearly Celebration of Passover

Midnight to midnight vs sunset to sunset

Tuesday		Wednesday		Thursday		Friday		Saturday		Sunday
13th day (us)		14th day (us)		15th day (us)		16th day (us)		17th day (us)		18th day (us)
Day 13th	Night 14th	Day 14th	Night 15th	Day 15th	Night 16th	Day 16th	Night 17th	Day 17th	Night 18th	Day 18th
	Preparation of the lamb and the Passover feast. Jesus was sentenced and crucified before sunset that ends their 14th.	The week-long feast of unleavened bread. It is also the 1st of the two high Sabbath days (The 2nd one is on the 21st day).		The week-long feast of unleavened bread continues.		The week-long feast continues. It is also their regular weekly Sabbath day of rest, and it starts at sunset of their 17th day.		The week-long feast continues and their "1st day of the week" begins. It is also the feast of firstfruits day. Jesus was resurrected sometime before Sunday morning dawn.		
3 nights and 3 days in the heart of the earth ->		1st night	1st day	2nd night	2nd day	3rd night	3rd day	Resurrection		

Israel is ahead of us on the calendar and their new day starts at sunset of each full day, unlike ours that starts at midnight.

Jesus died on the day of preparation of the Passover which was the 14th day of their 1st month **before sunset ended.** (Matthew 27:62, Luke 23:54, John 19:14, 31, 42).

The day after Passover is not just a regular weekly sabbath. It is a high sabbath day (John 19:31).

Jesus said he would be three nights and three days in the heart of the earth (Matthew 12:40).

Women went to the tomb on the 1st day of the week before dawn and Jesus had already risen from the dead (Mark 16:1-2, Matthew 28:1-7, Luke 24:1-3, John 20:1).

Their 1st day of a new week that comes after Passover (14th) is celebrated as the "feast of firstfruits" (Lev 23:1-14). Jesus is the "first-fruit" from the dead (1 Corinthians 15:20).

All the different activities are so important in understanding who Jesus is, and why God required these times of remembrance each year. They all pointed to his first Son, who was the Passover lamb that was slain for our sin (John 1:21, 1 Corinthians 5:7, 1 Peter 1:19).

The 12th chapter of Exodus is a pretty good reference for the timing of everything they observed. It gives the instructions that the Israelites were to follow regarding their release from Egyptian bondage. It all started days before their actual release from Egypt.

On the 10th day of their 1st month, they were to pick a firstborn, first year, male lamb without blemish and keep it until the 14th day of their first month, when it was to be sacrificed. (It was called the Passover lamb.) They were to apply its blood on the doorpost, roast the lamb with fire, and then eat the flesh of it in that evening along with unleavened bread and bitter herbs. They were to leave nothing left over in the next morning, and to be ready to leave in a hurry. While they ate the Passover meal in the nighttime, the Egyptian firstborns all died at midnight.

God said "this day shall be a memorial" for their future (Exodus 12:14). They were to celebrate it with a feast throughout their generations on the very same day each year which was the 14th day of their 1st month.

They celebrated the Passover with a yearly seven-day feast called the feast of unleavened bread. They were to eat the unleavened bread for seven days. And, on the 1st day and the 7th day of the feast they were to do no work except for what they must do in order to eat. These two days (1st and 7th) were referred to as "holy convocation" days. They were the yearly, special "high sabbath" days in the celebration. These holy days could fall on any day of the week, depending on the day that the Passover celebration began.

Jesus died on their Passover day (the 14th day of their 1st month), the day just before a special or "high" sabbath day of rest and feasting (Luke 23:52-56, and John 19:14, 31).

An important piece of information that should be noted is how different the Jewish calendar days are laid out than ours. Israel is several hours ahead of us. Their calendar day starts at the setting of the sun and goes through to the next setting of the sun (Genesis 1:5). In other words, their 24-hour day starts at nightfall and goes till the next nightfall, unlike our calendar day which starts in the middle of the night or midnight. Their 14th day (Passover) ended at sunset and their 15th day began at sunset. They could have their day of preparation for the Passover end at sunset, as they began their day of holy convocation and feasting with the unleavened bread.

Some of the verses say that the feast of unleavened bread started on the same day that they killed the Passover (Mark 14:12 and Matthew 26:17), and other places in the bible say the week-long feast of unleavened bread started on the 15th day and went until the 21st (Leviticus 23:4-21) and Numbers 28: 16-17). Their 14th calendar day and their 15th calendar day are back-to-back in our same day, according to the different timelines around the world (see chart for explanation).

In summary and from what I understand, there was at least eight calendar days of celebration starting on the 14th day of their 1st month (Passover), and Jesus was crucified shortly before sunset on their same day that the lambs were sacrificed and prepared for the Passover feast.

What does it all mean?

I was trying to figure out why we celebrate good Friday and Sunday as the two days that Jesus died and then rose again "on the third day". Jesus compared his own death and resurrection to the story of "Jonah and the whale." Jonah was swallowed into the belly of a great whale and then spewed out three days later (Matthew 12:40). Jesus said that he, himself was to be "three days and three nights in the heart of the earth" So, if Jesus was crucified on a Friday, how could he have been three days and three nights in the heart of the earth but be raised again somewhere before the dawning of Sunday morning. It does not add up!

We have to put together different pieces of scripture to find out the probable days of the week that he really died and rose again. We can count backwards in the calendar to figure out the day of his death and the day of his resurrection.

First of all, Luke 23:56 and 24:1, Mark 16:2, John 20:1 and Matthew 28:1 all agrees that Mary Magdalene, the 'other Mary' and a few other women prepared spices and ointments to anoint the dead body of Jesus. But they first had to wait and rest on the sabbath day according to the commandment. Their weekly sabbath day ended on the last day of the week, or Saturday at sunset. The scriptures all also agreed that the women went early the <u>next morning</u> after the sabbath day to the tomb. (They all may not have gone to the tomb together since some of the stories vary just a little.) But the scriptures point out that it was their <u>1st day of the week</u> (or Sunday morning) when they went to visit and found the empty tomb (John 20:1).

Jesus showed himself alive on this particular Sunday. Matthew 28:1-9 talks about an earthquake, the angel of the Lord, and then Jesus himself speaking to some of the women.

We can roughly determine the day that Jesus died by backtracking from their 1st day of the week, early morning (Sunday). This was the time that the women came to the empty tomb. There is a lot of estimated guesses of when Jesus died. To, me with all the clues in the bible, Wednesday seems to be the best fit.

Jesus rose to new life on a special first day of the week, which was the day that they celebrated their <u>first fruits of the harvest</u>. "firstfruits" is described in more detail in the book of Leviticus (Leviticus 23:10-11, 12-15).

During this time, the people were instructed to bring a small bundle (or sample, or tenth) of their first fruits from their harvest of barley, and a perfect firstborn young lamb for a burnt offering to the Lord. The priest would present the first fruits from the harvest by waving them before God. God would accept it as a thanksgiving offering for their great harvest. Only then could the bringer of the offering enjoy the rest of their harvest for themselves. The people celebrated the things that God caused to spring up out of the ground into new life. If it sounds familiar, it is! It is also found in Malachi 3:10-12.

<u>Jesus became the first human to be born from the dead on the day of the firstfruits</u>. **1 Corinthians 15:20 says, but now is Christ risen from the dead, and <u>became the firstfruits</u> of them that slept.**

We all die in Adam, but in Christ we shall all be made alive (1 Corinthians 15:20-23). Jesus was the first born from the dead. He ascended into heaven to present himself to the Father and was accepted. So now, all his harvest of fruit (or souls) is accepted (Matthew 9:37-38, 13:30, 37-39). **In John 12:24 Jesus had said, "Except a corn of wheat fall into the ground and die, it abides alone: but if it dies, it brings forth much fruit."**

The Israelites were referred to as God's "firstborn" in the story of Egypt (Exodus 4:22). They were literally delivered out from death. And "SO WAS JESUS, even more so!" He was raised from death itself. The body and the blood of the firstborn lamb redeemed the Israelites in just that one night. But all the earthly lambs in the world could not permanently set mankind free from the curse. God was showing his people that they needed a redeemer, and that it was possible to be redeemed through a substitute. He was slowly revealing his own Son. We can see that God had planned ahead and prepared the way for his Firstborn, who was to be the first born out from the womb of an Israelite women.

Jesus was the one to take the place of all the lambs that had to die as a sacrifice. He would permanently redeem and offer all nations permanent Sonship if he is celebrated and accepted.

CHOSEN

———⌑———

LESSON 53

An earthly father could have had more than one firstborn son depending on the circumstances. Abraham had two firstborns, one through Sarah his wife and the other through Hagar her concubine (Genesis 16:1-16). Isaac, who was the firstborn son of Sarah was chosen by God to provide the bloodline link that would eventually lead to Jesus, even though he was not the very first born to Abraham. It didn't matter that Abraham and Sarah diverted from God's original plan and made it happen themselves through another woman's womb first. What mattered was that God had already said that Sarah was his chosen vessel to bring about Jesus. Sarah had a part in his plan!

By tradition, if a son was the very first son born of a father, he was eligible for the birthright inheritance. He could receive the double portion of inheritance and be the leader in his father's place (like Jesus is with his Father). We found out that sometimes there were extenuating circumstances that changed the right of the firstborn son to another throughout the Old Testament.

Jesus was the very first Son of God and he was the first to open the womb of Mary (an Israelite woman) chosen by God. He qualified in both cases because he was God's firstborn and Mary's firstborn.

The mothers that led to the birth of Christ seem to be chosen on purpose by God. He was making sure that his word, his prophecy about his seed that would defeat the devil was going to come to pass. I believe that there was something special he saw in each woman that he picked. His own Son was to come through the womb of a particular woman of his choice.

Sarah was the woman chosen to continue the bloodline by God, even before Abraham had any sons. (Abraham did eventually have six more sons through his next wife Keturah, after Sarah had passed away.)

All throughout the Old Testament, there was quite a bit of focus on firstborns and firstborn rights. Abraham's son Isaac and Isaac's son Jacob (now called Israel) were both considered firstborns to God, even though they were not born first of their own fathers. God called Israel his firstborn son. So, if you think about the things that happened between some of the sons like Isaac and his older brother Ishmael (who was born first, Genesis 16:1-16), and Jacob or Israel and his older brother Esau (who was born first, Genesis 25:21-34), the firstborn rule seemed to have a connection through the women of God's choice too (Genesis 25:23).

Let's quickly review some of the women's involvement with the birth of Jesus from in the beginning when the prophecy began.

Adam's wife, Eve – She was naïvely tricked by the Serpent. From her womb came her first two sons, Cain and Abel. This is where Satan began his mission to stop and destroy her seed that would crush his head. He caused them both to be disqualified in his attempt in stopping God's plan. Neither one of them were eligible because one was killed by the other. Eve's third son, Seth became the line that Jesus would eventually come through.

Abraham's wife, Sarah – God had told Abraham that he would have a child through <u>her</u> even though they were already old. Sarah thought that God had restrained her from having the child and that maybe she could obtain it through her maidservant, Hagar (Genesis 16:2). She had wanted a child so much that she had her husband sleep with her maidservant to get it. But Hagar was not God's choice. The child was not to come from her womb. God had said that the child was to come through Sarah's womb (Genesis 17:15-19, 18:10-14). So, the child was not dependent on Abraham's actual firstborn son through Hagar. But Sarah's firstborn son, Isaac was a seed that led up to Jesus. She was God's choice!

Isaac's wife, Rebekah – When Isaac had grown up, Abraham had sent his servant to go to the land of his kindred to choose a wife for Isaac (Genesis 24: 7, 12-15). When the servant got there, he asked God to help him find the perfect wife. Rebekah was the first woman to come out to where the servant had been praying. God picked her as the one to marry Isaac, and for his seed to come through. When she gave birth to twins, the firstborn son (Esau) sold his birthright to his brother (Jacob) for the meal. God had already told her when she was pregnant that this was to happen. Jacob became God's firstborn by the transfer of the birthright when Esau gave it to him. Jacob's seed led to the birth of Jesus in the future.

Israel's (or Jacob's) first wife, Leah – Even though Jacob fell in love with Rachael, he was tricked into marrying Leah (her older sister) first, before he could marry Rachael. Leah was the chosen one of God in this case. She was not loved by Jacob as well as Rachael and tried to get her husband to love her more by giving him children. I believe she felt unloved, and God acknowledge it.

Her first three sons sinned against their own father, so the lineage of Jesus Christ came forth from her fourth son, Judah. Jesus was from the tribe of Judah. Even though the first three sons were disqualified, God still chose the womb of Leah.

Judah's second wife, Tamar - Judah first married a Canaanite woman who died after she had three sons. Tamar was a young woman who was originally given to Judah's first son named Er, as a wife. Er was very wicked, so God killed him! Then Judah gave Tamar (his daughter-in-law) to the next son named Onan according to their tradition. Onan would not make any children through her because (by tradition) her child would be claimed as his dead brother's child, not his own. God was very displeased with his decision and he died too (Genesis 38:6-26)! When Judah's third son Shelah had grown up, (by tradition) Judah should have given Tamar to him, but he didn't.

Here is the unusual twist to the story of what happened next between Judah and his daughter-in-law. By tradition, she should have been passed down to his only son left. Judah would not give her to him because he was afraid that he would also die. He must have thought that the death of his other two sons were because of her. He must have thought of her as a jinx. To make a long story short, Tamar became pregnant with twin boys from Judah, himself. He ended up taking her as his own second wife to make things right with her.

The birth of their twins was an amazing story in itself (Genesis 38:27-30). When she was in labor, one of her sons poked out his hand long enough for the midwife to put a scarlet thread around his finger. The thread was to identify him as the firstborn. But then he retreated back into her womb and the other child came out first. The son who came all the way out first was Tamar's firstborn. He was named Perez and he became a part of the line leading to Jesus. Tamar was the one chosen by God.

So far, the seed to come was not always dependent on the actual first son born of the Israelite father, like with the case of Abraham and Sarah's concubine. Some of the firstborn sons failed, and their birthright ended up into the hands of a brother. However, if you noticed, God had a hand in changing up things in each woman's life to eventually bring about his Son. The women's sons were either her firstborn or given the title of firstborn because of the eldest brother's disqualification. So, from Abraham's bloodline leading up to the tribe of Judah, there was a significant pattern that involved particular women. In the case of Mary, there wasn't any earthly man involved in the conception of Jesus. Mary was God's final choice to put his own son!

So, I was wondering, was God hiding his seed that was to eventually be born? The devil may have been focused on the sons themselves, especially the firstborn in trying to track the DNA trail of Jesus to come, so he could destroy him. It seemed like he consistently went after the firstborns to ruin their credibility with God or get them destroyed. I could be wrong, but I believe God switched things up so much that it became impossible for the devil to trace him. Even when Jesus was finally born, King Herod ordered all the children under two years old to be killed that were in Bethlehem. But an angel warned Joseph in a dream, so he and Mary fled with the baby Jesus and hid in Egypt until the king had died.

You may want to brace yourself for my conclusion of this lesson.

The history in the Old Testament shows us very important concepts regarding the firstborn's birthrights here on earth. First, I hope we agree that the Father of Jesus was in and with the body of Jesus here on earth. **Jesus said so himself, when he said, "I and my Father are one (John 10:30-37-38). And, he said "the Father dwelleth in me" (John 14:10).** I hope that you also agree that Jesus as the firstborn Son of God, who was born here on earth, should be the rightful heir to whatever belonged to his Father.

The children of the earthly father in the Old Testament received their actual inheritance when the father died. **When the father died, it meant that the father was no longer here in bodily presence.** The spirit and soul of the person does not cease to exist when the body dies! To die, is to leave the body! Here is my big question that I want you to think about! Since the body of Jesus contained the Father and the Son, did the Father of Jesus die on the cross, when Jesus died? **Well, of course my answer is a big "NO" because he is an eternal Spirit.** Did he leave the body when the body died? My answer is yes! There was no life left in the body of Jesus. If this was true, everything should have been turned over to Jesus as his Firstborn son (under the firstborn rights), when his Father left the body. He was the only true Son of God. But, of course, Jesus left the body too. Oh wait, he was then restored back into his original body! So, does whatever the Father own here on earth now belong to his Firstborn Son?

Jesus said, "All power is given unto me in heaven and in earth" (Matthew 28:18). God's firstborn earthly son received his birthright blessing. All throughout the bible, until God's own Son was finally born as one of us, he had been preparing the legality of his Son's eternal birthright. He made it legal here on earth!

In the story of Egyptian bondage, when God had spoken to the Pharaoh, he spoke as if Israel himself was still alive, here on earth and in his earthly body. Why did God call the Israelites by their own father's name when he said, "Israel is my son, even my firstborn …Let my Son go that he may serve me?" We already established that God claimed Israel has his own firstborn. And, the truth is, Israel is alive and in the presence of the Lord Jesus in heaven! If God can refer to the Israelites by the name of Israel himself, then he can refer to the Christians by the name of Jesus himself too. He could have just as easily said, "Jesus is my Son, even my firstborn …Let my Son go that he may serve me." God is still demanding this to the enemy of our soul for us because we are born again under the name that belong to his firstborn Son.

God claims those associated with his firstborn Son as his firstborn. And, just like the strangers and half-breeds that were accepted as an Israelite, we are grafted into the spiritual body of Christ. The Father knows us through his own Son's Holy Spirit living within us. **Jesus said, "I am in my Father, and you in me, and I in you" (John 14:20). As Jesus is, so are we in this world (1 John 4:13, 15, 17).** He joined us as one under the name of Jesus making God our Father. We are chosen by God to be his children.

"Jesus is my Son, even my Firstborn …Let my Son go!"

I wonder if the Father said something similar, when Jesus descended into the lower parts of the earth. Did he say something like this to Satan regarding those who were waiting for their redemption?

IF MY PEOPLE

LESSON 54

God made a promise that is still true today. **In 2 Chronicles 7:14 (KJV) God said, "If my people, which are called by my name, shall humble themselves, and pray, and seek my face, and turn from their wicked ways; then will I hear from heaven, and will forgive their sins, and will heal their land."**

This was something that God had said in the Old Testament. There is a story behind his statement that I would like to explore.

Exodus chapter thirty-two says that while Moses was on Mt. Sinai with God for forty days receiving the ten commandments, the people began to wonder what happened to him. Some of them freaked out and reacted foolishly. They thought their leader either abandoned them or something terrible must have happened to him.

They started to remember back to what they had witnessed regarding their captivity days. They had observed the Egyptians practicing their ungodly religion of idol worship. They had remembered that the Egyptians gave credit and allegiance to their false gods for everything happening in their own lives. The Israelites had been exposed to these practices. It had become common place under their circumstances, while they had been slave workers in Egypt.

They told Aaron (the brother of Moses and high priest) that they wanted him to make a molten calf, so that they could worship it and claim it as their own god similar to what the Egyptians had done. They had forgotten that these false gods did nothing to protect and save them from their bondage. They also did not take into account that these false gods gave the Egyptians no protection from the plague of death or from being destroyed in the Red Sea. Aaron made the molten calf from their golden earrings, and he created an altar for them to sacrifice their burnt offerings (Exodus 32:1-23). They began to celebrate the golden calf with food, dancing, and worship.

When God saw what they were doing, he became angry and wanted to destroy them. Moses had to intercede to change his mind. Then when Moses came down from the mountain and saw for himself what they were doing, he was so angry that he threw the tablets of the law written by God down and broke them.

Moses stood before all the people and asked for those who were on the Lords' side to come forward to him. All the sons of the tribe of Levi came forward. Moses directed them to kill all the others directly involved in the treason, so the Levites obeyed (Exodus 32:26).

Form this event, God had said that he was taking the Levites instead of all the firstborn males of each tribe for his own purpose. **God said in Numbers 3:12-13, "...the Levites shall be mine...".** God reminded Moses that all the firstborn males had already been redeemed as his, from the time they had been delivered from Egypt and that the tradition of the Passover was still to be carried out every year.

Aaron and his sons (who were of the tribe of Levite) were put in the highest position as priests while the other Levites performed their own assigned duties to help in the traveling wilderness church.

There had to be times and places set up to perform all the different activities. There were daily, weekly, and yearly rituals and sacrifices performed for many different reasons.

While traveling through the wilderness, the people of God had to live in portable tents that they could just pack up and go when they needed to continue their journey. God established the Levite priesthood and a portable housing as his dwelling place too, among the people. It was called the Tent of Congregation. The Israelites were all asked to bring materials that could be used to build the different things needed in and for God's own temple. The response from the people was more than enough to put together a dedicated temple for their God.

+++++++

In the far-off distant future, King Solomon who was the son of King David constructed the first stationary building in ancient Jerusalem called the Holy Temple. When it was completed, he then prayed and dedicated it to God. He asked God to hear all prayers made toward the temple (2 Chronicles 6:1-40).

In the next chapter, it says that as soon as he concluded with the prayer, fire came down from heaven and consumed the burnt offering and sacrifices. It says the glory of the Lord filled the temple. All the people saw the fire that came down from heaven and bowed down to the ground in reverence and gave God worship (2 Chronicles 7:1-3).

They began to rejoice with song and music and feasting for many days. The Levites supplied the instruments for music and lead the people in worship and devotion and the priests sounded the trumpets. When all the things were done in the dedication of the temple, the people were sent back home to their own tents "glad and merry in their hearts" (2 Chronicles 7:10-11).

The Lord appeared to King Solomon and said that he had heard his prayer. He accepted the temple as his dwelling place and as a house of sacrifice. He also said a very famous quote known among those who lived through great times of revival and healing. God makes a promise for those who seek his face.

2 Chronicles 7:14 (KJV), "If my people, which are called by my name, shall humble themselves, and pray, and seek my face, and turn from their wicked ways; then will I hear from heaven, and will forgive their sins, and will <u>heal their land</u>."

In 2 Chronicles 7:15-16, God also said that his eyes and his ears would be open to prayers made in his temple. He has chosen and sanctified his dwelling place and that his name, his eyes, and his heart shall be there continuously.

Jesus was and is God's temple, his dwelling place. Jesus resides in us and that makes us God's temple. God hears all prayers directed through his Son. Your prayers do not have to go through any of the Israelite sons, Levites or any earthly priest. He hears all prayers from those who turn back to him, those in captivity and even the strangers. The church is the body of Christ in the world! The church has a job to do if it wants to see loved ones come to Christ. It has a job to do if it wants to transform the world. We have to start with ourselves and meet God's condition of seeking his face. If we do, he promises to heal the land.

THE REAL HERO

LESSON 55

When Jesus started his healing ministry, he was seen performing great miracles for everyone that needed it. He brought healing and cleansing to those who asked him.

In Luke 5:13, a man who had leprosy came and fell on his face before Jesus and begged. He said, "Lord, if it be your will, please make me clean." Jesus touched him and said, "I will! Be clean!" The man was immediately healed, and the leprosy was gone. God's firstborn Son, Jesus can make us clean. And that includes healing, protection, and deliverance. And if you take notice, he did say that it was his will to heal and that he was following the instructions and will of his own Father.

The things that God was teaching his people throughout time was his way of establishing his redemption plan. The life or holy and pure Spirit of God that was in the body of Jesus secures our redemption. What the Israelites did while in Egypt to receive total deliverance from their enemy is our example to follow. They partook of the lamb and hid behind the protected door that had been covered with the blood of that lamb. We seek God by feasting on (or soaking in) his presence. As we do, God says to us, "You are redeemed, and the shed blood of my Son has covered you. You are mine!"

We had belonged to him in the beginning before the fall. Redeemed means that God takes back what was his.

In Luke 20:36 (KJV) Jesus said, "Neither can they die any more: for they are equal unto the angels; and are the children of God, being the children of the resurrection."

When I look at all the information about God, I see that he wants to be a loving Father who redeems his own before catastrophes, like in the story of the Egyptians and Israelites. The Israelites were spared while the Egyptians were not. The Israelites were the ones to let God be in charge and decide things for their own lives on that particular day.

Even on their journey through the wilderness, after they were saved from bondage, they had to continue their trust in God to get them through and out of the wilderness. There thoughts had been conditioned by their bondage. They needed to clear-out those fearful thoughts, so that fear would not affect their decisions and actions in a negative way. Their thoughts had been poisoned by their past and had caused their faith to faulter into creating a manmade molten calf as their god. They did not know how to let go of those thoughts of bondage and trust God at his word.

I thank God that he gave us Jesus! Jesus is our buffer and our safeguard. The old thoughts and images can be rooted out and left to die in our wilderness experience. We can create new thoughts, images, and dreams, as we forget the past, and focus on our journey into a new life of freedom. The Father expresses his thoughts to us through Jesus. We see through the words and actions of Jesus that he loves us and would do anything for us. He proved it by going to the cross. We have someone like us to lead us into his kingdom of joy and peace.

The first man Adam could not redeem or save his own children from the effects of sin. He needed someone to redeem him from his own predicament first, and so do we. Adam needed to be cleansed and redeemed by someone higher in authority than himself.

God (the Godhead), the highest authority possible, existed eons before Adam. In the bible, Jesus was called the second Adam. He was born of God which made him higher in authority than the first Adam, who was not born of God. The Son had literally come down from his highest position in the heavenly's to rescue us from an evil invisible enemy that could not be seen. As one of us, Jesus then crossed over the threshold into death itself, so he could totally destroy the devil's stronghold on the departed spirits of mankind who had been waiting for the promised Messiah. He proved himself our hero and got promoted. He was crowned with glory and honor and restored back to his rightful place in the Godhead as the Son of God. There may be fictional stories about hero's who rescue mankind, but Jesus (our God) is the real and true hero!

Isaiah 9:6 (KJV), "For unto us a child is born, unto us a Son is given: and the government shall be upon his shoulders: and his name shall be called wonderful, counsellor, the mighty God, the everlasting Father, the prince of peace."

THE BREATH OF GOD GIVES LIFE

LESSON 56

We don't know how angels were created, but we do know how man came into existence. Adam was called a son of God because he was the first to be made into a being of our kind from God himself. He was made from the dust of the earth but did not come to life until God breathed into his nostrils the breath of life. Then he became a living soul.

We can't live without the breath of life. Even the unborn child receives oxygen and expels carbon dioxide through the umbilical cord of its own mother until it takes its own first breath. All living things here on earth need something from the air to breath and survive. When we look at those who had drowned in the flood and the Red Sea, their lives were driven out from their bodies because of their inability to breath! We cannot live without whatever is in the breath of God.

It is interesting that breathing life into a person was something that Jesus did too, just like when Adam received his first breath. In a previous lesson, I briefly mentioned that after Jesus had risen from the dead and met with his disciples, he breathed on them as he told them what it meant. He said that he was giving them the Holy Spirit (John 20:22). It was definitely something they didn't already have or else he would not have breathed on them.

Please, don't think it silly to question what I am about to tell you. If you look at some of the viruses (like Covid-19) that have spread through the breath of someone with the virus, you know something can be transferred. It can be contagious and dangerous, and it can travel into the bloodstream. So, in the case of Jesus, did something good be transferred by his own breath to those he breathed on?

I don't understand it all, but I believe something good happened to the disciples of Jesus when he breathed on them. They were given the same authority that his Father had given him. They were to be leaders in starting up his church. He had already exercised this power and authority, now it was their turn through the same Spirit.

Jesus gave us the Holy Spirit, so that his own presence could be in us to help us fight the good fight of faith. And, to rid us of the power behind sin for ourselves and the lives of others. We can walk in peace, security, and overall well-being, if we fully grasp the significance of having him live in and with us. So, I see it this way, it is better to accept him than to reject him, for he is the essence of all life.

THE ANTIDOTE

---◆---

LESSON 57

The invisible presence that Jesus gave to his disciples came from his breath. Just because you can't see something, it doesn't mean it isn't there.

If we consider what we have learned so far about the coronavirus we can see that it can be transmitted or transferred by just a sneeze or touching something that has been exposed to it. It can also be transmitted from the breath of one person to another without them touching each other. It is a real thing and has been seen under a microscope even though we can't see it with the naked eye.

I have a couple of question that I want you to think about regarding the virus. Can a person get the virus just from touching something else that a sick person touched? And how long does the virus stay active?

When the church first started up, it started up with all kinds of ordinary people. They were people from different backgrounds. For Instance, Luke was a doctor, Matthew was a tax collector and some of the others were fishermen like Peter.

A little while after Jesus ascended into heaven, Paul who had been a persecutor of the Christians, became a very dedicated supporter for Jesus after his conversion. He performed many miracles. He had such a strong anointing on his life that after he would minister to others, handkerchiefs and aprons that he had been wearing during services, were taken to the sick and oppressed. The diseases and the evil spirits departed from those who touched his garments that were brought to them (Acts 19:11-12). Paul didn't even have to physically be there to heal them, and neither does Jesus!

What about with Paul? Was the anointed power of God seeping from his pores as he sweated, while preaching under the anointing? Did the healing power of God saturate the handkerchiefs or aprons that Paul was wearing? And did it stay active long enough to give healing to others? Did the substance of faith in healing linger in his clothing? I don't know, but the bible tells us that it worked, and people got healed and delivered.

What would Jesus do if he was physically here to heal, deliver and carry on his Father's mission? He would touch people, like when he touched a blind man's eyes and healed them. Other times he would just speak the command for healing. Sometimes people would touch him and were healed. The practice in the New Testament church is to pray for one another, lay hands on each other for healing, and to speak to the sickness, disease, or spirit to command it to leave. (Mark 16:18, Acts:28:8). We are to do what Jesus did!

The blood of the lamb and the lamb itself saved the Israelites from the plague that affected Egypt and killed all their firstborn sons. In a manner of speaking, the Israelites received the vaccine from the lamb, so that they would not be touched by the plague. The lamb represents Jesus Christ who is the real lamb of God.

As of this writing, the world has just faced a pandemic brought on by an invisible enemy. Health professionals had talked about certain drugs that would stop the pandemic from taking more lives.

Science has found a way to extract newly created antibodies from the blood of survivors. They first test for antibodies in the recovered patients and then develop a vaccine from their antibodies. These antibodies can be given to critically ill patients to help their body in the fight for their lives. The body does have the potential to heal itself, but sometimes it needs help in doing so. When a patient recovers from the infection, it is a good sign that their body has formed the correct antibodies to kill off the virus in the future for themselves. Thanks to science, immunity can be transferred to another.

The corona virus is not choosey who it affects, and neither does the invisible enemy of sin that has infected humans since the beginning of our time. The corona virus can attach itself to anyone it comes in contact with, if they don't have the protective measures in place like masks, distance, cleansing or a vaccine. The biggest hope with the virus is that it will eventually and totally be wiped out. Sin killed Jesus! Let's just say that he got the death gene from humans. Let's pretend that sin is a virus, and we all have been exposed to it. We all will die eventually because it causes death.

I had mentioned earlier in a previous lesson that an anti-venom is type of antitoxin that comes from the blood of certain animals like a horse or a sheep (lamb)? It is created by injecting tiny amounts of venom into the animal, in order to bring about an immune system response. It becomes a purified, venom neutralizing, antibody product that can stop the venom from killing you.

Jesus, the lamb of God had all our sins placed upon him, and it was enough to kill him. But the good news is that he was the first to be risen from the dead. He left the virus called sin (the disease, poison, plague, the curse of death) behind on the cross to die. When Jesus died, the virus of sin could not survive without his living body as its host.

When Jesus was given his life back, he had full immunity to the virus of death. Sin like the virus was conquered on the cross and in the grave, not Jesus. He has the power or antibody that defeats death itself. His destiny to live forever was already established before he was even born. God was making the antibody to death itself to give to us. Jesus presented his own pure blood full of the antidote into the holy place of God and proved its effectiveness at cleansing the virus of death. This, is what he offers to us! Don't be afraid of his vaccine!

When I first got saved, it took a while until I felt comfortable with this new thing called salvation. It even scared me a little bit. I was afraid that I might feel or experience something weird and out of the ordinary. Some of my experiences from the past had affected my belief. Some of these ideas came from movies, fictional books, documentaries and even from watching cartoons. I had been influenced by fear of the unknown, so it was hard to trust the Spirit of God enough to feel his presence. It was a slow learning process. But once I let him into my mind and heart, I felt his peace, comfort, and love.

I had to learn to trust him with my life! He has the vaccine and there is no more fear of death, itself! He knows us, and he is patient and slow to anger, because he is our Father. God had inspired writers of the bible to refer to him as Father, so that we can relate to him and come to him. So now every time I think back to that day that I came to him out of desperation, and he accepted me, I thank him all over again. I know now that "HE'S GOT THIS"!

ALL WORDS MATTER

"You May Just Get What You Say"

———— ◆ ————

LESSON 58

Jesus had said that "man shall not live by bread alone, but by every word that proceeds out of the mouth of God" (Matthew 4:4). He also said that every idle word that we speak, we will give account in the day of Judgement. For by our words, we will be justified or condemned (Matthew 12:36-37).

There are numerous scriptures in the bible that say the just shall live by faith (Romans 1:17). God considers us righteous when we commit ourselves to him. Hebrews 11:1-35 summarizes some of the awesome stories from the Old Testament where God counted different people as righteous, just because they believed him at his word. **Without faith it is impossible to please God.** However, this also means that the reverse is true. With faith, he is well pleased and rewards us as we diligently seek him (Hebrews 11:6). His written word is powerful enough to build and strengthen our faith to believe and trust him in everything.

We can ask God for his wisdom if we want his help for any situation, but we must ask him without wavering in faith. **"For he that wavers is like a wave of the sea driven with the wind and tossed about. For let not that man think that he shall receive anything of the Lord. A double minded man is unstable in all his ways (James 1:5-8)"**. A spirit of doubt or skepticism can get in the way of receiving an answer from God. In the "Message Bible" translation, it says to ask "without a second thought" of any other option.

If we expect God to answer us, we have to be actively listening and watching for his response. It may come through any of a number of ways. One way that he responds to us is when we search for the answer in the bible. He can also respond to us in a thought, or through someone else who just happens to blurt out the answer. It could also be revealed to us through a life experience. God uses many ways to teach us something or to give us his wisdom and knowledge. We should honor him with our complete trust by expecting him to respond. It could be right in front of our faces, and we could miss it! His word says to ask him in faith, and he will give an answer (1 John 5:14-15).

So how can we be confident that whatever we ask and believe God for will actually come to pass? How do we activate our own faith? God's word says that we live by faith through what we say! Believe it or not, the answer lies within our own words. Do we believe every word that comes out of our own mouths?

Life and death are in the power of the tongue (Proverbs 18:21). For he that will love life, and see good days, let him refrain his tongue from evil, and his lips that they speak no guile (1 Peter 3:10).

God's written word tells us to be mindful of what we speak (Psalms 34:13, Matthew 12:36-37, 15:11, Ephesians 4:29, and many more). Thank goodness that everything we say does not come to pass automatically. This area of our being is the most powerful and problematic area that we have. Words have power! We need to be picky with every word that comes out of our own mouths.

We need to practice speaking only positive, inspiring, and encouraging truths. In doing so, we eventually cause our minds to accept and believe the good things that we say and pray for. As we speak, we hear our own words, and cause them to affect our thoughts again. Speaking, reinforces or strengthens thoughts. If we speak negatively influenced words, even to others, our words affect them as well as ourselves. Our words have the power to influence the imagination.

A good example is in what we say to our own children without thinking. We have to realize how much our words are impacting and shaping their world.

Every word that we speak does something good or bad. When we work on choosing wise words to say before we say them, and are focused on guarding our own thoughts and imaginations, we are resisting the enemies influence and submitting to God. We are causing our words to powerfully work in our favor.

Angry thoughts and words can be used as weapons of destruction and can be very hard to control! Most of the time, they lead into judging others. I have been there and done that myself. Unpleasant thoughts can unleash a powerful force of emotions through what we speak. For an example, "You made me mad" is a famous expression of putting the blame on another for your own anger. It all depends on how we react to feeling a negative emotion.

Proverbs 15:1-4 tells us that a <u>soft answer turns away wrath</u>: but <u>grievous words stir up anger</u>. The tongue of the wise use knowledge aright: but the mouth of fools pours out foolishness. The eyes of the Lord are in every place, beholding the evil and the good. A wholesome tongue is a tree of life: but perverseness is a breach in the spirit. Ephesians 4:26 tells us that we can be angry about something, but to sin not. Let not the sun go down upon our wrath: neither give place to the devil.

Jesus said, "Judge not, that you be not judged" (Matthew 7:1-5). It is never a good idea to lash back or criticize another for their flaws without first considering the consequences. Jesus said that it is hypocritical to point out your brother's small flaw when you have an even bigger flaw yourself (Matthew 7:2-3). An angry force that speaks judgement can flex its muscles in an attempt to play God. It can be very difficult to restrain and control words, in order to keep from cursing another. I like what the "International Children's Bible" says about judging (or criticizing and blaming) others. It says that the forgiveness you give others will be given to you.

All negative words matter! I am not just talking about swearwords either. Words expressing strong disapproval and disrespect, or words of doubt and mistrust do not help in turning a bad situation into a good one. These actions apply not only to cursing others, but cursing or condemning things too, when they don't do what we expect them to do for us. We should not be practicing the negative attributes of the curse on anyone or anything and that includes ourselves.

Sometimes, we have to remind ourselves that we have been redeemed, in order to counteract any negativity of our thoughts about ourselves and others. Jesus himself said that the measure of judgment that we use to judge others, is the same standard of judgement that we must also live by ourselves (Matthew 7:1-5). I believe that Satan (our invisible enemy) has used this as a weapon against us more than ever to cause hate and division. Is it our place to speak out to condemn another? Are we guilty of the same things? Evil itself is what we are to judge, condemn and defeat in this world. And, at the same time, we should remember that we ourselves have some of the same kind of shortcomings as those we judge. God has pardoned us for our shortcomings, and we should be more careful to do the same to others. We all have a right to redemption.

While Jesus was preaching and teaching during his ministry, he saved a woman from being stoned to death for her sin. She was brought before him after she was caught committing adultery. He used the moment to teach about condemning others. The men who brought her to him were trying to find a reason to accuse him of speaking against the Mosaic law. They wanted to see if he would follow the law that says she should be stoned (John 8:3-10). Jesus (in all his wisdom) said to them, "He that is without sin among you, let him be the first to cast a stone at her." Not one person was worthy enough themselves to condemn her, so they all walked away, except Jesus. Jesus gave her the best response of them all. He spoke to her and said, "Neither do I condemn you! Go and sin no more!" We all have faults and make mistakes, but Jesus was sent to bring us healing through forgiveness.

The world is being shaped by what all people say. There are good and evil voices of influence out there. We can help to shape and affect the world with our own voices (James 3:2-10, 14-16, 17). We are supposed to be a light to the world. **James 3:10 says, "Out of the same mouth proceeds blessing and cursing, and these things ought not be."** Words have been known to cause wars! Taming the tongue really is one of the hardest things to do. When we say or act out to express our negative feelings to curse anything or anyone, even if no one else hears us, we are attaching the curse to our own lives, because we are the ones that said it. We are the ones who gave what we said power and substance by pronouncing judgement that affects our own lives.

All words mattered when Jesus was sent to die on the cross. There was a mixed crowd of people that showed up for the court case that was held against him. There were those who had heard bad things about him from their own religious leaders. Jesus was accused of blaspheming their God as he claimed his equality with God and that God was his Father. It was a true statement that God was his Father, and he did speak about it quite often. There were others at his hearing that had believed his claim, but their voices were not heard. He was put on trial for the very words that he had been speaking as he ministered to others.

The dedicated followers of the religious leaders trusted the decision of their leaders since their leaders were the experts in the laws of Moses. The people accepted their judgement as the truth and joined them in the accusation. These leaders had been trying to find fault with Jesus and couldn't. Their accusation was based on the truth twisted into a lie. They were jealous of Jesus having so many followers and hated him without any good cause. They wanted to be known as the representatives of God over and above Jesus, and they didn't believe that he was who he said he was. Even though the religious leaders thought their judgement against Jesus was justified and in their best interest, it wasn't.

They didn't believe a mere man could be an actual earthly son born of God himself. Maybe they also thought that a mere human being could not be good enough or could be any closer to God than themselves. They believed themselves to be the middlemen between God and his people, not Jesus. They were thinking in terms of their occupational relationship with God and not Sonship. They thought themselves to be the CEO of God's establishment, and they were in a sense. But Jesus as God's Son was part-owner of his own Father's family business. Perhaps they could not believe or even comprehend what Jesus was saying, because they were blinded by their own jealousy. The truth was that Jesus had been sent to earth to claim his own Fathers' kingdom.

The religious leaders had actually cursed Jesus to die with their own words when they said, "let him be crucified" and when they said, "let his blood be on us and on our children" (Matthew 27:11-26). They even made a choice to free a murderer instead of Jesus. With their voices, they spoke their desire to let a sinful man who was to be put to death go free and crucify Jesus instead. It was symbolic of why Jesus came in the first place. His innocent blood makes atonement for the iniquity of others, so that they could be free. **In Leviticus 17:11 of the Old Testament God had said, "For the life of the flesh is in the blood: and I have given it to you upon the altar to make atonement for your souls: for it is the blood that makes atonement for the soul."** In the New Testament, the shed blood of Jesus makes atonement for our souls, as well as for our children and our children's children.

In the process of condemning Jesus to death, and by their own words, they were confirming God's will and words without even realizing it? According to Leviticus 17:11, the blood of the animal sacrifice made atonement for the soul every year. It was a shadow of things to come. The blood of Jesus that God gave us by giving us his Son, makes atonement forever (Hebrews 10:11-14).

When the accusers of Jesus spoke what they spoke, did they link themselves with the curse of death when they said, "Let him be crucified" and when they said, "Let his blood be on us and on our children" (Matthew 27:22, 23 and 25)? If you look at other versions of the bible like the Message bible, it tells us that they said, "We'll take the blame" and in the New Living translation it quotes, "We will take responsibility for his death". Was it their fault for the death of Jesus? Better yet, with their own words could they have claimed Jesus as the sacrifice?

Jesus had never committed any crime but was crucified anyway. Those who had him put to death really owed him his life back. But after his death, they could not have brought him back to life, even if they wanted to. The deed was done! He died at the hands of the religious leaders who were judges of the Mosaic law.

They cursed him to die under their law. But Jesus had a right to live according to the law (Matthew 5:17-26). Did they disobey the law themselves by killing an innocent man? If they would have realized the error of what they had just done, they would have known that they broke one of the commandments themselves that says, "Thou shalt not kill".

They had done Jesus wrong even though they were in the same ministry as he was, God's! **Jesus had said in Matthew 5:24 that the remedy for breaking a commandment against your brother was to be reconciled to him.** So, according to the law, they really did need to ask for his forgiveness and give him his life back but, how could they? They had already killed him.

Jesus had said he came to fulfill the sentencing of the law of "sin and death" under the Mosaic law (Matthew 5:17). 1 Peter 1:18-19 tells us that we have been redeemed from the curse, by the precious blood of Christ (as a lamb without blemish and without spot). The leaders spoke and confirmed the blood sacrifice of Christ (the Lamb of God himself) into a reality for all of mankind. They made it happen without even knowing it. They said it with their own words of "Let him be crucified, let his blood be on us and on our children."

We can say "his blood be upon us" meaning "he is our sacrifice", and we give him his life back by allowing him to live in and through us. God supplied us with the blood and the body of Jesus as an atonement for sin if we accept it (Romans 5:9-19). We are no longer under the death sentence of Adam and Eve. Jesus himself (the person inside of his own body) willingly gave up his own earthly birthright to life itself, so that it could be given to us, who still live here in our own bodies.

As our leader, he took the responsibility for our shortcomings. I would not want any of my own family members to have to die for me for any reason, especially for something I did. It would be one of the hardest things to bare. It would not make any one of us feel any better about their death. But in the case of Christ dying for us, he lives for us too! It is so much easier to trust God himself, our creator, the one who can handle anything, the one who is all knowing and all-powerful, omnipotent, invincible, and unstoppable to figure out a way to take care of the problem of sin for us. He is a genius!

Adam and Eve did not have God in their presence at the time of their fall, when Satan snuck in and tricked them. But now, we all can! Greater is he that is in you, than he that is in the world (1 John 4:4).

You can't change the fact that Jesus was the Son of God or God in the flesh (1 Timothy 3:16). If we confess Jesus as the Son of God, who came from God, we are saying that the accusation spoken against him at his trial was a lie. And we believe everything that he said was the truth. Did he ever at any time while on the cross admit any wrong-doing? Did he ever say, "Okay, I give up! I am not the Son of God, so please let me live." He told the truth as he had always done and then he died for it. He said he is the only way to the Father. He is the way, the truth and the life and his truth makes us free from the law of sin and death (John 14:6 and John 8:32). He is God in the flesh as he is God in our flesh!

Everything that God had said through his Son Jesus was spoken for us all. God knew his book would be passed along down throughout history. Most of what he said and did, we can believe for ourselves regarding healing, deliverance, love, patients, our future with him and many other truths. He gives us lessons on living! We accept the truth that the death of Jesus and his offering to the Father makes atonement for our own souls. And, as our high priest, he had asked his Father to forgive us. It has already been done. Through the words of Jesus, we are reconciled to a God that remembers our sin no more (Romans 5:9-10). All words that Jesus spoke, even to his Father, mattered!

THE INFLUENCE OF A HELPMATE

Adam, the keeper of the garden that God had created was told not to eat from the tree of knowledge or he would surely die (Genesis 2:15-17). At this point in time, Eve had not been created yet from his body. When God had told Adam about the consequences of eating from the tree, Adam had not yet committed any crime.

After Eve was created as Adam's helpmate, she became a carrier of Satan's words and thoughts about the tree and relayed them to Adam. Neither one of them believed the words of God that he had spoken to be true anymore about eating the tree's fruit, because it had now been mixed with a lie from Satan.

Genesis 3:6-7 states that Eve picked the fruit from the tree, but they both ate it. Between the time she took it from off the tree and the time they ate it, it didn't seem like anything had happened yet. They did not receive knowledge of their nakedness and hide from the Lord, until after Adam believed what she said, and they both ate the fruit.

Eve was first deceived, and Adam (the keeper of the garden) followed. They both became tied to the crime. Eve may have been the first to act on the crime, but Adam was the one who came into agreement with the words that deceived her. He put aside the word or warning that God (the owner of the garden) had said.

It was Adam's negative faith in what God had said that created a problem. Only when Adam took the wrong thought and acted on it, did he cause the crime to become a reality. Satan became their god because they let his words matter to them over and above God's words. They both now needed a dependable redeemer, savior, adviser, protector - a helpmate. Eve, as Adam's helpmate, first accepted the false information to damage Adam's faith in God, and it hurt them both.

Satan tries to cause his thoughts of deception to rule in our thoughts if we let him. He mixes his own thoughts that he wants us to think, say and act upon with ours to cause evil intention.

God, on the other hand, speaks to us through our spirits! He gives us his Holy Spirit (which thinks with the mind of Christ) to be our helpmate. The Holy Spirit can communicate to God without interruption from our own minds that can be influenced by evil thoughts. He can distinguish right from wrong, even when we can't. He knows our weaknesses and our strengths. He is our internal helpmate!

The prayer language is an extra benefit that we can use in helping us communicate properly. When the followers of Jesus were baptized, they began to speak it through their prayers and in prophecy (Acts 2:4, 18 and Acts 10:44, 46). Even Paul used it to his advantage (Acts 9:17 and 1 Corinthians 14:18). Our vulnerable minds may be unfruitful or unaware of what is being said in prayer to God as the words bypass our carnal thinking. We don't always know what the Spirit says to God on our behalf, but he knows what we need to say.

What if after Eve had taken the fruit from the tree, she ate it, but Adam did not? How could Adam have fixed the problem with his wife? Would she have to be destroyed or was there a way to help her? Adam could have taken responsibility for her sin and paid the price for her sin? But she would still be left vulnerable to Satan's influence, especially after Adam's death. And besides, how would the human species survive. The death sentence had to be delayed in order to keep mankind from extinction. They both eventually died, after they had many descendants. The fact is that Adam did cross the line and partake of the same fruit that she did, so neither one of them could save the other anyway. They both needed help!

Somewhere along the line, something had to happen to reverse the curse of death. Jesus was the only human that was given rights from God over and above Satan, Adam, and Adam's descendants. We can't give our own life up to redeem our own life, but the Son of God can, and did! Jesus had never attached himself to the crime of sin and judgement, before he had died, so it could not get a stronghold on him. The law of sin and death that accuses, had nothing to condemn him with. So, the influential voice of sin itself that influenced Adam, and then later tried to influence Jesus was totally defeated. Jesus had done the right thing before he went through death's door to nullify the curse. We know this because he himself was the first to be healed and set free from the pangs of death that the curse brings, when he was raised from the dead.

Jesus as the risen Christ became the first of a new kind that can be produce after his kind. The Holy Spirit was his lifeline, his Spiritual companion, who made sure that he would not give in or be overtaken by Satan like Adam was. This same Holy Spirit can help us to be overcomers like he did with Jesus.

ADAM'S HELPMATE (EVE) VERSES JESUS'S HELPMATE (HOLY SPIRIT)

Eve - Adam was put into a deep sleep, so that God could take a substance from his body and use it to produce Eve's body. She was made from Adam and then given to him as a helpmate. She also became the carrier for Adam's physical seeds.

Holy Spirit - Jesus was first born or conceived with the help of the Holy Spirit (Holy Ghost) (Matthew 1:18, 20). The Holy Spirit then came down from heaven to be the Son of God's helpmate. This happened when Jesus was filled with the Holy Spirit at the beginning of his ministry (Luke 4:1). The Holy Spirit was his helper, close friend, companion, and team worker. The Holy Spirit was with Jesus all the time, especially when he was confronted by the devil while in the wilderness.

As for Eve, the Lord wasn't presence in the garden when the incident of the tree and the serpent happened to Adam and Eve. They had no idea that the serpent meant them harm. If the Lord could have been their all the time with them, would the outcome have been different?

The Holy Spirit is given to us as a helper and comforter (John 14:16-20). He is the Spirit of truth who does not listen to Satan. He knows better, Eve did not.

Here is my whole point regarding the Spirit of God as our helper. Adam was given a helpmate and his helpmate was tricked by a different voice other than God. Adam's helpmate Eve needed a helpmate. We are given a helpmate that will only listen to the voice of God. And he is with us and listens to us all the time, as we need him. Satan cannot use the Holy Spirit like he did with Adam's helpmate. Satan cannot get between our spirit and the Spirit of God because God's Spirit envelopes or covers our spirit.

Romans 8:9-10 says that we are not in the flesh, we are in the Spirit, if the Spirit of God dwells in us. I see it this way! The Holy Spirit that comes to dwell in us carries, surrounds, guards, protects our spirit, while he is in our bodies. He loves and protects our spirit like a father does for his own child. Our spirit is not just left vulnerable and alone. Our sprit is carried and surrounded by his Spirit that lives within our bodies.

THE WORDS OF JESUS MATTER!

At the death of Jesus, the actual real sin and crime committed at the cross was against Jesus. He had never said anything that wasn't the truth, and he was who he said he was.

The religious leaders did not believe his words to be true regarding his Sonship with God. They could not grasp the concept! They did not believe that God could have an actual earthly son.

They had not seen the proof of the resurrection because it had not happened yet. What was crucial for them was what they believed after his resurrection.

If you don't believe that Jesus was raised from the dead (after three days in the grave), how can you believe God could raise you from the dead? How can you believe that you can be brought back to life after death, if you haven't known it to happen first to someone else?

The real evidence of the death of Jesus had changed. There was no dead body anymore! People saw him alive! Many became believers after Jesus had actually rose from the dead and spoke of things pertaining to the kingdom of God for 40 days, before his more permanent ascension to his Father (Acts 1:3). Mankind may have taken the life of God's Son from him, but now he has him back. The sentencing that was noted against Jesus could not permanently kill him and can never be carried out again.

We don't have to have a guilty conscious for claiming his death as a recompense for our sins. He is alive and well! He is the most perfect human being, ever! We are literally made sons and daughters because of our ties with him. There is no curse or sentencing for those who accept his concept.

Forgiveness was spoken into our existence by his death and resurrection. Even the leaders themselves needed to be forgiven and redeemed from their own ignorance. They had not accepted Jesus for the man he really was, the Messiah. But the truth is, he was the chosen and anointed man of God to be their leader, even though they rejected him. For those who reject him, they are responsible to pay their own price for their own sin. For those of us who accept his death and his resurrection, we are tied to his death and his eternal life. **Paul said to reckon ourselves to be dead unto sin, but alive unto God through Jesus Christ our Lord (Romans 6:11).**

The words of Jesus matter! They matter more than anything else! He paved the way for our forgiveness when he spoke it. **He had said, "Father, forgive them for they know not what they do" (Luke 23:34).**

Hebrews 8:12 God said, "For I will be merciful to their unrighteousness, and their sins and their iniquities will I remember no more.

ALL WORDS MATTER!

Our own physical bodies have nothing to do with our salvation, except for what we speak with our voices. **Romans 10:9 says that if we confess with our mouths the Lord Jesus and believe in our hearts that God has raised him from the dead, we shall be saved.** Our own voices matter!

For us, we can now say, "Thank you Jesus for letting them curse you to die, so that I can be free"! Thank you for speaking words of forgiveness to the Father, so that I can be forgiven! Thank you for being my voice (my advocate, my redeemer) in heaven before my Father!

If we want good things to happen, then we need to be careful what we say. Words are powerful and productive, so we have got to take out all the cursing (and negative speaking). We should not let condemning thoughts take control and cause us to speak them. It is not our place to judge and condemn, and it confuses our own minds about our relationship with God. God is a God of love! Do we really wish bad things to happen to others who God loves too? If so, then are we any better than those who first wanted to stone the women caught in adultery or those who condemned Jesus to die? God is our source, and we have to be in agreement with him, his words and his wishes.

Whatever we say, our minds agree and thinks "Alright, if that is the way you want it, I will try and make it so". Thank goodness everything that we say does not come to pass like it does when God speaks! I am glad that it works that way! We are safer in speaking words that are in line with his word.

If we want our words to be fruitful in the right way, then we need to stop the cursing in all things, except the things that come against God himself. We should strive to speak blessings instead. The curse has already been dealt with through Jesus.

I can't tell you how many times I have had to practice the right thing in this principle of cursing and blessing over and over again. I am still a work in progress. When I say something that has a negative impact, even accidentally, a thought comes to my mind that I probably should not have said it. I am trying to stop insulting others, even under my breath. I remember that I could be attaching the curse or blessing to my own life, because I was the one who spoke the words into existence.

God helps us when we work on renewing our minds with his faith-based substance and thoughts. Thank goodness, God forgives us when we ask him to. Thank goodness he can help us in taming the tongue for it is almost impossible to do on our own. I am now practicing speaking good things, even when I am upset. I am trying to train myself to believe that the good words I say will come to pass. And, if I want to believe that God will answer my prayers, I need to believe that all words have power and that all words matter, even my own! All words bad or good do influence and affect our own faith! Sometimes, I have to counteract what I just said by saying something positive. I even thank God for immediately reminding me of this principle. Other times I just take note for the next time. I feel God is working with me in renewing my mind and changing my speech for the better. He will help us as long as we want him too.

What comes out of our mouths can light fires, or give fuel to an already burning fire, and some of those fires can burn bridges. We may need or have to cross that particular bridge a little later. When we see or hear something we don't like, we should look for the good in the situation to bring it out in the open. And, if we can't find the good, maybe we should say nothing at all. And, if we have to burn a bridge, we need to be choosy of which bridge to burn or find better ways to get across that bridge.

In the story of Job who lost everything, he never burned the bridge to God. So, God gave him double of what he had before Satan had spoken false words of accusation against him. Satan had used the power of words to attack the relationship between God and Job. I know I have mentioned this story repeatedly, but I just want to emphasize its importance. It has a powerful message regarding twisting of the truth. Job had prayed continuously over his first set of children, just in case they were to sin against God in some way. God saw the good in his prayers, but Satan did not. Satan knew that God had put a hedge of protection around Job and his family, as well as blessed him richly. Until Satan stepped in to accuse Job of possible treason against God, the relationship between God and Job was perfect.

Satan hears what people say. Once words are spoken, he uses them to twist their meaning in his favor. A good example is what we see in some of the news media platforms. They have been known to embellish the content of different stories. It is hard to know who to believe anymore! Some reporters do not just tell the facts, they target people that they either hate or love. They work to persuade their audience into believing in their own opinions. Words that others speak can be twisted and embellished in order to sell a story. Satan is known to do the same thing. He is attracted to words that he can twist and use as fear tactics against us all.

Did Satan hear Job expressing his concern for his children, as a fear-based prayer of anxiety, distress, and worry? Did he put his own little spin on what Job prayed to distort its intended meaning? Did he use the "what if" card of his own evil device, when he tried to convince God that Job did not trust him enough with his children? Was Satan focused on how he could make Job's prayer request into a curse? Did Satan, like the news media, twist the meaning of the prayer for his own purpose? Did he take a weakness of Job and bring it before God? Was he attempting to condemn Job's good deeds of offerings and prayers? Did Satan use Job's own fear about his children against him?

Satan tried to get God to move against Job to "destroy him without a cause" (Job 2:3). He was trying to get God to unjustly judge Job. But Job was a righteous man and did his best to please God. So, Satan set a challenge before God and dared him to strip Job of everything he had blessed him with, his wealth and prosperity, as well as his children. He wanted to prove to God that Job would turn on him and "curse him to his face". Satan was trying to damage the good relationship between Job and God, just like he had done in his own relationship with God.

Satan has been trying to stop (or at least slow down) God's spoken word of judgement over his own life, because of his own fear of his future. But his greatest fear is about to come to pass (Revelation 20:7-10)!

He took legal action against Job to advocate his own defense. He used the fear of judgement that Job portrayed in his prayers over his children to support his own case. He wanted God to allow him to fulfill Job's worst fear. Did Job have times of doubt, and don't we all? Satan was hoping that Job would completely turn on God like he himself did.

He thought that he could trap God into taking action of either one way or another through his devious plot. He thought that Job would rebel, and then God would either have to destroy him or pardon him. Satan thought that if Job were to rebel when he lost everything, and God were to pardon him, then God would have to do the same for his own rebellion. Satan was trying to make a case that he himself should not be destroyed if Job also failed to be faithful. But he was wrong, Job never rebelled!

Who was in heaven to defend Job? Jesus wasn't born yet. Job had to stand his ground himself from here on earth, while Satan was in the presence of almighty God pleading his side of the case against him. How could Job defend himself? Who could prove Job's faithfulness, even in the midst of devastation, except Job himself?

This story shows what Satan himself has been doing with his time left. He has been trying to prove that mankind should be charged as an accessory to his own crime. He has been trying to trick people with his con job. But Jesus has already paid the price and covered us for being an accessory to his crime. Satan has been seeking for a loophole that will give him a way to escape from his own sentencing. He thinks that if God were to pardon us for our rebellious attitude, then he himself should be pardoned. He wants to hold us hostage to change his own set destiny.

James 4:7, Submit yourselves to God, resist the devil and he will flee from you.

We have to resist and keep resisting Satan's cursed ways. We have to make the choice not to imitate him in cursing what God has made. Even the angels of God know not to accuse or pass judgement like Satan does (2 Peter 2:11). Michael, the archangel of God, when contending with the devil over the body of Moses after he died, did not bring a "railing accusation" against him. Instead, he said, **"The Lord rebuke you" (Jude 1:9 and Zechariah 3:12)!** We are to be of one mind, having compassion and love, not rendering evil for evil, railing for railing. We are to avoid evil itself, do good and seek peace whenever possible.

When David confronted Goliath for battle, he came against him in the name of the Lord of hosts, the God of Israel (1 Samuel 17:45-47). None of his intentions were for his own selfish desire. He spoke up to defend what belonged to God. He was angry for the right cause. His claim was that Goliath defied (confronted and challenged) God, when he came against God's people. He knew and spoke that God would deliver Goliath into his own hands. And he gave all the credit to God, when he said, "**All the earth may know that there is a God in Israel who delivers his people, for the battle is his.**" David knew that God was the Lord of all the heavenly host of angels and that he was in charge of the battle.

If God be for us, who can be against us (Romans 8:31)?

In a battle, we have to be persistent in submitting and surrendering to our leader until it becomes natural. Even our own military has to learn to submit to the orders of their leader, for their own good.

As we put on the armor and place the shield of faith in front of us, the enemy is reminded that we have been redeemed and that there is a higher power supporting us.

Let the redeemed of the Lord say so, whom he hath redeemed from the hand of the enemy (Psalms 107:2).

Jesus defeated Satan with "It is written"! He used the scriptures like a sword in battle, as he spoke them out of his own mouth. He spoke up against the ideas and plans that Satan was trying to plant into his heart (Matthew 4:4-10). He was not about to bow down to Satan and he spent his life warning others! Jesus tells us what the first and greatest commandment is, and that it gets the support of God as our loving Father (Matthew 22:36-38). Jesus is our example to follow!

Life and death or in the power of the tongue and we really are conforming to what we speak over ourselves. We should speak God's truth to ourselves until it becomes a part of us. We should be careful of what comes out of our mouths because we may just get what we say. **ALL WORDS MATTER!**

OFFERING LOVE

———◆———

LESSON 59

Love is not just a feeling; it is something that we do! It is certainly something that God does all the time and we should be thankful that he does! There are lots of things that God has already blessed us with that we take for granite. He already did his part in giving us access to all his blessings, when he gave us his Son. A grateful heart in all things is highly acceptable to God and it gets his attention. Acknowledging God for all good things can bring more good things. Offerings of thanksgiving are mentioned all throughout the bible, and they are sure ways that we can come before him to express our love and gratitude. It is something that we do!

Matthew 6:33 tells us to "seek first the kingdom of God, and his righteousness; and all these things shall be added unto you." What things is Jesus referring to in this scripture? Matthew 6:25-32 explains (by example) what he is talking about. He says not to worry about food to eat or clothes to wear for our Father knows that we have need of these things. He explains that the fowls of the air do not have to sow or reap or store their food away in barns. It is already supplied for them in nature by God on a daily basis. For us, God knows that we have need of things like food, clothing, and shelter. But these things are not the only things that we need. This scripture tells us to put him first in all things for he has more knowledge of what we need than we do.

In Mark 11:24 Jesus said, whatever things we desire, when we pray, BELIEVE that we receive them, and we shall have them. Speaking out our prayer request while adding his own words helps us absorb and believe him for the things that we need.

Psalms 100:4 tells us that when we come before God, we are to first **"enter his gates with thanksgiving and into his courts with praise."** We offer God our thanks in advance as we enter his presence. While we are there, we give him a gift or token of our love when we praise him. **Psalms 37:4 says, "delight in the Lord and he shall give you the desires of your heart."**

Thanking God in advance for his love, counsel and wisdom, food and shelter, good health and healing, success and prosperity, deliverance, freedom, or anything else that we may need, is a good first step in receiving the desires of our hearts.

God's kingdom of love is full of the faith substance (spiritual matter or elements) needed to sustain life. **Faith is the substance of things hoped for, and the evidence of things not seen......Through faith we understand that worlds were framed by the word of God, so that things which are seen were not made of things that do appear (Hebrews 11:1, 3).** Life itself comes from him and it is his gift of love to us!

Let's look a little deeper into the importance of the different offerings that God had required of his people. Why were they so important to God in the bible? How does thanking him in everything release power to bless our prayers? How does the substance of faith work to cause good things to appear from things that we can't see like the scriptures says? What does God use our offering for?

The biblical principle regarding the blessing and the curse are tied to the offerings, as well as God's own Son. In previous lessons, I explained some of the things that I have learned about this topic. The giving of tithes and offerings (in Malachi 3:10-11); the Feast of Firstfruits (in Leviticus 23:4-14, 20 and Proverbs 3:9-10, etc.); and Jesus (1 Corinthians 15:20), who gave himself for us as an offering, are all interrelated.

Without God's own offering of grace and mercy first, the curse would have overtaken our world to destroyed it, all because of mankind's sinful and selfish desires for power. The ultimate offering that is keeping the world from total destruction has already happened. It happened when Jesus was nailed to the cross on Passover, in order to rise from the dead on the day of the Firstfruits (1 Corinthians 15: 22).

If you remember, the Feast of Firstfruits was the thanksgiving celebration looking forward to a full and abundant harvest. It took place during the week-long Passover celebration every year. At this particular time of the celebration, God's people presented a small portion of grain called the sheaf offering. It was the <u>first</u> offering of the new harvest in any given year and presented on the first day of their week.

Details in Leviticus 23:10-14, tell us that this grain offering from the fields, and a perfect unblemished young lamb among other things, were given to the priests. The priest would then burn the lamb on the altar and wave the sheaf offering before God in expectation of his acceptance. The people were required to give their offering to the priests **before** they could enjoy the rest of their new grain to be harvested.

If the people wanted the rest of their individual crops to flourish, this was the way to ask. I believe the waving of the sheaf was a thanksgiving offering of faith in advance for a bountiful harvest (Leviticus 23:10-11, 15-17). **Proverbs 3:9-10 says, "Honor the Lord with your substance, and with the <u>firstfruits</u> of <u>all your increase</u>, and <u>your barns will be filled with plenty</u>."**

God appreciates a thank you and loves a cheerful giver (2 Corinthians 9:7). As the people gave their thanksgiving offerings and or tithes throughout the year they would succeed in all areas of their lives. **God had said that he would open the windows of heaven to pour out an abundant blessing (Malachi 3:10).**

Malachi chapter three explains the result of giving or not giving, so that we can see how offerings through the priest affect our lives with either a blessing or a curse. The first two chapters of Malachi are mostly about the priests, who were the presenters of the offerings to God. It was their job to make sure that the offering was the best they could present to him, and they failed (Malachi 1:6-8, 10-14 and 2:1-8). In chapter three, when God told his people that they had robbed him with their tithes and offering, he included the priests in his accusation (Malachi 3:8-9).

Jesus is our high priest who represents us before God. He made sure that our offering would be presented to his Father in the best way possible. He makes our offering holy, for he has already been in the presence of the Father! Our offering is cleansed by his own blood. Isaiah 53; 2-12 described Jesus as someone who grew up as a tender plant and as a root out of dry ground. His soul was made an offering for sin and now as our high priest, he shall justify many.

Without the principle of sowing and reaping through the sacrificial offerings, there would have been no Jesus. In the New Testament, Jesus was referred to as the firstfruits of a new kind, born or birthed again out from the depths of the ground (1 Corinthians 15:20-23).

The principle of sowing and reaping shows that God's one seed offering, his own Son could produce a multitude of good seed for his harvest. Jesus the firstfruits, was the true bread of life producing seed that came from God's own offering first (John 6:47-51, 63). God even spoke it into existence in the beginning of time starting with Adam and Eve.

Jesus, as the Son of God became the perfect offering for firstfruits (representing mankind). In the process of his offering up himself, Jesus gave his own Father something more perfect than any other mortal man could even begin to give. Jesus presented good seed that his Father could use to reproduce more like himself.

There is no curse against those that take part in his harvest because Jesus paid for them with his own life. When Jesus was cut down, he took the "handwriting of ordinances" that was against us, out of the equation of the blessing and the curse, as he was cursed and nailed to a cross, himself (Colossians 2:14). He gave 100% of his life for mankind instead of just 10%. Jesus satisfied the sentencing of the curse for our sake, and in our stead, if we accept his offering of love for ourselves.

The curse has run rampant on the earth because of our own ignorance, our own doing, without us even knowing it. **Jesus asked God to forgive us for we "know not what we do" (Luke 23:24).** Even top leaders all over the world don't know all the answers in doing the right thing, but God does!

God gave us an earthly king to lead and guide us. He is the one who belongs on the throne, for his mercy endures forever (Psalms 136:1-3 through 23-26). God's mercy endures through his Son, Jesus Christ.

Jesus gave his own life up to bless ours. We can receive the blessing without having to go through the same process that he did. We don't have to physically die first. We don't have to wait until we die and go to heaven to get it. If he, as our firstfruits was accepted by the Father, so are we. His physical death settled the issue of the curse, and we are pardoned. All that is left in the equation is the blessing.

Jesus said, "Except a corn of wheat fall into the ground and die, it abides alone: but if it dies, it brings forth much fruit (John 12:24)."

Jesus did not go into the depths of the ground to suffer forever in our place, but to take his Godly position over death, hell and the grave.

Revelation 1:17-18, "Do not be afraid; I am the first and the last. I am he who lives, and was dead; and behold, I am alive forevermore, amen. And, I have the keys of hell and death".

Jesus has all keys of authority and power. He has the keys of hell and death. And, he has the keys to the kingdom of heaven (Matthew 16:18-19). These keys can bind or loose, open or shut gates (doors or realms) between heaven and earth. He gave keys of authority and power to the church. Jesus said that the gates of hell shall not prevail against it (Matthew 16:18-19 and Matthew 18:18). We need these keys!

Jesus talked a lot about the kingdom of God. He gave many examples to explain how wonderful it was. Romans 14:17, says it has everything to do with righteousness, peace and joy. Mark 4:26 says that the kingdom of God is as if a man should cast seed into the ground. Philippians 4:19 says God shall supply all your needs according to his riches in glory by Christ Jesus. John 3:3 says you must be born again to see the kingdom of God. Matthew 12:28 told his disciples to heal the sick and say the kingdom of God is come unto you. Luke 10:9 says that if devils are cast out, it means the kingdom of God has come to you. The kingdom of God is among us by his Holy Spirit. God is everywhere through his Spirit.

Here is just a taste of what is gradually taking place and will be completed someday in the future.

Daniel 2:44, And in those days of these kings shall the God of heaven set up a kingdom, which <u>shall never be destroyed</u>: and the kingdom shall not be left to other people, but it shall break in pieces and consume all these kingdoms, and <u>it shall stand for ever</u>.

We can boldly access the throne of God through the name of the Son of God. He is the only best offering that we can truly rely on. He has already been accepted as the ultimate offering and God approved!

In other words, we can pray and talk to God knowing and believing that his desire is to be our Father, like he is with Jesus. God sees us through his Son's Spirit who lives within us (Romans 8:23, 1 Corinthians 15:20-23). We have Sonship! This Sonship is the spiritual relationship that cannot be broken between the heavenly Father and his Son. That is why our prayers go up to the Father, when we say them "IN THE NAME OF JESUS"!

The offering was part of God's plan in slowly establishing his intimate relationship with us, breaking the curse and releasing his blessing of Fatherhood. He sowed the seed of his Son in the earth and is now reaping from what he has sown.

So, if all that is left is the blessing for those who belong to the Son, then we can get something incredible in the deal! The word blessing means we get "divine favor through his Spirit." We are also blessed from the inside out with his love and invisible presence. We may not be able to see the Holy Spirit, but we can experience good results from his presence.

He is a real being even though he is invisible. The only way we can pray or communicate with our Father is by our invisible spirit, who is recreated by his invisible Spirit.

We can't always instantly or physically see what he is doing to bless us, while he is doing it. It is a supernatural action that starts in his realm or kingdom that we can't see, hear or touch with our physical bodies. It is made from hidden things. **Hebrews 11:3 tells us that things which are seen were not made of things that do appear.** It is not seen by our natural vision until it manifests or matures into a physical substance (of atoms and molecules), big enough for us to see or even touch. It is like the seed that is planted in the ground. We can't see it, until it eventually springs up into a beautiful plant and begins to produce fruit. It is amazing how faith operates. We can see and experience the results as time goes by.

Jesus had given or offered to his Father exactly what his Father wanted more than anything else in the world, genuine Spiritual Sonship for the rest of us. Through Jesus, we are connected with God as our Father. We have a right to the blessing that is promised to his Son, who gave of himself 100% for us.

God shows us what he thought when his Son pleased him. **He said, "Prove me now herewith, if I will not open you the windows of heaven and pour you out a blessing that there shall not be room enough to receive it. And I will rebuke the devourer for your sakes, and he shall not destroy the fruits of your ground; neither shall your vine cast her fruit before the time in the field" (Malachi 3:10-11).** God blessed Jesus with this principle, and he wants to do the same for us.

Jesus got back what belonged to God in the garden. He got back the authority over good and evil, blessing and the curse. The story of seed time and harvest in Malachi did not come first, but the story of Eve and her seed did.

Jesus said that the fowls of the air neither sow or reap, nor gather into barns because the heavenly Father feeds them. Then he asked the question, "Are you not much better than they?" He also said to consider the lilies of the field and how they automatically grow (Matthew 6: 26-33). God takes care of his own!

God offers back to us the blessing of being his sons and daughters if, we associate ourselves with the offering of his Son. It is associated with a new beginning that promises blessing instead of the curse. Jesus was and is God's gift of love to us.

FIGHT THE GOOD FIGHT OF FAITH

Bible Lessons in Warfare

❖

LESSON 60

Jesus never gave up on fulfilling his special assignment to prove the love of his Father. He was determined to remain brave until the end of his life in doing the right thing. He could have asked his Father to give him more than twelve legions of angels to rescue him from being killed, but he didn't (Matthew 26:53-54). He was harassed, rejected, mocked and spit upon, and then he was put to death despite the good work that he was doing.

After Jesus had ascended into heaven, some of his followers also went through similar persecution. They were warned not to preach Christ anymore. But they did not let the threats stop them from doing what they knew was right. Jesus, Peter and Paul knew to cast down all thoughts of the imagination that stood against the knowledge of God. This included the condemning thoughts spoken to them from others.

Paul never let any condemnation or shame of what he had done to the Christians before his conversion effect his going forward. He had to put it behind him. He knew that he was now doing the right thing and did not care what others said or did about it.

Jesus never gave up in the face of opposition from others, and neither should we. He knew who was really behind all the harassment that he endured. We all know what it is like to be harassed, since we have experienced it at one time or another ourselves. Satan is the father of strife! When we feel persecuted, we should realize that we may just be dealing with an invisible presence (behind the scenes). He is trying to cause strife and division, to get us to give up and give in.

For where envying and strife is, there is confusion and every evil work (James 3:16).

For we wrestle not against flesh and blood, but against principalities, against powers, against the rulers of the darkness of this world, against spiritual wickedness in high places (Ephesians 6:12).

There are different types of beings besides us. They exist somewhere out there among us in God's infinite creation. They are doing mindboggling things that we are unaware of. We can't possibly believe that we are the only ones who exist.

There could be those more advanced than us, who may be trying to help or hurt us. A lot of the stories in the bible speak of angels, demons, and spirits. Adam and Eve, Enoch, Noah, Abraham, Moses, King David, Jesus, Peter, Paul, and others all had encounters with some of them in their lifetime. There are great stories of how God and his angels have gone to battle on our behalf, with either another person or other beings.

Satan and his evil warriors have been trying to wear out the saints with exhaustion. They are working their agenda behind the scenes of our lives in an attempt to destroy our future. Fear and anxiety of an unknown future can stress us out to the point that our feelings and our health are both affected. The pressure can cause us to react in a negative and self-damaging way, and we could end up releasing words that we ought not say. We can actually cause more problems for ourselves. We can actually attract more harm and misery that can hinder any blessing that God might want to get to us. The enemy wants us to respond and stay stressed out, while God wants us to live in peace!

The Israelites that God had brought out of Egypt are a good example of what stress can do. They had been through a terrible trial! They had a hard time staying persistent in resisting their past thoughts of bondage. The stress of it all kept them living by their past oppression and fear.

While they were in the wilderness, they complained a lot about how uncomfortable things were for them. There was an issue with the water that God had to make drinkable, the manna from heaven, and the qual that they got tired of eating. They even complained about the leadership of Moses, after he had worked so hard to convince the Egyptian king to let them go. Their stress showed up in their complaints.

The people voiced their fear of going forward into the promised land. They saw that the land was good, but they were afraid of the people that lived there. They became so stressed about it, that they began to talk foolishly. They went so far as to say, "If only we would have died in Egypt or in this wilderness!" They were saying that they would rather die, than to face another traumatic event. They were giving up even before they got there. They imagined the worst would happen and said so. They said that they believed they would fall by the sword, and that their families would be taken captive, if they went in (Numbers 14:2-4).

They, themselves ended up wandering in the wilderness for 40 years until they all had passed away, according to their own decision to not go in. It came out of their own mouths. God told them that they would have what they said, and they did (Numbers 14:28-29). So, learn to watch what you say!

Their confession did not line up with what God had planned for them. He did not tell them that they would fall by the sword, and that their families would be taken captive (Numbers 14:2-4). He wanted to bless them with the land and was planning to make sure that it happened. But their stubborn and rebellious attitude took precedence over what he had intended for them.

God would not let it come to pass for their children's sake. They could still take part in his plan to move forward. Out of all the adults, Joshua and Caleb where the only ones who were all fired up about going in to conquer the promised land. Joshua, Caleb, and the children under 20 years of age still had a chance to go in.

When the children began to move into and take over the promised land, they became too friendly with the idol worshippers in some of the cities. The worshippers had a practice of giving their own newborn babies as a sacrifice to the underworld gods in an effort to appease them! Is that insane or what! In killing their own children, these idol worshippers were robbing their own children of their right to live, to have a voice in the world, and to make their own decision in choosing life or death. The Israelite children forgot what their own parents went through in Egypt. They were being exposed to idol worship just like their own parents were. When they mingled with these nations, they were taken in by the constraints of these nations, their political powers, and their belief systems.

The Israelite children began to lose their foothold over their enemies as they started to mingle with them. But believe it or not, they were actually obeying God's command to leave some of the idol worshipping nations unharmed (Judges 3:1-2). I was surprised! I wondered, why did God want his people to leave them alive, if he had already known them to be a stumbling block to his people? So, I asked him why, and as I read the rest of the chapter, he showed me the answer. He used their enemies to teach them to war against what is ungodly, and to not accept it. Does God sometimes use the enemy to teach the difference between accepting what is right verses something that is wrong? It looks like he does according to this part of the story!

The Idol worshippers were tricked into letting false gods be their god. The Israelite children were starting to get caught up in the idol worship, but soon found out that it was a way that led to destruction.

They were realizing that something wasn't quite right with the belief system of these people. They saw for themselves that it was a very depressing experience and realized the error of their ways. They wanted out! They had learned not to want it for themselves. They were learning some lessons the hard way.

God had to teach them to fight back the stronghold of their enemy, not to embrace them. God wanted them to get rid of the danger, even if it meant they had to go to war to do it. We win our battles with God's presence first and foremost, as we submit to him and resist the enemy.

Sometimes, God teaches us how to fight and win our battles, and other times, he wins our battles for us. There are numerous stories of him intervening in the battles for his own people. He would fight for them when they would sincerely turn to him. The whole point of the wars in the Old Testament was to take down the stronghold of evil, and to establish the kingdom of God over time. Jesus said, "The Father's kingdom and his will, will be done on earth as it is in heaven (Matthew 6:9-13). It will be done with or without those who do not want to fight for his cause.

There were times in the bible when God's people won their battles by just praising him. He would then take care of their opponent. There is a fascinating story about a king named Jehoshaphat, who was told that a multitude of enemy soldiers were coming to kill them all. He proclaimed a fast and prayed to God for help. **God responded through a Levite prophet and said, "Be not afraid, nor dismayed by reason of this great multitude; for the battle is not yours, but God's!"** God intervened before there was even a battle. While the people were singing and praising him during their fast, he caused their enemies to turn on and kill each other in confusion. After it was all over, God's people just walked into the camp and collected so much plunder, that they could hardly carry it all (2 Chronicles 20:1-25, 27). The battle was won for them while they were all busy giving God praise.

In another story that I mentioned in an earlier lesson, God revealed a plan to bring peace instead of a battle. It was a story about the prophet named Elisha. The Syrian king was planning a sneak attack on the king of Israel and so God revealed to Elisha where the camp of the enemy was hiding out. Elisha went and warned the king of Israel where the camp was, and the king was able to avoid that area.

When the Syrian king found out that it was Elisha who had revealed his location, he sent a great army to go get him. At night, they surrounded the city where Elisha and his associates were staying. When one of Elisha's men woke up the next morning, he saw the great army surrounding the city. He became fearful and asked Elisha what they should do. Elisha told him that he had no reason to fear. He then asked God to open the young man's eyes, so that he could supernaturally see that the mountain was full of horses and chariots of fire to protect them. There was a multitude of God's angelic army standing to defend them, if needed. (2 Kings 6:9-23).

Then Elisha asked God to blind the enemy soldiers as they approached him, so that he could led them into the hands of the king of Israel. Once they were led to and standing before the king, Elisha then prayed for God to take away their blindness. They were now the ones surrounded.

Instead of the king of Israel killing them, Elisha advised the king to feed them and send them on their way back home in peace. There was no blood shed from a would be battle at that time.

Sometimes, I believe God leads us to defuse a battle with love and kindness. Scripture says that if your enemy is hungry or thirsty feed him. In doing so, this can make him feel ashamed or humbled. The bible says that God will reward you for your effort in portraying his love to them, without having to compromise your beliefs. (Proverbs 25:21-22 and Romans 12:20). **Romans 12:21 says, be not overcome of evil, but overcome evil with good.**

God does not want us to mingle with or accept the ideas of those whose belief system is contradictive to his. We need to know what his belief system is, in order to discern the difference. The first commandment is to love the Lord, God with all our heart, soul and mind FIRST, and then love our neighbor. There are so many ideas of evil intent spreading all throughout the world. The good news is that God's ideas are also spreading all throughout the world. Rather we like it or not, we are all in a spiritual and mental battle. If something does not line up with the things of God, then don't accept it for yourself.

The formation of man-made laws should be based on God's view of how things should be. As ideas become law, they affect us all alike! Why do you think there is so much conflict? There are too many opinions or views to deal with! We can't seem to agree on how life should be! There really is only one way that works, and someday it will be the only way. But for now, we have to take a stand, because God's opinion is all that matters, if we want to keep our freedom!

So, how do we fight the good fight of faith against an unseen enemy?

First of all, purging our conscience is important! We must learn to cast out the wrong kind of thoughts that are not our own. We must not own them! Most people accept ideas from others, just because it seems reasonable and popular. We have to determine its purpose. Why is the idea right or wrong, and how does it affect God's principles of life? How does it hurt me, as well as someone else?

We have to know what to fight for, and what to fight against. We need the right tools and weapons. The bible is not just some storybook for entertainment. God meant it to be teaching instruments to live by. We gain knowledge (fact and truth) and wisdom (to make wise decisions) through the scriptures! The words of God gives us spiritual and mental strength, power, and ammunition.

Real life stories of what others have already experienced with God have been preserved throughout history. God's words give us the confidence and courage to go forward. His word has been given to us for spiritual protection and peace of mind. I hope I have given you enough information to be aware of how God thinks, feels, reacts, and loves his people.

We can learn what to do in any situation through his word. We can either take similar action or learn what not to do. It is his invisible armor, and it works from the inside out to guide our conscience in the right direction!

Psalms 100:4 tells us to "enter his gates with thanksgiving and his courts with praise." *This is how we supernaturally enter the throne room of God. The success of some of the most famous bible characters is that they dwelt in the secret place of the "Most-High". We can't see this place in the natural. It is a place between God and us, where no weapon formed against us can prosper or penetrate our spirit man. The devil does not want anyone to learn about our greatest weapon, praise!* ***God inhabits the praises of his people (Psalms 22:3).***

The story regarding the massive army that was coming to kill King Jehoshaphat and his people, shows us that praise can be used as a weapon against the enemy (2 Chronicles 20: 17-19, 22-24). Praise gets the attention of God.

I was thinking, maybe in the case of Job, what could have been a better prayer for his children? Did Satan hear Job's prayer, and then use it as a weapon to cause division between Job and God? Could he claim that Job did not trust God with his own children? Job was in a horrible spiritual conflict with an invisible enemy and didn't even know it. What if Job had just given a prayer of thanksgiving for all he had, instead of what he could lose?

How could Satan have used this type of prayer and twist it around into a faithless prayer? I don't think he could have!

I know that Satan cannot condemn any of our prayers anymore, because Jesus settled the court case that the devil has brought against us, by his own death, once and for all. Our faith is in Jesus! We can now approach God as our own Father, instead of as our judge. God is our Father through the Sonship of Jesus Christ. This goes for all who accept Jesus from the past, the present, and the future (Romans 1:7, 1 Corinthians 1:3, 2 Corinthians 1:2 and many more).

The real challenge is to rescue people and not to fight each other. We can't just go to war and start wiping each other out! Who would be left? The battle must be won by liberating others. Sometimes people don't have a clue that they are bordering trouble for themselves. The battle in God's courtroom has been won, now the rest of the plan is to spread the love of God to the captive and set them free.

The Lord is my strength and my shield (my faith partner); my heart trusted in him, and I am helped (Psalms 28:7).

THE OFFERING OF THANKSGIVING IN EXCHANGE FOR MIRALCES

The Invisible Works of God

—◆—

LESSON 61

God has given mankind evidence of his invisible presence all throughout history. He had given the Israelites in the Old Testament physical evident of his presence by the miracle of the Red Sea occurrence, and by taking up residency with them through his own dwelling place (his own earthly tent) in the wilderness. Eventually, the evidence of God's presence was manifest in his earthly Son Jesus, who performed many miracles to show us God's intent of good will, mercy, and love. The invisible God has a voice. We can't see God with our physical eyes, but we can hear him speak. We have his words <u>written</u> and passed down throughout history that tells us of his existence.

God spoke as himself through a visible man named Jesus. We can't see Jesus now in the natural, but we can know that he exists by divine revelation and scripture. Believing in his invisible presence is a miracle in itself. Jesus was God's ordained miracle worker who blessed others. He said that it was his Father who did all the miracle works through him (John 14:10-11).

Jesus called himself the bread of God, and later the true vine.

In John 6:33, 35 Jesus said, "For the bread of God is he which cometh down from heaven and gives life unto the world. <u>I am the bread of life</u>, he that comes to me shall never hunger and he that believes on me shall never thirst."

In John 15:1, 5 Jesus said, "<u>I am the true vine</u>, and <u>my Father is the husbandman</u>. I am the vine, and you are the branches. He that abides in me and I in him, the same bringeth forth much fruit. For without me you can do nothing."

It is interesting to note, that by some of the miracles Jesus performed using bread and wine, he proved that he could take the ordinary or natural and make it supernatural. He used the bread and wine, to teach others the principle of God's invisible but real blessing.

Early in his ministry, his first recorded miracle was turning water into wine at a wedding party, when they had none left (John 2:1-10). The ruler of the feast was impressed with the wine that Jesus had made from the water. He even made a comment that it was better than the wine which was served at the beginning of the wedding.

Jesus also performed miracles using the bread. At one time, Jesus had multiplied five barley loaves of bread and two small fishes to feed thousands (Matthew 14:14-21, Mark 6:34-44, Luke 9:11-17 and John 6:2-13). There was so much of the bread left over that it filled twelve baskets full after everyone was fed.

I thought it was also interesting that in the four different versions of the same story with five loaves and two fishes, most of the wording was the same, except for in the book of John. For example, Matthew 14:19 says "**Jesus looked up to heaven and blessed the bread**", before giving it to his disciples, who then distributed it to the crowd of people. In John 6:11, it says that Jesus "**gave thanks**" before he gave it to his disciples to feed the multitude.

Jesus had repeated this same type of miracle more than once. It is reported twice in the book of Matthew. First in Matthew 14:19 and then again in Matthew 15:36. This next time was with seven loaves and a few fishes, and they still had food left over.

In Matthew 14:19 Jesus looked up and blessed the bread and in Matthew 15:36 it says he gave thanks. So, they must mean the same thing. Jesus had presented an offering of thanksgiving in exchange for a miracle.

In the first story, the small amount of food of five loaves and two small fishes became enough to feed thousands. The food had belonged to one young man in the crowd (John 6:9). He gave all the food that he had brought with him, as an offering to Jesus, in order to help feed multitudes. It became his offering. It became something that Jesus could start with, to bless others. Jesus lifted it up (like a sheaf offering) to give God thanks in advance of feeding the multitude. It became a firstfruits offering to be multiplied for the sake of all those needing nourishment. They were all fed from the hands of Jesus. And there was more than enough bread and fish left over after they had all eaten.

At his very last supper and just before his death, Jesus had showed his disciples a realistic way of remembering his life, death and resurrection through communion (Luke 22:17-20). He handed them the cup of wine and the bread and told them to drink the wine and eat the bread in remembrance of him. The last time that Jesus had handed them food was when he multiplied the seven loaves of bread and a few fishes to physically and miraculously feed thousands. By this communion he showed once again, the importance of the thanksgiving offering of FIRST **blessing and giving thanks** to the Father in advance.

Luke 22:17-20 (KJV), And he took the cup, and <u>gave thanks</u>, and said, "Take this and divide it among yourselves: For I say unto you, I will not drink of the fruit of the vine, until the <u>kingdom of God shall come</u>." And he took the bread, and <u>gave thanks</u>, and brake it, and gave unto them saying, "This is my body which is given for you: this do in remembrance of me." <u>Likewise</u> also the cup after supper saying, "This cup is the New Testament in my blood which is shed for you."

Jesus associated the communion offering to the miracle of life and rebirth that hadn't happened yet. In this communion supper, Jesus was educating them on how he was going to be like the young man who gave up his lunch as an offering to affect multitudes. The wine represented his blood that was to be shed for the remissions of sin and thereby initiating the new covenant, and the bread represented his body that was about to be broken for many (Matthew 26:26-28, Luke 22:17,19, 1 Corinthians 11:24-26 and Revelation 1:5).

Jesus mentions the kingdom of God that was to come after his resurrection and that he would not sup with them until then. He had said in Luke 17:20-21 that it was not some physical thing that could be observed, when it comes. But that the kingdom of God would reside from within.

He was about to give his own blood and body as the thanksgiving offering, in advance of God responding back with new and better promises. It all has to do with the kingdom of God! 1 Corinthians 4:20 says the kingdom of God is not in word, but in power! NLT version of the bible says, For the kingdom of God is not just a lot of talk; it is living by God's power.

The communion celebration is powerful! It is like feeding our spirit man a supernatural dose of his power for miracles. It is a real thing! It affects our faith consciousness!

Jesus had presented himself through his death as an offering of thanksgiving to his Father in advance of, and in exchange for miracle working invisible power that comes from the kingdom of God.

I believe Jesus knew how the principle of blessing and thanksgiving worked and he worked it. The miracle of him multiplying the bread to feed the multitude shows why we should remember him. He shows his connection with the kingdom of God for miracles that he made possible for us all. God is a God of more than enough.

ON EARTH AS IT IS IN HEAVEN

Matthew 6:9-13(NIV), Our Father in heaven, Hallowed be your name, your kingdom come, your will be done, on earth as it is in heaven. Give us today our daily bread. Forgive us our debts, as we also have forgiven our debtors. Lead us not into temptation but deliver us from the evil one.

You can't go wrong in praying this prayer, because Jesus said this is the model prayer for us all. It is a prayer of blessing and will come to pass rather we believe it or not. When Jesus said to say the words, "your kingdom come, your will be done, on earth as it is in heaven" he is saying "All will be well" like it is in heaven. When you say what the "WORD" says to say, you are putting yourself right in the middle of his will for the future.

There were a lot of teaching moments where Jesus used sowing and reaping to explain Godly kingdom principles. He explained how our earth <u>will be</u> made "as it is in heaven".

In one of his lessons, he said that the kingdom of heaven is likened to a man who sowed good seed in his field. While he slept, his enemy came and sowed tares among his wheat. Later, when the blade of wheat began to spring up, he also noticed the tares. He decided to let them grow up together. Then he would have the reapers gather the tares first, bind them up and burn them. He did not want any of his wheat to be lost, while the tares were being uprooted, so he waited until harvest time. Then the reapers could safely gather the wheat into his barn (Matthew 13: 24-30). Jesus explains that the good seed are the children of the kingdom (Matthew 13:38). The tares are the children of the wicked one (or devil) who sowed them. The harvest is the end of this world system, and the reapers are the angels (Matthew 13:36-43).

From what this scripture says about the good seed and the tares, we can see what the most important job in the whole world is. It is to help in the spread, cultivation, and multiplication of his good seed that he is trying to birth in others, so he can add them to his own harvest. **Jesus said, "Every plant which my heavenly Father has not planted, shall be rooted up" (Matthew 15:13).** You must be born again.

Jesus wants us to represent the Father and his love to others, like he did. God can transform the unprofitable, corruptible, and bad seed by death and rebirth. He can replant it in his perfect, fruitful, and fertile kingdom. The curse cannot raise up out of the ground with the seed if Jesus has paid the price for it. If the curse has been dealt with, then what's left is the blessing. In Malachi, God said "I will bless", and through God's offering of Jesus, he says "I did bless." It is up to us to believe and accept his offer. We can offer our bodies as living sacrifices, so that Jesus can continue his miracle works through us.

Through Jesus, we can stop owing a debt that we do not owe anymore. We can use bible stories to defeat and cast out imaginations that can hurt us, as well as hurt others. We can get divine revelation, as well as perfected knowledge on how to deal with difficult situations just like he did.

Throughout history God had spoken his inspired secret weapon into the world through prophecy. He hid and protected his seed from Satan until it could be implanted into mankind. He used the laws of the firstborn rights, the priesthood, and the womb of his chosen women to personally give us his own invisible image. He was already claiming what was and is his, when he said, "Let my Son go" to the pharaoh of Egypt. He redeems us from the enemy of slavery and permanently gives us Sonship.

God demonstrated his ability and desire to restore life in a story of the dry bones (Ezekiel 37:1-14). Ezekiel was a Hebrew prophet who had an unusual encounter with God. God showed him things about the future of Israel by an incredible illustration. The Lord God carried him into a valley which was full of dead men's bones. He then told Ezekiel to prophesy to the dry bones and command them to listen. God said he would restore the flesh and muscles to the bones and cover it all with skin, as Ezekiel prophesied his words into existence. Ezekiel spoke to the dry bones what he was told to say, and suddenly there was a rattling noise from all across the valley. Ezekiel watched as the bones of each body came together. He watched as the muscles, flesh and skin formed over the bones. But there was no breath in the bodies as of yet.

God told him to prophesy to the four corners of the winds to breath on the bodies to give them life again, and he did. They came to life and stood up as a very great army.

God showed the prophet something about Israel. He was telling of the destruction and then restoration of the people and land of Israel.

We have this story of Ezekiel's prophecy handed down throughout history. God is the one who restores life to the dry bones. He can open the graves of the spiritually dead and put his Spirit in them, so that they can live (Ezekiel 37:14).

Hebrews 4:12 (KJV), For the word of God is quick, and powerful, and sharper than any two-edged sword, piercing even to the dividing asunder of soul and spirit, and of the joints and marrow, and is a discerner of the thoughts and intents of the heart.

Proverbs 3:5-10 (KJV), Trust in the Lord with all thine heart and lean not unto thine own understanding. In all thy ways acknowledge him and he shall direct thy paths. Be not wise in thine own eyes: fear the lord and depart from evil. It shall be health to thy navel and marrow to thy bones.

God became one of us physically (through flesh and blood), to be expose to sin like us. He created the antibody against sin for us. He is the invisible Spiritual life-giving version of the communion. We partake of his perfected and Spiritual body when we partake of his wine and bread.

Jesus said, "For the bread of God is he which cometh down from heaven and gives life unto the world. I am the bread of life, he that comes to me shall never hunger and he that believes on me shall never thirst.

I am the true vine, and my Father is the husbandman. I am the vine, and you are the branches. He that abides in me and I in him, the same bringeth forth much fruit. For without me you can do nothing" (John 6:33,35 and John 15:1, 5).

God used a natural physical body to defeat a supernatural enemy. He defeated the devil with his secret weapon at the cross, in the heart of the earth, in the tomb at the resurrection, in the highest court and finally in his own throne room. The devil's weapon was the nails that nailed Jesus to the cross. But the greater weapon was the man that was nailed to the cross.

Jesus had said, "If I be lifted up, I will draw all men unto me" (John 12:32).

The battle will be won over the earth and his blessed kingdom will stand forever here on earth because of what he did. Thank goodness, we are not judged based on our own goodness, but his! I pledge my allegiance to the Lamb of God who makes us part of the Father's kingdom!

MY HEAVENLY FATHER

(Conclusion)

---❖---

LESSON 63

It takes faith to believe in an invisible Father that you can't see. What if you could come to the deep realization that God is not just God, but he is also your own Father? If you have accepted his offer of Sonship given through Jesus, you are spiritually rebirthed as the heavenly Father's own child. You are not born again physically, but spiritually with a new personal relationship birthed from his Spirit into yours, making him your Father.

What if you could have a loving relationship with him deeper than you could ever have with your own earthly daddy? Our parents are only human and make mistakes too, just like us, and they are not all knowing like God! We don't always discuss everything about ourselves with them, but we can with our heavenly Father. He knows it all anyway! Jesus referred to God as "Abba, Father" (Mark 14:36). It is a relationship based between the heavenly Father and his child. It is a more intimate relationship with God as our father.

Galatians 4:6, And because ye are sons, God hath sent forth the <u>Spirit of his Son</u> into your hearts, crying Abba, Father.

Would you be more inclined to get to know him, to find out who he is, how he thinks and what he thinks about you, if you were to realize that he is a Father more to you, than your own daddy?

If only more people could just grasp the meaning of what being born again really means! They would know that as a loving Father, God wants to bless them in all good things. He has been trying to be our Father for thousands and thousands of years, even though he is invisible.

We learn what love is through our relationships. God gave us each other so we can experience what it is. We can feel good feelings about those around us like our children, our parents and our friends. Our relationships with others can help us understand his love even though he is invisible.

Jesus explains the love of his Father by telling a story about the prodigal son and his own father. A young man went to his father and had asked for his inheritance to be given to him. He wanted to go out and explore the world around him. He left his comfortable surroundings of family and friends and went out to a far-off country. He squandered every bit of his inheritance in riotous living. There arose a famine in the land and the only job that he could find was to feed the swine. He would get so hungry that he wished he could eat the same garbage that the swine was eating. He finally came to his senses and took the long journey back home in hopes of just being able to get a job working for his father. His father was so happy to see him, that he gave his son the best robe he had, put a ring on his finger and shoes on his feet. That night his father gave him a spectacular feast to celebrate his homecoming (Luke 15:11-32).

The father of the prodigal son honored his son's decision to venture out on his own, and I am sure his father wondered if he was okay. God lets us make our own decisions in life. He hopes we make good decisions because he loves us with a fatherly love. Just like with the prodigal son, our heavenly Father will always be happy that we turn back to him, even when we make mistakes. The father of the prodigal son didn't see or dwell on his son's fault. He just saw the son that he loved spending time with.

God sent a part of himself to us to reestablish his <u>relationship with us</u> and make it invincible. God may seem like a big scary God, but he came to us as an innocent lamb through his Son. He proved his love through physical means even though he was invisible. His Son was the visible and physical evidence of his presence. God gave us an earthly and bodily image that we could relate to. We can see and hear and know who he is. We can see within our own imagination his love because he proved it through the life, death, and resurrection of his Son. He showed us what our future can be by showing us the resurrection of his earthly Son.

Through the Son, we learned about his Father. Jesus showed his unconditional love for his Father and trusted him completely with his life. He was a good son and was willing to help his Father win the love of the rest of us. I believe Jesus knew that he would not be lost. He knew he would be able to be with his Father again forever. There is no other love story that could compare to their love as Father and Son. They had to go through the hardest thing that anyone could ever endure. In their relationship with each other, God also proved to us that he can take away our pain and abuse like he did for his earthly Son Jesus. He proved he loved his firstborn Son and gave him everything. It also proves that he loves us and wants to bless us with all his good things.

I want to remind you about the firstborn right in the Old Testament because Jesus had been born as an Israelite under the law of Moses. If Jesus was bound by the laws in the Old Testament, then he had a right to the firstborn's inheritance either way you look at it. He was Mary's firstborn son and Joseph's first son by his marriage to her. And he was the firstborn Son of God. Mary came from the lineage of King David and his son Nathan. Joseph came from the lineage of King David through his son Solomon. With this knowledge, we can now put a few more pieces of the mystery puzzle together. We can get an understanding why God established the firstborn right in the first place. He was establishing a law here on earth that would affect his own Son, who was to be born in the future. The Father made a way that his own Son would inherit it all. The promise of the inheritance for his Son was hidden in the Israelite bloodline.

What two things did the bible say that the firstborn son had a right to? He had the right to a double portion of all the father had. He was to rule over all the rest of his father's people. The firstborn right was symbolic of God, the Father and his "Firstborn Son" and his right.

If we accept the Spirit of Christ in us, then we are called by his name. God had referred to the whole group of Israelites as Israel himself, after Israel had already died. When the Israelites were held in bondage for over 400 years, God had given Moses a message to tell the king of Egypt. God called the Israelites "My son" (Exodus 4:22-23). His message to the king was, "Israel is my son, even my firstborn……let my son go", as if he, God himself, was their Father. So, this tells me that in God's mind, this is the way he thinks about the whole group that associates themselves with his actual firstborn Son that came out of the Israelites.

In the beginning, the Lord God was creator of Adam and the garden. He was not Adam's daddy. Maybe this was the way Adam thought of God. There was no father and son relationship established yet. Adam was so afraid after his sin; he hid himself from God. Jesus on the other hand, did not hide himself from God as his Father. He may have not wanted to die on the cross, but he trusted his Father to take care of him somehow. He did not distance himself from his Father, when he faced his most difficult trial.

God set out to prove his love to mankind, so that mankind would accept him and come to him, not hid! God is not automatically our Father, and we are not automatically his children. We have to acknowledge him as so. Throughout history, he started building his foundation of Fatherhood for us, and it became a reality through Jesus.

How can the world know the magnitude of God's great love, if he is invisible to them? How can they know what an invisible Father has done for them and is still doing for them, without some kind of evidence that can be acknowledged through the physical senses?

We need to hear and see in our imagination his stories. We still need to create new stories for the world to hear and see. Be Jesus to the Father, as well as be Jesus to others, so that they can see the miraculous things that a loving Father could do for them. He was good to those who sought his presence, and for those who rose up against his children of faith, he would rise up against them. Love is of God and **God is Love (1 John 4:7-19)**! There is no fear in his perfect love because love casts out fear! Love protects, listens to, gives advice, secures the future, and take care of the present needs for those that belong to him.

God made this world for us, not the devil. When Adam and Eve sinned against him, Adam put the blame on Eve. Eve put the blame on Satan. (He was the tempter that triggered their disobedience.) The wrong voice or message was given to them. Satan messed with their minds to cause confusion and distrust about God.

God said to the serpent, "because YOU have done this, you are cursed…." Whose fault was it and who started the problem? God did not come against Adam and Eve personally, he was telling them the truth of their consequences, and how he planned to fix things. **Through Jesus, he says, "Neither do I condemn you, go and sin no more" (John 8:11).** With Jesus, we can find that we are no longer naked before God. He has put a ring on our finger and clothed us in his righteousness like the story of the prodigal son (Isaiah 61:10 and Luke 15:11-32).

Do you believe you were a victim, or do you believe it is all your fault? God knows who is to blame! It helps you in forgiving yourself or others when you really know who is behind all the chaos. Yes, you should admit your shortcomings, but don't keep them. Don't take Satan's blame! It is the devil working behind the scenes to condemn.

Stop hiding from God, take his forgiveness and place the blame right back on the devil. Resist and rebuke the enemy! Order the adversary to stop! You are the body of Christ and have authority over him because you have Sonship!

Get a Godly anger and cast the enemy out and away from your own life and from others you care about. This revelation of resisting and rebuking by what we speak can make a big difference in our lives. I was glad that when I first got saved, the preacher had me rebuke the bully or devil from my life.

Your Father gave you the right and the power to do it. If Adam and Eve would have known any better, they would have rejected Satan's words and said so themselves. Now we know better, so be persistent!

When you accept God as your Father, then know this – **"AS YOUR FATHER, HE LOVES YOU AS MUCH AS HE LOVES JESUS**! As Jesus is to the Father, so are we! We have OUR Sonship through Jesus!

For God so loved the world, that he gave his only begotten Son, that whosoever believeth in him should not perish, but have everlasting life (John 3:16).

ABOUT THE AUTHOR

Author, **Phyllis Cook** - Pastoral Certificate and Associate degree in Applied Science. I would not be here today if it wasn't for God reaching out to me in my darkest hour like the loving Father that he is. I tell my story of how I was set free from mind-altering assaults of defeat. These thoughts kept me from living my best life. I know what it is like to be a victim of anxiety, depression, and fear because it almost destroyed my life When I finally accepted Jesus Christ, I learned how to disregard and stop the lies of enemy forces from becoming a reality in my life. I began to replace them with the thoughts about God's love. I came to the realization that God really does love me and has got my back. The more we learn about him, the more we feel his love, and the more we feel his peace. God is so good! It is never too late to find out who he is and how to have a better life now!

www.ingramcontent.com/pod-product-compliance
Lightning Source LLC
Chambersburg PA
CBHW081327090426
42737CB00017B/3047